D0027160

THE UNTOLD STORY OF
THE TRAGIC 1979 FASTNET RACE

LEFT FOR DEAD

2ND EDITION

30 YEARS ON – THE RACE IS FINALLY OVER

NICK WARD
WITH SINÉAD O'BRIEN

BLOOMSBURY
LONDON • NEW DELHI • NEW YORK • SYDNEY

FOR CHRIS

THE FINAL CHAPTER 'NEVER SAY NEVER' IS
DEDICATED TO MY DEAR 'AUNT' BETTY,
MISS ELIZABETH EYELS, 1921–2010, AND TO
A GREAT MAN OF THE SEA, WILLIAM BRYN
FOULKES, 1940–2010. BLESS THEM BOTH.

Published by Bloomsbury Publishing Plc
50 Bedford Square, London WC1B 3DP
www.bloomsbury.com

First edition published in hardback 2007
First paperback edition 2008
Reprinted 2009
Second edition published in paperback 2010
Reprinted 2012, 2013, 2015

ISBN 978-1-4081-2816-9

This book is produced using paper that is made from wood grown
in managed, sustainable forests. It is natural, renewable and recyclable.
The logging and manufacturing processes conform to the environmental
regulations of the country of origin.

Typeset in 11.25/14.5pt MetaPlusNormal by
Palimpsest Book Production Limited, Falkirk, Stirlingshire.

Printed and bound by CPI Group (UK) Ltd, Croydon, CR0 4YY

Contents

One

Breaking the Silence

It is over 25 years since I sat alone at a bedside table with paper and pen supplied to me by Treliske Hospital in north Cornwall. Then I thought it important to record the facts, as I knew them, while they were still vivid in my mind. I was tired and overcome, but the words wrote themselves. The date was 15 August 1979 – the day after the most shattering event of my life. This last quarter-century has given me plenty of time to reflect on the longest 14 hours of my life, which I shared with my friend and crewmate Gerry Winks aboard the yacht *Grimalkin*.

Four days before, on 11 August 1979, I had set sail on my first ever Fastnet Race, part of a crew of six men: David Sheahan (owner and skipper of *Grimalkin*), his son Matthew Sheahan, Gerald Winks, Mike Doyle and Dave Wheeler. All of us on *Grimalkin* were excited and proud to be taking part in this 600-mile offshore classic. The race began in near-perfect conditions, but on day three the unforeseen happened – *Grimalkin*, along with many of the other yachts, got caught up in the deadliest storm in the history of modern sailing.

The Fastnet Race disaster of 1979 claimed the lives of 15 yachtsmen, including two of *Grimalkin*'s crew, David Sheahan and Gerald Winks. What happened during Fastnet '79 has been much written about, including a great deal of intrigue about the circumstances in which Gerald Winks and I were left for dead, abandoned by our shipmates, at the height of the storm.

I have seen little or nothing of the other three surviving members of *Grimalkin*'s crew, Mike Doyle, Dave Wheeler and Matthew Sheahan, over the last quarter-century. The few days we spent together aboard *Grimalkin* have been written about, discussed and debated in the yachting press, on television and by the media. But we, the remaining crew, the survivors, the four of us, have not spoken collectively, either in public or privately. I have always felt there has been some bad feeling, some uneasiness between us. Recently, during a television documentary, I heard Matthew say that he had felt 'closure'. Like me, I am sure that he too, along with Mike and Dave, has his own perception of the events that took place on that god-awful August day.

In the months following the disaster I gave several interviews. I know now that I never portrayed my true feelings nor gave the full story. I was a 24-year-old man in deep shock and in no position to evaluate my situation objectively. Much of what I read about the circumstances surrounding my story caused me such pain that I simply wanted to block it all out. In 1980 I took the decision not to be interviewed again on the subject. Since then, every time a television company, a film company or a journalist has knocked on my door asking for an interview, I have declined.

That was until September 2004, when I was approached

by a documentary filmmaker called Sinéad O'Brien. She had by chance heard a story of how a young man had been abandoned with his crewmate in the Irish Sea. Of course, my first reaction to this approach was one of unwillingness. Now, though, I had begun to write for myself, not specifically about the Fastnet Race, but personal thoughts in the form of a journal. I discussed this new approach at length with my wife Chris, and then I agreed to meet Sinéad. She was interested in pursuing the story for a documentary or feature film, and had come across a video clip in which I was pictured with my dead crewmate Gerald Winks at my feet. The footage was taken moments before a Royal Navy Sea King helicopter rescue. Watching the streaming video on my computer screen brought back immediately, all too vividly, a slice of time buried but not forgotten. I was shocked, overcome – and glad that Chris was with me. Over the next few months, Sinéad, this bright, young, vibrant, tenacious Irish woman, was to tease out memories from me, some long covered up, almost denied. In front of this stranger I began to purge myself of 25 years of pent-up emotions.

After much indecision I decided to concentrate my latent emotions into a book – to finally put down on paper the feelings of anger, torment, helplessness, despair and pure bloody-minded frustration I had felt while trying to survive the near impossible.

Sinéad was able to explain to me the best way to embark upon the project. It was not long before we became partners in this book. My co-writer's input from the very start has been inspirational. I recognised her talent and enthusiasm immediately. Once she realised I had a story to tell, Sinéad brought her incisive style and her structuring skills to the writing of this book. She showed me how to add without veering off the line – the line of being true to myself. Without Sinéad this story would have been left as a private journal, unpublished.

This book is as much for Gerald Winks as it is for me – for if it were not for him, I would not be here to tell this story. This is the, until now, untold story of what became of Gerry and me on that day, 14 August 1979. This is my 'closure'.

NICK WARD, 2007

TWO

The Jewel in the Crown

I was born in the little south-coast village of Hamble, in Hampshire. I was the youngest of four children, three boys and one girl, and my upbringing was pretty much the usual for a small village by the sea. Hamble is no ordinary village, though; life in the village is inextricably bound to fishing, sailing and, in particular, yacht racing. Some of the finest national and Olympic sailing champions were born here, sailed here or are connected in some way with this place. If you are born in Hamble, it is inevitable that the sea or sailing will play some part in your growing up.

And certainly my father, Pa, instilled in his three sons from a very young age a love of the water and all things nautical, particularly sailing. My first sailing lessons were at the age of four in a pram dinghy Pa built for me during the winter of 1959/60. In the garage of our home, I would sit in a wooden rocking chair watching Pa plan and shape the plywood dinghy. The love, care and attention he put into building it were extraordinary. Perhaps because I was the youngest and he was that much older when I was growing up, Pa had the time to do things for me he had not had for the others. I know I spent far more time with him than my siblings had, and although I adored both my parents, Pa and I had a particular, wonderful affinity. Many nights I fell asleep in the rocking chair to the sound of him sawing, planing and nailing, then to be carried to bed in his arms. He was well built, six foot two, and for as long as I knew him had white hair, and an untipped Senior Service cigarette in his hand. Articulate and well read, he captivated me with bedtime stories and tales of the sea. He read me many tales, classic accounts of ships and their crews sailing the southern oceans and rounding Cape Horn. I wanted to be there, with the characters in the books. I can remember the absolute thrill I felt when we launched the dinghy down at Hamble quay the following spring – and also the crowd that it drew. Pa had named her *Fred* after my uncle – for no particular reason other than he couldn't really think of anything else – but I recall someone from the crowd calling over to him, 'You can't call her *Fred*.'

'We'll call her whatever we like,' said my father, straight-forwardly, to the heckler. 'Won't we, son?'

Standing alongside *Fred*, knee-deep in water, I waited for Pa to lift me in. Then finally, with the crowd cheering, I was off on my first sail in *Fred* with Pa. I felt like a sailor heading off to the southern oceans to follow his dreams.

Over the summer of 1960 Pa taught me the basics of sailing, how to tack up and down the river – as ever, he taught me with great care and attention. At such a young age I had no fear and my confidence grew quickly. I revelled in the water and everything about it, sometimes taking risks that Pa strictly warned me against. One of the first rules he instilled in me was that if the dinghy capsized, I was to stay with it.

'Stay with the boat, son. Hang on to it, never leave her – she will save you.'

This beautiful navy-blue and snow-white dinghy was my first love. And I had fallen not only for *Fred*, but for the river too. These lessons with Pa began a life-long passion.

While I was still a very young boy, I heard about the Fastnet Race from my next-door neighbour, Dick Langton, a seasoned offshore sailor. Dick had competed in three Fastnet Races, and he told me of the notorious stretch of water between the mainland and the rock, and all the variations in weather he had experienced, from being totally becalmed to being rained and hailed on. He described the stunning sunsets you could witness off the south coast of Ireland where the Irish Sea and Atlantic Ocean met, and how he'd never seen anything like them. I used to slip under the fence, dash into his front room and plead with him to tell me more. He told me of lightning, thunder and summer gales, but he also told me that, while no part of the route was easy, it was all worth it – the finish and the reception at Plymouth justified every minute of the 'hardship'. His hearthside stories gave me an idea of how important this race was. In my young mind it began to take on mythical form.

Pa had also increased my appetite for the Fastnet by taking me when I was seven years old to Cowes Bay on the Isle of Wight, a stone's throw from where we lived in Hamble, to see the race's start. This was in the early 1960s, and Pa drove the launch *Snapdragon* for Eileen Ramsay, a famous marine photographer. Even at this age I was aware of the significance of this great race, that it was the last in a series of five that make up the Admiral's Cup competition, the world championship of yacht racing. To this day the Fastnet Race is considered to be the jewel in the crown of offshore races.

It took just under an hour to travel across the Solent to Cowes. We anchored in the bay and waited. This Fastnet Race start, the first of many I was to watch in the coming years, enthralled me. Hundreds of yachts filled the bay. The atmosphere, the feeling of being there, made the hairs on the back of my neck stand up. I stood by Pa; typically, he didn't miss the chance to give me a nugget of sailing advice. 'One hand for yourself, one hand for the boat, Nicholas,' I remember him telling me. And I promised myself that one day I would be among the boats on the start line, that I would see for myself what this race was all about.

As I grew older sailing became my whole life, an integral part of my being – or at least that's how it felt for a teenage boy without a worry in the world other than would the weather be OK for that night's racing. I couldn't get enough of it. I loved every minute I spent afloat. All other activities – social, academic or otherwise – were secondary, or based around sailing. I was racing at least three days a week. I dashed home from school to take part in Wednesday evening races. On Fridays I couldn't wait to get out of school because weekends meant uninterrupted, intensive sailing. I belonged to the Hamble River Sailing Club, a great club on the banks of the river Hamble, which over the years has produced more champions and medal-winners than almost any other club in the country. When I wasn't in school, most of my time was spent in, on or around the river. If I wasn't involved in club activities, I was still on the river, earning pocket money by helping Ray Sedgewicke, the Hamble ferryman.

Pa was soon taking me round the country to open meetings, trailing our dinghies and winning a few cups and medals on the way – for my club and, much to Pa's approval, for myself. I had a long apprenticeship in dinghies before I made my first Channel crossing in my early teens and started to race small keelboats offshore. Hamble and Cowes were my playgrounds, my schools of race training and seamanship.

School life was also pretty good fun. Many of my school friends were involved in sailing. I like to think I was a fairly normal, well-balanced schoolboy, who had hopes of doing well in my O-level exams and going on to do something connected with the sea or the river. I was sure of my future; it seemed simple then. I was dead set on a career in the merchant navy. I was also very clear about which offshore races I wanted to race in. I reckoned 17 was the right age for my first Fastnet. On completion of that I would move on to the Sydney to Hobart Yacht Race and the Bermuda Race. But the Fastnet was to be first. I was intent on that.

At the age of 15, in my fifth and final year at secondary school, I had an unexpected setback. I suffered a brain haemorrhage. The previous day I had been playing hookey, along with my good friend Mark Parkin. We had enjoyed a very long walk to Titchfield Haven, a small, popular tidal inlet with a picturesque harbour that dried out at low tide. It was a very hot March day and by the time we had walked back again I had a nasty headache, which fortunately eased off by the time I went to bed.

The next day, 24 March 1971, was again hot. This time

I attended school. In the afternoon I played a hard-fought game of hockey and was exhausted after it, more exhausted than normal. School friends told me afterwards that I collapsed on the hockey pitch, but this I don't recall. I simply remember having a violent headache, like a migraine but worse. As usual I caught the bus home, but unusually when I got there went straight upstairs and to bed.

My headache got more severe as the evening wore on, so severe that I starting to bang my head against the woodchip-wallpaper-covered wall of my bedroom to try to stop the pain. I was sick several times. Turning over in bed, I tried supporting myself with my left arm and it collapsed beneath me, useless. The vision in my left eye became blurred, as if there was a screen being erected on my left side, blocking things out. My curtains were closed because I couldn't bear any light. Soon I had lost all sensation in the whole of my left side. An ambulance was called.

I was taken directly to the Royal South Hants hospital in Southampton. Ma was with me. I felt every bump the ambulance went over, and its flashing blue lights and the sound of its siren hurt my eyes and ears. I remember looking up at Ma as she squeezed my hand and gently rubbed my forehead. I had never seen her like this – there was fear in her eyes. I began to understand that my condition might be serious. I was transferred to the Wessex Neurological Centre.

The next day my condition deteriorated further and I was rushed into the operating theatre for an operation that lasted around three hours. I found out months later that I was given no more than a fifty-fifty chance of survival. Ma and Pa didn't – couldn't – tell me this at the time. There was never an explanation of exactly what had happened, only that some abnormal blood vessels were found, which I had probably been born with. Brain haemorrhages are sudden in onset and can occur at any time of life.

My life was on hold. I was in a world ruled by doctors and physiotherapists. I spent months in hospital, and found out that the longer-term side effects of my haemorrhage were a left-sided weakness and epilepsy. I felt as if life, barely begun, had passed me by. All my hopes, dreams and ambitions were thwarted. I had to struggle to relearn basic skills, such as walking. If it hadn't been for my family, I could not have got through this. And as well as their support, I had a special form of therapy awaiting me – sailing.

It was one year later, in the spring of 1972, that I plucked up the courage to sail again. I went on the river with Mark. It was weird at first. I was reluctant; people had gathered on the quay to wish me well and I did not want to make a fool of myself. Christ, here I was standing knee-deep in water that felt particularly cold on my left side – as if someone had poured liquid nitrogen on it – cold, cold, cold. Then I thought: bugger it – I can't back down now. I had something to prove to myself. Sod it, here goes. I struggled over the transom and sat in the dinghy. At once, it was as if I'd never been away. This was no problem – familiar territory – I could cope with this.

Mark jumped in and off we went, not far, but far enough. Brilliant, absolutely brilliant, sailing again. I can do this, I thought; I was born to it. Next stop: racing. But for the moment at least I was back on the river again, dinghy sailing. This first sail was so confidence-building that it fired me up like never before. I was now determined, doggedly so, to prove to myself that I was still good enough and could achieve my ambitions, even if perhaps not as quickly or in the way I had once foreseen.

So I was back into sailing, alternating it with work on the river. I worked in a riverside chandlery, the biggest around, which at this time supplied most of the well-known ocean-racing yachts. Soon I was also boosting my income delivering boats, locally and abroad, gaining sea time and experience and travelling with one of the best delivery skippers in the business. Most weekends I was sailing and racing competitively offshore. I had given up my dream of joining the merchant navy, but I had made a life for myself on the sea. I had no complaints.

By 1977 I felt ready to do the Fastnet Race, but most skippers like to retain their crew for a full season and I wasn't able to make the commitment that year. In June 1979, however, I got my chance. I was asked by David Sheahan, one of my customers, to join him as crew for the forthcoming Channel Week series of races. I was thrilled. I took up the offer without a second's thought. David's racing schedule and requirements matched my availability. In fact, if they hadn't, I would have made damn sure they did. I knew that by participating in and finishing this series the boat and her crew would automatically qualify for the Fastnet Race. This could be the year! I would have to prove myself to David and his boat first, but it was a start, at long last, and not just any start – a Fastnet start.

By this time I had gained enough experience for people like David actively to seek me out to crew on their boats. I didn't know David well at that time, only that he was an accountant in his mid-40s; I was better acquainted with his son, Matt. I often saw Matt in the dinghy compound, in the changing room or out racing his sailing dinghy on the Solent. I knew that his father owned and raced a 30-foot-yacht called *Grimalkin* – she was quick, and sister ship to *Silver Jubilee*, the world-cup-winning boat of 1976. *Grimalkin* was the type of boat I was used to sailing, and most importantly David seemed a man to trust. When he asked me to join his crew, he already knew my physical capabilities, my strengths and my 'weaknesses'.

Less than a week after taking up his offer, I got a letter from David. I remember the excitement I felt when I read it: Channel Week would be a good introduction to his boat, he said, 'in contemplation for the longer Fastnet Race in August'. This was getting more and more real. He signed off by saying that he would keep in touch with me either through Matthew or directly as more details became available. I was getting to know Matt better too. At 17, he was confident and self-assured, articulate and sometimes outspoken. Stocky in build, around five feet eight or nine, he was strong and athletic. I didn't regard Matt as a really close mate, but we were friends who shared a goal and a passion.

The first race of the series began on Friday 6 July. It was the well-known 165-mile offshore race from Cowes to St Malo. *Grimalkin* sailed with a six-man crew, which after one early change of crewmember settled down into a line-up of me, David, Matt, a guy I knew called Gerry Winks, and two others, unknown to me: Mike Doyle and Dave Wheeler. Mike and Dave were crew that David had advertised for locally, in Surrey. Matt knew the boat best and Dave and Mike fell in with Matt's lead and my experience; David's reason for asking me aboard. Gerry, at 35, was also highly experienced.

David Sheahan was one of the best skippers I had crewed

for. He was extremely good-humoured, and appreciated effort and attention to detail on board his boat. His manner towards the crew was always calm, almost avuncular. In many ways David reminded me of Pa. They never met, but if they had, I know they would have got on famously. They were both polite and courteous men, neither would 'put up with any nonsense', ashore or afloat, but each had a great sense of humour. David, a handsome man, was even of similar countenance to Pa, but shorter, around five foot nine, and of slighter build. His large glasses emphasised the slimness of his face, and a hint of grey showed in the medium-length darkish hair under his sailing cap.

The great thing about this week's racing was that I had the chance to work with and get to know the rest of the crew. Matt was almost simian in his agility in front of the mast, always eager to get the best from *Grimalkin*. But there were times when he became frustrated and gave in to 'stroppy' behaviour – which the rest of us found quite amusing. It never seemed to take him long to recover from these mini tantrums. He adored and respected his father. There was an equality in their relationship, too – they were like best mates as much as father and son. Gerry Winks was second-in-command and navigator – he proved to be a good watch leader and excellent back-up for David. He was a large man, around 14 stone and well over six feet tall, but surprisingly softly spoken, and affable, with a great sense of humour. I took to him at once.

Mike Doyle was a likeable young guy who smiled a lot. By his own account he was fairly experienced and certainly during these early races he seemed confident and sure-footed aboard. He was tall, dark-haired and had an incredibly deep voice, which I was sure he used to great effect in chatting up women. He also had a large repertoire of jokes and was good at raising a laugh from the crew.

I had rather less time for Dave Wheeler. He had a good nature but was somewhat young in outlook. I found out fairly early in the race that when put under pressure he developed a bit of an attitude problem. But he was also funny. He had a never-ending supply of filthy jokes, and he also broke wind constantly – more to his own delight than anyone else's. I don't know how many times he said to me during those first races: 'Pull my finger, Nick, the cartilage is stuck.'

I would pull, purely to keep him happy, knowing what the result would be.

'Ah, that's better,' he'd say, and laugh his head off.

Now and then, particularly if there wasn't much going on, it was hard not to get swept along with Dave's silly jokes. It was lavatorial humour, unsuitable for David's ears, but I do remember on occasion laughing so hard I nearly fell overboard. At times Dave had to be reminded by the skipper that he wasn't just along for the ride. Looking back now, I can see that he was young, very young – about 19 – and while his intentions were good he possibly *was* just along for the ride.

This first race passed without incident, and apart from my neck ache, brought on by working the spinnaker most of the day, I enjoyed it. On the leg across the Channel to St Malo we had the pleasure of seeing a fantastic all-colour summer sunset. Sitting on the rail watching this magnificent colour scheme paint itself in front of my eyes brought back what Dick Langton had told me years before about the Fastnet sunsets. If we qualified for the race, I hoped those sunsets would appear for us too.

One evening, later in the week, when plenty of drink had been taken and spirits were high, our goodnights became an unending imitation of the closing scenes of an episode of *The Waltons*. Dave, of course, started it off with a loud fart, followed by, 'Goodnight, Johnboy,' and a lot of schoolboy-like giggles.

'Night, Mary Ellen,' said Matt.

Then Mike pitched in, with his deep voice. 'Goodnight, Grandpa.'

I replied, 'Goodnight, Elizabeth.'

A belching competition ensued – the beer having its effect – and this went on until David could take no more and called it to a halt.

Overall we had had a fantastic week's racing in July. *Grimalkin* performed well. We endured some close racing, some success and also our share of bad weather, which *Grimalkin* and her crew stood up to without difficulty. We sailed together well as a crew. All in all, compared to our competition – and for that matter other boats I'd crewed on – I felt that David's crew was a good mixture of experience and youth. And apart from the usual friction caused by such proximity, there was absolutely no animosity on the boat.

Although we were forced to retire from the last race, David judged the week a success because we qualified for the Fastnet. He entered the boat, and confirmed that I would be in the crew. I knew, finally, that it was a certainty that I'd be on the 1979 Fastnet Race start line. I felt great; everyone did. We had a few beers that night too, and sang *Grimalkin*'s praises until we could sing no more.

David decided not to compete in Cowes Week, preferring to concentrate on Fastnet at the end of the week. This suited me well. It meant I too could concentrate on the main event, the race I had been waiting for, aspiring to, for years.

A couple of weeks before the Fastnet Race, David Sheahan sent a letter with detailed preparations for the race to each member of the crew of *Grimalkin*. He was very specific, allotting individual responsibilities, duties and domain aboard. He also included a watch schedule. This sounded clinical, but it established our roles aboard. I was really pleased to read that I would be off watch for the first 12 hours of the race. All I would have to do was hand the crew sandwiches. I was no cook – David had already 'awarded' me *Grimalkin*'s burnt spatula, the result of my labours in the galley during Channel Week, but I was fine with this. I'd much rather be trimming a sail than cooking.

David ensured that his boat met with every single one of the stringent safety precautions set by the race organisers. He did not skimp on anything. He was so methodical that as well as ensuring the boat was in a state of perfect preparation, he also ensured that we, his crew, were the same, even insisting we all pay a pre-race visit to the dentist to check everything was in order. Not too many skippers went to such lengths. He was a perfectionist – which is why I loved sailing with him.

During the week before the Fastnet, I checked the weather daily. The conditions seemed perfect for later in the week. I couldn't wait to get on board and set off on the 608-mile-long race. Starting off at Cowes, the race continues westwards along the English coast until it passes Land's End. Its course then takes it up and across the approaches to the English Channel and into the Irish Sea, rounding the southernmost point of Ireland, the Fastnet Rock lighthouse – known

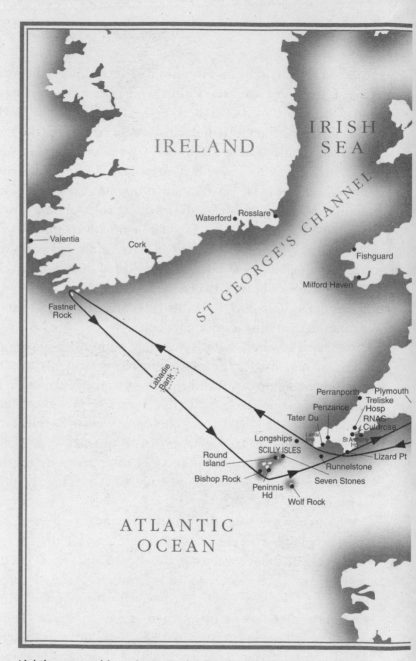

Lighthouses and key places on the Fastnet Race route.

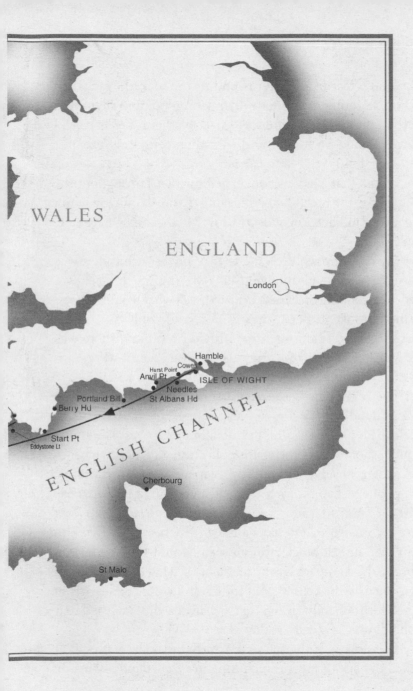

WALES

ENGLAND

London

Hamble

Hurst Point Cowes
Anvil Pt ISLE OF WIGHT
Portland Bill Needles
Berry Hd St Albans Hd

Start Pt
Eddystone Lt

ENGLISH CHANNEL

Cherbourg

St Malo

as Ireland's 'teardrop'. After rounding the rock, the race then backtracks, going inshore to its finishing point in Plymouth off the famous breakwater. No part of this route is easy. I knew it would be tough, and in sailing terms my greatest challenge, but I was ready for it.

I think that Ma was concerned for me. Throughout the week before the race, she kept saying to me, 'Now, you won't forget your medication, will you, love? Put it somewhere safe, won't you?'

My epilepsy required me to take phenobarbitone twice daily – an anticonvulsant drug. This was the one thing I never needed reminding of. I knew only too well what would happen if I did not take it. But I suppose Ma could only picture the worst. What if I did forget, or mislaid it? What if there was bad weather and I had a convulsion? Ma and Pa were both well aware of the many risks involved in offshore sailing.

The night before the race I stayed at home in Hamble with Ma and Pa. We ate an early supper and watched a bit of television. Pa got out his stamp album. He was passionate about his hobby, annotating his collection with his own beautiful calligraphy. He was adding a Japanese commemorative stamp, one he had recently bought, a version of the Japanese artist Hokusai's famous woodcut entitled *Behind the Great Wave at Kanagawa*. It depicts a huge wave topped with white foam that almost blocks the view of Mount Fuji. I admired not only the stamp and its immaculate setting on the album's page, but also the yellow-gold Indian-ink words beneath it in Pa's beautiful handwriting. Just as I always did, I wished that my hand was as steady and accurate as Pa's.

The next morning, after an early breakfast with Ma, I packed the last of my kit, including my wallet and my neatly bottled-up medication. I was glad of the substantial breakfast Ma had given me. It helped quell my nervous anticipation. I closed the bedroom door, stroked our black cat Tom, who lazed on the windowsill of the landing, then went down the stairs to the hall and the open front door. Pa waited in the drive in his white Escort estate. I got in, then wound the window fully down to say goodbye to Ma. She leant in and said simply, 'Take care, won't you, love.'

As Pa slowly drove off I turned in my seat and saw Ma framed by the high privet hedge either side of the gate. She smiled broadly and gave me a huge sweeping wave.

Pa drove me the half-mile or so to Hamble Point where *Grimalkin* was berthed. We didn't speak in the car, which wasn't unusual. There was often companionable silence between us. He was deep in thought and I knew that he was concerned for me, but, typically, he did not voice it. We reached the marina. Only five minutes away was *Grimalkin* and my starting point to the Fastnet Race.

I retrieved my kit bag from the boot. Pa got out too and we shook hands rather formally, then he put his arm briefly round my neck. 'Do as your Ma says – take care.'

He went to lean, arms folded, cigarette already lit, on the railings of the marina. I walked away, turning and waving once. Pa's white hair made him easy to spot.

It was early in the morning of Saturday 11 August 1979, and the next four days were going to change our lives irreversibly. This was the start of a 600-mile odyssey for *Grimalkin* and her crew – a journey that people would speculate about for decades to come.

Three

Watches and Lighthouses

I strolled along the wooden decking in Hamble Point Marina. Across the river I saw Warsash, the village opposite Hamble, the red roofs of its sailing club and the Rising Sun pub so familiar. The tide was coming in and the sun reflected off the surface of the water, bright and glinting, dazzling me. My boyhood haunt; I had skimmed stones from the bank of the creek adjoining the marina countless times. I walked past the chandlery, which buzzed with yachtsmen, all with last-minute requests for charts, books and other provisions. I knew this chandlery and the manager, Chris, well.

'Hey, Nick ... good luck! By the way, I'll have that cartoon ready for you when you get back.'

Chris had promised to draw a caricature of me leaning against the huge old oak tree outside the chandlery. He was an excellent artist.

'Cheers, mate.'

I turned and began walking the length of F pontoon. It was busy with crews preparing to sail: some on the Fastnet Race, others just going out to watch the start. The excitement I was feeling seemed to run through the entire marina. There were more boats than usual, of every colour and size, every berth seemingly taken. The atmosphere was electric, Fastnet electric – I felt it, could almost taste it. I certainly smelt it too – someone was frying bacon. I also heard the sounds of rapping halyards: wire against aluminium, the background music in any marina. I passed a yacht with familiar faces on board, three guys sitting in their cockpit drinking coffee and smoking. They were customers of mine, and also off on the race in what looked like their new OOD 34.

'Hey, Nick,' one of them hollered. 'What do you think your chances are against us?'

I couldn't help smiling at this. 'Well, we'll just have to see!'

Seeing these guys smoking reminded me I had a half-full packet of Marlboro Reds in my pocket; they had to be transferred into my kit bag as David forbade smoking on board. Despite this, Matt and I did light up occasionally, unknown to our skipper. I was a light smoker; perhaps five a day. Five or six days' abstinence wouldn't hurt me. Be nice to know I had some on me, all the same.

Thoughts of nicotine vanished as ahead of me, berthed at the end of the walkway, I glimpsed *Grimalkin* – I could see her mast, her rigging and most of her light-blue painted decks. This 30-foot boat was not long-keeled, heavy nor of a traditional design. She was light, buoyant and wide – designed and built according to the complicated International Offshore Rule (IOR). Ron Holland, her designer, had created a yacht for speed and comfort. Getting closer, I could see her blue-painted transom. I loved the shape of her transom. Ron must have been thinking of a woman when he drew those lines. I also saw her white hull with her name beautifully painted in dark blue script. She was a fantastic-looking boat. All of a sudden, my mouth was dry; I needed a drink, caffeine, tannin at least.

I saw Matt was in the cockpit – I knew at once it was him because he was wearing his green tartan flat cap. It did nothing for him whatsoever but despite some serious ribbing from the rest of the crew he always seemed to have it on. David stepped down off the deck and greeted me with a friendly smile and a firm handshake. Four people stood alongside the boat – I immediately recognised Gay Sheahan, David's wife, and Matt's younger brother and sister, but not the fourth person. Gay introduced her as Gerry's wife, Margaret. She seemed excited, but nervous. Her hair was dark and her face was pale, not tanned like Gay's. Just past her I saw Mike and Dave busy on the foredeck, coiling rope and untwisting halyards. I was the last to arrive.

'Just going to stow my kit bag below,' I called over to them. 'I'll join you in a minute.'

Matt grabbed my kit bag for me and Gerry helped me over the guardrail and on to the deck of the boat. Once I was aboard, Gerry threw me a wry smile.

'Glad you could make it . . . Mr Ward.'

Redhead Gerry had a very dry sense of humour. We had clicked the first time we met. I smirked back at him.

'Wouldn't have missed it for the world, Mr Winks.'

Matt threw the kit bag back in my direction, nearly knocking me over – he and Gerry seemed to find this hilarious.

'Come on, guys . . . we need to keep going.' This was

David, calling us to order. We all responded to our skipper's command.

I started unlacing my brown Docksides shoes, and as I did so I noticed that, like Matt's tartan cap, they were pretty odd-looking. I had got them when I was 16 at Dick Langton's suggestion, and I hadn't raced without them since. What a superstitious breed sailors are. Pa had told me that green was an unlucky colour to carry on board and since then I had never had anything green among my belongings while on a boat. Many other things are deemed unlucky too – to race on a Friday is one, to change a boat's name, to lose a bucket at sea, even whistling on board could bring bad luck. Worst of all was to have someone die on board, and then to sail with the dead body. I had no doubt that every sailor on this race – all 2,500-odd of them – carried some sort of lucky item and had rituals he or she carried out, unnoticed by their crewmates. I had several, even my habit, when stowing shoes, of ensuring that the left shoe was in front of the right one.

I pulled on my nonslip waterproof sea boots and climbed down the vertical six-runged companionway ladder into the cabin. Once down there I inhaled *Grimalkin*'s familiar smell, the unique blend of natural and man-made materials that gives any racing yacht its individual identity. This was a scent that always put me at ease. With the foredeck hatch open, *Grimalkin*'s cabin looked bright and welcoming. It was not the largest space to share with five other blokes but I'd had experience of smaller boats and this was light and functional in comparison. I saw to my left the galley's little stainless-steel sink full of mugs – I had mistimed my arrival by at least a quarter of an hour.

To my right was the navigation table, with the VHF radio and echo sounder just above. As well as the VHF, David had two other radios on board: the Callbuoy and an AM/FM radio receiver; he was leaving nothing to chance. Two folded charts were laid on the table's hinged top. It looked like David had been plotting our course. I took a moment to observe the ruled line from Hurst Point, halfway down the Solent. The line was not straight, so I knew he must have been working out wind and tidal variations. Beside the charts a pilot book was open at the page for Portland Bill and its lighthouse, almost halfway along our course, its notorious rip one of the most important tidal points in the race. David had scribbled some tide times, routes and weather information on a waterproof pad alongside. Opposite the navigation table was the port quarter berth. The bunks were made out of strong blue material laced to aluminium poles that were supported by brackets from the deckhead. Each had a PVC-topped, waterproof stowage bag for personal items. The shelves above the galley were filled with cans and jars of food, retained by wooden slats – every available space was used.

As I unpacked my kit bag, placing my oilskins, harness and lifejacket into the full-height hanging locker, I began to visualise our forthcoming trip by means of the lighthouses we would pass, just as I always did on races. It was a memory map, going westwards from our start off Cowes, like David was doing on the paper charts. I have no idea whether this was something that others sailors did – I have never asked – but this was my way of plotting a journey. A bit like humming a well-known tune, I started running through the names:

'Hurst Point, the Needles, Anvil Point, Portland Bill,

Berry Head, Start Point, Eddystone Light, St Anthony's, Lizard, Tater Du, Longships, Wolf Rock, Seven Stones/ Sisters, Peninnis (Scillies), Round Island (Scillies), Bishop Rock and finally Fastnet Rock Lighthouse before turning back.'

It amazed me how they rolled off my tongue. I knew that we would not necessarily pass each one in this order because wind, tide and weather conditions would dictate changes, but it felt good that my map was firmly in place. I placed my medication safely on the shelf above the port bunk and, as I climbed back up into the cockpit, thoughts of lighthouses evaporated. The rest of the crew were hard at work preparing and rigging the boat, so I got stuck in too.

We had planned to leave Hamble Point at 10.30am, leaving plenty of time for our 13.20 start time. On the foredeck Matt and I unpacked *Grimalkin*'s number-one genoa from its sail bag, while Mike and Dave attached sheets with tight bowlines. We then attached its halyard to a welded, stainless-steel eye on the pulpit, for easier access later when hoisting it out in the Solent. We folded or rather 'flaked' the genoa against the stanchions, fixing the elastic sail ties with care.

'Hold on to your bollocks, guys,' said Dave.

Dave could always be relied upon for juvenile comments. This could be irritating, but today the mood was too good. As we carried on rigging *Grimalkin*, the banter got sillier and sillier, particularly between Gerry and Dave, whose high spirits led them to talk in Donald Duck voices. They lisped and rasped away like two mad men.

We rigged the mainsail in the same way as the genoa then we flaked it, flat as we could, to prevent it from flogging in the breeze before hoisting once we were in open water. One of the last jobs we did was to tie the dodgers: specially made, white, flexible PVC panels that bore *Grimalkin*'s sail number – K5637 – in black 15-inch-high letters. We fixed them to the guardrails with 3mm line, threading the line through brass cringles in each corner, attaching one dodger halfway along each of *Grimalkin*'s sides. These identification panels were a requirement of the race organisers and rescue services alike.

Once we were all prepared on deck, David called us into the cabin. As on all our previous races, he was meticulous in explaining where everything was – from the safety equipment, such as fire extinguishers, the first-aid kit and flares, to food supplies and the quantities of water we could each use. The boat's water tanks held 25 gallons and we were to be frugal in using it: daily consumption no more than three gallons. As he had stated in the typed instructions sent to each crewmember before the race, he again stressed that we had six gallons of diesel, allowing 24 hours' running time for the engine. Under race rules the engine could be used only for charging the main batteries, powering the navigation lights or for the assistance of fellow competitors in distress. Under no circumstances was the engine allowed for providing any forward motion while in competition.

With the serious instructions out of the way, David simply wished us all good luck. He was as excited, as exhilarated as the rest of us were, but in a very British way. David was not one for hype – he hated bullshit. He was just a decent, down-to-earth bloke.

Then it was time to say goodbye. Not knowing Gay that

well, having only met her three or four times before, my
goodbye to her was pretty formal, as were Mike's and Dave's.
On the few occasions I had been in her company, she had
always been fun, with a great sense of humour. She was a bit
like a younger version of my own mum, and I suspected that,
like Ma, she was anxious, seeing off not only her husband
but also her son. With Mike, Dave and I back on the deck,
David said goodbye to Gay and his other two children, and
Gerry said goodbye to Margaret. Margaret was noticeably
more emotional than Gay.

David, hugging his wife tightly, said, 'I'll see you in
Plymouth.' It was a bank-holiday weekend on our return and
David had planned a family cruise. Gay now pulled Matt into
a group hug and I overheard her say to them, 'Now, you two
. . . you must look after each other.'

David reassured his wife that everything would be OK,
then got back on board, turned to the crew and said,
'Everyone ready?'

Without another word we singled up, untying the bow
and stern spring ropes, leaving us attached to the pontoon
with one bow and one stern line. David was now standing
at the helm with the tiller in one hand and the engine throttle
lever in the other. He said the magic words, 'Cast off,' then
Matthew quickly pushed on *Grimalkin*'s bow while Dave
pushed at her stern, slowly easing her clear before jumping
on board. As we quietly slipped away, Matt's younger brother
followed as far as he could, holding onto the barnacled pile
at the end of the pontoon. I was reminded of the times I'd
waved my own father and older brother off on races when I
was too young to take part.

'Have a good race, Matt,' he shouted to his older brother.

Then he waved frantically. 'See you, Dad, see you in Plymouth.'

We motored away down the Hamble, David, Matt and Gerry waving farewell to their families.

We soon made our way towards the mouth of the river – I was sitting forward, on the cabin top, my back against the mast, watching and listening to everything around me, determined to absorb every minuscule detail of this, my first Fastnet Race. Even the gentle rush of water against the knuckle of *Grimalkin*'s forefoot as she sped along sent a shiver down my spine. To me the most wonderful sound in the world – apart from Joni Mitchell – is the sound of a racing yacht's bow moving through water, sometimes gently slapping, sometimes forcefully crashing. Hearing the boat's beautifully straight bow, sharp as a knife, slice easily, effortlessly into the gentle chop was magic. I knew that sailing was something I could never get enough of, ever.

Further downriver we passed the old Fairey Marine slipway, where so many famous aircraft, yachts, seaplanes and powerboats had been launched over the years to cross the Solent from Hamble to Cowes. The Hamble River's most prominent feature, its Spit, a shingle bank marked by a tall black post called Spit Pile, was half uncovered, glistening mud exposed for a short time before the tide returned. All around was familiar territory: my playground, the safe training ground in which I had been taught to swim, sail, row and scull – almost in preparation for today, it seemed, for this race.

We passed Hamble Point buoy, then, a quarter mile further on, Coronation buoy, where on 21 July 1962 Chris Bell, a dinghy sailor from HRSC, my club, had drowned.

Chris, 21 years old, a good friend of my eldest brother, had been a great sailor, full of potential. The following year a race was established in his memory – the Chris Bell Trophy – which still runs to this day. As we motored by I thought about his headstone in Hamble's cemetery. It said, simply, 'Claimed by the Sea'. We surged on and I turned round and looked through *Grimalkin*'s light grey exhaust smoke at Hamble. Holding onto the end of the main boom, I said my own farewells.

The weather was sunny and fairly warm and *Grimalkin* created her own breeze. As we rounded Calshot Spit, two miles out, the sails were hoisted but we continued to motor-sail for a distance while the wind picked up and filled the sails. There was wonderful silence as David killed the engine and *Grimalkin* accelerated, responding quickly to the trimming of her sheets. Crouched over the port genoa winch, I played the sheet a while. Matt altered the sheet lead to get a better shape in the sail. We made sure the opposite lead, the starboard one, was altered in the same way. This was great; this was what we all went sailing for. Matt was revelling in it already. He was sitting on the top rail of the pushpit, looking forward, as *Grimalkin* made her way hastily over to Cowes as if she, too, was impatient for the start.

We were cracking along, and within an hour or so we reached Cowes Roads, off the Isle of Wight. The sight as we edged towards Cowes was breathtaking – it was one of those picture-perfect moments where you stop yourself blinking for fear of missing anything. This spectacular view took me back 17 years to my first-ever experience of a Fastnet start, as a spectator with my father. The mouth of the Medina River, the entrance to Cowes, was filled with yachts and powerboats celebrating both the start of the Fastnet and the finish of Cowes Week. Some of the yachts flew their colourful spinnakers, and photographer-laden Press boats zigzagged their way at speed through the gathering fleet in hope of getting the precious, money-making image. With all this commotion the normally calm water was chopped up. *Grimalkin* was holding her own, coping with the wash and the chop well, responsive to the helm.

We saw the larger classes, class 0, the maxi yachts, such as *Condor of Bermuda*, at 78 feet. She had been moored and based on the Hamble since her return from the previous year's round-the-world race, when she had been jointly skippered by Robin Knox-Johnston and Les Williams. For this Fastnet she was skippered by Peter Blake, New Zealand's equivalent of one of my sailing heroes, Eric Tabarly. *Tenacious* sailed past us, 41-year-old media mogul Ted Turner at the wheel of his white, 61-foot sloop, looking as cool as only a Fastnet-course record-holder could. I saw *Morning Cloud* through the crush of boats around us. You couldn't miss her – this 44-foot yacht looked truly magnificent, almost regal, as she glided through the choppy water in our direction. As she got closer to us I caught a glimpse of Dick Langton on the foredeck, working hard as usual. Dressed in his crew kit of white trousers and light blue top he looked very professional, very cool. I yelled across to him.

'Good luck, Dick.'

He saw me and waved. As *Morning Cloud* passed by close to us, the whole crew, all six of us, stopped and watched. I could hear the incessant clicking of cameras as photographers on smaller boats pursued her, vying for position to get the best shot. Seeing her in all her glory I knew that she and her owner, former prime minister Edward Heath, and crew deserved all the respect and attention they got. White-hulled, flush-decked, with a light blue boot-top and deck paint, she was the second largest of Britain's three-boat team. She looked good, stunning.

Everywhere I looked there was something going on. The sun glinted off shoreside windows. Cowes was looking beautiful; *Grimalkin* was looking cool too. Mesmerised, I managed to remember how Pa had taught me to be careful close to busy, manoeuvring boats, how to cope with their unpredictable wash, how best to cope with the strong tides and chop off the Medina's mouth. He showed me this by example, and much of what he had taught me, what I had learned on the river, in the Solent, had become instinctive, like a third hand, a third hand that most Solent-born lads possessed.

Gerry yelled, 'Below us, bear off a touch, David, there's a boat on starboard, we won't cross her.'

It was *Green Dragon* crossing us on starboard tack; not much in it but she had the right of way. *Green Dragon* was the fastest boat in our class and favourite to win. She was on form, and we gave her a wide, respectful berth, while keeping a close eye on her movements. David had told us that her crew were local and for their knowledge of the Solent's wind and tidal idiosyncrasies there were few, if any, better boats to shadow.

We milled around the start line, waiting for our 13.20 start and sussing out our competition, sailing close by, tacking under their bows, seeing how they were reacting. This gave David a benchmark. It was exhilarating for everyone, the hustle and bustle of pre-start manoeuvres – great, within the rules, fantastic.

'She feels good . . . the new halyard's got less stretch . . . it's easier to trim,' I called over to Matt.

We were so close to our competition that sometimes the slop of seawater generated by a tacking boat would spatter *Grimalkin*'s genoa or slop into the cockpit. The clack of a winch, the noise of sheet ropes running through blocks, all were evidence of the hard-working crews around us. We were enveloped; our muscles were flexed, tested. Throughout this period we ensured that David was aware of *Green Dragon* and her position at all times – one of us relaying to him exactly when she was tacking, making a move to one end or other of the start line. She was easy to spot – as the name suggests, she was painted an emerald shade of green.

We then practised our start a couple of times, lining up transit points from the shore and the outer distance mark, checking for bias at one end or the other, sailing along the line and putting in a few practice tacks. These practice tacks, although second nature to us all, still had to be done because we knew that after the start there was a long beat to windward, against the wind. David's instructions from the helm were brief and to the point. As on any racing yacht there was no need for talking. Energy was better used on rope, winch or concentration. Choreography between a good skipper and crew is fluent, requiring only the nod of a head, a look or sometimes the pointing of a finger. But so close to the competition, raising an arm or pointing to a buoy or another boat was taboo. This could indicate a change of tactic or an altering of course. It was a game of chess, with nothing given away to an opponent.

'Hey, David,' said Gerry, 'we need to come up a point or two.'

Acknowledging Gerry with a quick nod, David called to me. 'Nick, ease off the genoa sheet, then keep it slack, I want to bear off.' He called out further instructions. 'Gerry, quick on those runners. Nick, help Gerry out if we tack . . . let off the windward backstay. Matt, keep your eyes peeled – ease the main, will you?'

David was now able to gauge and prepare for our start. The breeze was light to fresh so we set full sail and then sat in wait. David, Matt and Gerry counted off the minutes and seconds on a stopwatch. Mike, Dave and I kept an eye out for boats getting too close that could inhibit our start. David was immersed, concentrating like a batsman at his crease, waiting for the next ball. He glanced behind him, tiller in one hand, a small hand-held compass in the other, looking for the transit point and the RYS line.

The starting gun fired. *Grimalkin* was one of the first boats across the line, vying for position with *Green Dragon*. Using little rudder movement and letting the sails do most of the work, David had timed our class-five start to perfection. The first tack we put in was a slick one. Dave described it as 'shit hot' – and he was right. Timed again to perfection, there was no need for Matt to go forward or for Mike to clear the genoa or for me to use the winch handle. No mechanical advantage was needed as it was all done by hand – we were in the groove. *Grimalkin* rolled nicely through the eye of the wind, carrying her way, losing no speed while tacking.

'Keep it up, this is great,' yelled David.

He was not afraid of mixing it and before long we were in some closely fought duels with French competition. We recognised a double-chine-constructed half-tonner from last month's Channel Week. She was built of aluminium and was light and fast. Her crew, mostly young and cool-looking, got so near we could smell the smoke from their untipped cigarettes. One of them smiled as they put down their helm, tacking away inshore. Matt, holding onto the forestay, nimble as a mountain goat on *Grimalkin*'s angled, slippery foredeck, eyed them closely. We won the encounter. Matt smiled at his dad and gave him the thumbs-up.

'Good call, Matt,' shouted David in reply.

Close-call tacking was fantastically exciting, especially if the crew worked as one – easing, clearing, tailing and winching the genoa, each of us had more than one job to do. As we steamed along we kept clear of the French boats by either bearing away round their sterns or tacking away in another direction. It was close, and every tack counted, but we were smooth and more often than not came out the better.

I could see *Green Dragon* slightly ahead, her varnished transom like a target as we made our way down the Solent, close tacking through the tidal gate of Hurst Narrows. I also saw Hurst Point lighthouse, number one to tick off on my memory map. The afternoon sun made it glow, which I remembered not only from sailing past it so often, but from boyhood visits by car with Ma and Pa. There had been a castle and lighthouse on this point since the mid-1700s, essential even then for the safe passage of warships, entering and navigating up the Solent to Portsmouth Harbour.

We were now well up with the competition and had earned third place as we passed the Needles. This lighthouse, number two on my memory map, with its white, needle-shaped, contoured chalk cliffs, is one of the most striking sites round the British coast.

We were concentrated, working hard on the many short

tacks along this last stretch of the Solent before reaching the buoy marking its entrance. Excitement gave energy to aching muscles as we diced with the many other boats in class five. Between tacks, interrupted frequently by what seemed alternating shouts of 'Starboard' from *Green Dragon* and from us, we changed position, from third to second to first, back to third, tack by tack behind another French boat and *Green Dragon*. Like *Green Dragon*, David had chosen the island shore, and now other boats in class five, realising there was more wind and tide where we were, tacked across from the mainland shore to join us.

Within a few short hours we had left our very familiar home waters to join those of Christchurch Bay and the English Channel. By 6pm we had cleared the Fairway Buoy on the western exit of the Solent. The wind had dropped slightly but we were slipping along at a good speed, still maintaining third position in our class. The crew concentrated hard on the boat speed and sail trim, but we hadn't had a break since the start and we were all beginning to feel it. The muscles in my right arm were painful, making concentration harder to maintain. Dave was in the cockpit, drumming his fingers on the side deck and not doing much else, apart from breaking wind. I must have been less tolerant than the others as it was only me who appeared to be irritated by Dave. His occasionally childish behaviour might have annoyed the others too, I suppose, but being blokes we didn't discuss it. Only once had Matt mentioned to me that on a previous race, when Dave responded too slowly to a changing situation, David had bollocked him. But I could feel my blood rising, and under the incessant drumming I snapped.

'Jesus, Dave . . . give it a break.'

Dave laughed this off. 'Ohhhhh, feeling a bit touchy there, Nick?'

David butted in and instructed the crew to – in turn – take a break and eat some sandwiches. During my short break I relieved myself and grabbed a drink to help revive my tired muscles. By the time I returned to deck, the drumming had stopped – Dave had dozed off in the cockpit. Good, at least he was quiet. I sat on the windward rail with Matt and Mike, legs under the lower lifeline. It was standard practice for crew not tending sheets to sit in this position to gain maximum weight to the weather side, balancing the boat as she heeled into the wind. Also, *Grimalkin*'s cockpit seats were flat, narrow and hard – comfortable for no longer than five minutes or so. It was a racing boat's cockpit, one that encouraged the crew to either work or rest below. Apart from her bunks, the most comfortable place aboard *Grimalkin* was sitting on her weather rail. Our gaze was directed at our competition and at the soft, fast-receding coastline of the Isle of Wight, the flashing of the Fairway buoy and the lighthouse behind it. I kept a close eye on *Green Dragon*; so far we were doing fine, going nicely.

By 7.45pm the winds had become lighter. We sailed into Christchurch Bay. The visibility we had enjoyed beating down the Solent was now not so good. I couldn't pick out any lights or features and was unable to see the illuminations on Bournemouth pier. This was strange; I reminded my crew-mates that a month ago, on another race, we saw both quite easily. No one was concerned, just slightly frustrated that our progress was now slower.

Grimalkin's watch system started at 8pm on Saturday evening. The watch system we used was tried and tested, and used on most other racing boats. The system ensured there were always two people on watch at any one time, and that, in rotation, one person – excluding the skipper – always got a 12-hour period off watch. This meant that the crew would alternate four hours on deck and four hours below. The off-watch crew's duties included preparing meals and keeping the interior of the boat in good order, although the most important thing was getting adequate rest or sleep for the next four-hour watch. The on-watch crew's duties and responsibilities included keeping the boat on course – the course predetermined by the skipper or by the on-watch navigator. Any sail changes or altering of course might, in some cases, require waking up off-watch crewmates. Every hour, the on-watch crew were required to enter the time, the boat's speed, the barometric pressure, the course steered, the depth of water and other details into the boat's log, as well as taking note of any obvious changes in weather or tidal situations.

I was, as expected, off watch for the first 12-hour period, from 8pm on Saturday evening until 8am Sunday morning. I spent the first hour passing round sandwiches, washing up and making hot drinks. The wind began to drop as the evening got darker. We sailed across Christchurch Bay to Anvil Point Lighthouse, number three on my list. At 9pm I went below to rest. During this period some of my crewmates were up and down the companionway ladder, checking their gear, grabbing bars of chocolate or cans of drink.

As I lay in my bunk I could hear other boats around us: the ratcheting of turning winches, the unmistakable sounds of other crews. It sounded as if our competition were doing some sail changes. I found it impossible to sleep, frustrated at not knowing what was going on, so I got up. I joined the others on deck, who were altering sheet positions, changing sail trim, getting a fuller shape in the sails to accommodate the lightening winds and to keep our speed to maximum. By half past ten we had done all we could, anything else was wasted effort. Satisfied I could do no more, I went below, this time to sleep.

Four

Still Waters

At around 7.30 on Sunday morning, 12 August, I woke from a deep sleep. Still groggy, I stayed in my bunk a while. Across from me David was dozing in his bunk, having been behind the navigation table for most of the night – no doubt he was dreaming about tides on our westward-bound course. I wondered how we were doing, whether there was much wind. It didn't feel like it from here; the companionway hatch was open and not much of a breeze came in through it. I clambered out of my bunk and looked out of *Grimalkin*'s slightly mucky, condensation-covered cabin window and saw Dorset's coast-line for the first time. Although somewhat indistinct, there was no mistaking the green rolling downs of Hardy's Wessex.

Up on deck, I saw that not much had changed during the night. There was a slight mist yet to lift – it always took a while for the early morning sun to heat up and burn the last of it off. The sea was lazy and flat and the winds were variable, noticeably lighter. I peered through the misty, hazy morning light for signs of *Green Dragon*, and I could see none.

'It looks like we're doing OK,' called Matt from the helm. 'What do you think?'

Undecided, I found myself scanning the horizon for signs of any other of the class-five yachts. Matt and I agreed that it was a little odd that there were no other boats in our class around us. The only boats in view were bigger and longer. We never assumed anything during a race, but Matt and I felt justified in thinking, rather excitedly, that *Grimalkin* could well be up front of our fifty or so competitors in class five.

Matt updated me on the latest weather forecast: force 4 to 5 south-westerly winds were predicted for the morning, increasing to force 7 or perhaps 8 later in the day. This was at odds with the winds we were sailing in, which were no more than force 2, but that was not unusual – the conditions of inshore waters, particularly round the headlands and bays of the English Channel, could vary from the forecast, particularly in the warmer, less predictable months of July and August. I knew from delivering yachts up and down this coast that a south-westerly sea breeze sometimes did not fill in until hours after it had been predicted. It was because of anomalies like these that crewmembers with local knowledge were so vital when racing a small yacht. Therefore, although frustrated by the lack of wind, none of us were greatly concerned.

My first four-hour watch period was fantastic. I'd had a good few hours' sleep and I was ready for anything. It started well, with a cup of coffee made by my watch-mate, Mike. Around the same age as me, he was easy to talk to, self-assured, always with a joke to tell. I knew that, like Dave, he was not as experienced as the rest of *Grimalkin*'s crew, but I found him fine to work alongside – physically strong, sure-footed and able to cope with most situations aboard. We went about our routine, alternating half-hour turns at the helm with making adjustments to keep *Grimalkin* going as quick as we could.

Intermittently Matt poked his head up from the cabin, wanting to know what was going on. He was young, exuberant, full of energy and seemed to be awake nearly all the time. Sailing in his dad's boat meant so much to him, and he was enjoying his first Fastnet Race at least as much as any of us.

'Better than work, eh, Nick?' he'd say.

'You bet, mate,' I'd reply.

Then he'd drop back below, calling just before he disappeared from view: 'Give us a shout if you need a hand with anything.'

Not much happened during this watch except the passing of two ships, one a container vessel, the other a coaster. Both sounded their foghorns in the mist. They were a fair distance from us and posed no threat but the sound of their foghorns brought David back up on deck. He checked our course, which was spot on. There was no wind change so there was nothing we could do, actively, other than keep our eyes peeled for 'cat's paws', tiny ripples on the surface of the water indicating wind.

To pass the time we played I Spy until we ran out of things to spy. Then we just sat in silence. Despite the frustrating lack of wind, there was a certain peace to be enjoyed in these dead calm waters. I spotted the dark shape of a cormorant in the distance – it looked reptilian, with its long thick neck and hooked beak. This bird was a favourite of mine. I wanted to get a closer look but it was keeping well clear. The only birds close to us were gulls, either floating in the water or circling round us in flight. Watching one hover above me made me think of a book I'd read recently, *Jonathan Livingstone Seagull* by Richard Bach. I loved this book, especially this line, which I never forgot: 'For most gulls it is not flying that matters, but eating. For Jonathan, though, it was not eating that mattered, but flight.' The serenity of the moment was disturbed by a familiar sound – it was Dave relieving himself on the transom again. Mike and I couldn't help but laugh. Matt popped his head above deck to see what the commotion was about.

'Keep the noise down, will you? Dad's trying to sleep,' he said.

Near the end of my watch the sun was shining fairly brightly through the mist and my eyes were sore from squinting.

When Matt and Dave came up to take over from us, we all stayed together in the cockpit for a while. The mood was good as we talked about the race and how we were doing. Not for the first time a discussion began about seeing, then rounding, the infamous Fastnet Rock in a day or so. I thought about what Matt and I had discussed earlier that morning – if, as we thought, we were leading our class, and we all kept our heads, then there was every chance of a victory in class five.

With that uplifting thought, I gave the horizon a quick 360-degree scan before going down to my bunk. I rarely had trouble catnapping, day or night. David was not so lucky – I could hear the sounds of him retching into a bucket, over and over. I offered him assistance, which he politely but firmly rejected. Best thing to do was let him sort himself out. Despite the lingering smell I drifted off to sleep.

At around 3pm my sleep was disturbed by David talking to his wife Gay via the VHF radio. This was the first of several arranged calls David was to make to Gay, giving her updates as to our progress. I heard him confirming to her that everyone was well and not to worry about a thing. He finished with the words 'over and out'. I smiled at him; he looked much better now, a bit of colour back in his face.

'She's going to phone everyone and let them know we are all fine.' He winked at me. 'Give me a hand with this, Nick.'

I hopped off my bunk and helped David mop the bilges out with a sponge and bucket. One of our skipper's characteristics I admired the most was his easiness in doing any of the most menial jobs on board.

After this task, hands wet, I replaced the floorboard, stowed the bucket and sponge, dried off, and returned to my still-warm bunk. I rested for a while before going back on deck for my second watch, from 4 until 8pm. Again, not much happened. The visibility was not brilliant and the wind was still holding at about force 2, if that – frustrating. Force 3 or 4 would have allowed us to carry full sail and at the same time gain some speed. Mike and I coaxed *Grimalkin* along, gently trimming her sheets in the shifting puffs of wind that were difficult to anticipate on the gentle swell of the English Channel. Later that afternoon, as we rounded Portland Bill – number four in my mind's eye – we saw that our hard work was paying off. With improved visibility we were still able to pick out class four, class three and even some stragglers from class two, and there was still no sign of *Green Dragon* – good. There was every chance we were ahead of her.

I was off watch at 8pm, but due back on a double shift from midnight until 8am, so as soon as I could I climbed down the companionway ladder to get some sleep. Dave was at the bottom, stuffing some thickly coated Marmite toast into his mouth, about to come up to start his watch. He always seemed to be eating. How he stayed so thin was a mystery to me; maybe being tall helped. I noticed he had left me the washing up. I was irritated, but bit it back. As I replaced the lid of the Marmite bottle, I read the ingredients label. Bloody hell, I thought, celery extract – that's why Dave is so flatulent.

I rinsed the contents of the sink and climbed into my bunk. Shit. My medication. I almost forgot. I reached up for my pills, took a couple, then, for peace of mind, counted the number that were left – more than enough. Just as I was about to doze off, David called down from the cockpit for me to move to a bunk on the opposite side of the cabin. This was to balance the boat correctly – not an unusual request in light winds.

It was dark outside when I woke. I looked at my watch: 11.45pm. I had slept well. There were quiet, muffled sounds in the cockpit above me, so I knew the weather had not changed. I was surprised the wind had still failed to fill in, all these hours later. I got up and dressed. Moving by the navigation table I glanced at the charts and saw that I had missed the passing of lighthouses five and six – Berry Head and Start Point.

Up on deck David, Gerry, Matt and Mike were having what seemed to be a serious conversation. The complete lack of wind, coupled with our slow speed, was beginning to give rise to concern about whether our fresh water and food would last. Aboard a small racing yacht there is limited space for provisions. Some yachts sacrificed provisions, which took up weight and space, for an extra sail – which is what we had done. If these weather conditions continued there would be no chance of us finishing in the five days David had estimated. Watching the sails limply flopping around through the mist and fog, I knew this was a realistic concern. If this weather continued the race might have to be cancelled. As far as I knew, despite a few close calls, this had not happened in the race's history.

I could sense that morale was dipping somewhat. For the Fastnet Race to be postponed or called off would be more than a mere inconvenience. This race was something we'd prepared for, all six of us, physically and mentally. Our preparation and our qualification for this one race had been meticulously planned.

David went below. After scanning several different broadcasts, he found a forecast. This, along with the others we had heard over the previous few hours, now really began to puzzle us. The conditions we were experiencing conflicted entirely with what had been forecast. The forecasters sounded too optimistic, too normal. We did not have, as they had suggested at one point, force 5 to 7 south-westerly winds. Rather, we had wind strength zero and wind direction zero.

'What are they on about?' Gerry said, shaking his head.

I shrugged. 'Buggered if I know . . . what do you think, Matt?'

Matt and Mike were equally stumped.

'Let's not get into a panic yet,' said David, coming back

up. 'There's nothing that would surprise me about August weather.' It was a clear attempt to dispel the anxiety that was building up. He continued, 'OK, Gerry and Nick . . . concentrate on getting as much out of her as you can. And you guys, go and get some rest.'

The first part of my watch, from midnight until 4am, was with Gerry – I was glad to spend some time with him. Soon into the watch we passed by the Eddystone and St Anthony's lighthouses, seven and eight on my list, but we saw neither because of reduced visibility. We kept our eyes peeled in the black murk. Vigilance was needed in the busy English Channel. We were crossing shipping lanes and there was always the possibility of collision.

Gerry and I spoke at length about the flat, still, almost lake-like waters we were sailing in. We both agreed that we had never experienced anything quite like this, quite so odd. It would be so easy to run into another boat, yacht, even a ship. Noises were weirdly muffled, the moist fog acting like a silencer on our movements. I told Gerry it reminded me of old black-and-white films of Dickens novels. On a couple of occasions, despite our best efforts, *Grimalkin* simply stopped, completely becalmed. This usually brought David or sometimes one of the off-watch crew up, trying to see what was going on. When there was any wind, it shifted direction too. On the rare occasion we got near to a fellow competitor, we could neither tell what class of boat it was nor whether it was longer, as the navigation lights were blurred in the fog-bound darkness.

Gerry was telling me how he wanted to progress in offshore racing and how this, his first Fastnet, had been one of his abiding ambitions – much like the rest of us. Later, as the damp atmosphere worsened, I noticed that he kept rubbing his hands together, intermittently at first, then more frequently as the night passed. His joints were beginning to ache, he said. I knew that he suffered from arthritis, and that it was fairly severe for a man so young, so this didn't surprise me. He hadn't told me about his arthritis himself; David had mentioned it on a previous race. I was relieved for Gerry that he was off watch at 4am, and could rest and get some warmth back into his joints.

Just after 3am David climbed out from the cabin and checked the log. He went back below and then returned a few minutes later, announcing a change of course to take advantage of the tide. I looked at the written log entries – our last three hours of effort had seen us travel a distance through the water of 17 miles, an average of just under 5 knots. Matt came up on deck at least 20 minutes before his watch was due to begin and relieved a tired and aching Gerry early. No sooner had Gerry gone below than Matt leaned towards me and whispered, 'Any ciggies there, Nick?'

That question had been a long time in coming. 'Not on me. Anyway, your dad's up and about. He'd shoot me.'

Matthew winked at me. 'What he doesn't know won't hurt him. Come on, where are they?'

I relented. 'In the Tupperware box.'

Matt sloped back down below. At 17, he was unusually confident both in person and as a sailor, but with this he could be slightly petulant – not unlike me. Our common bond, if there was one besides sailing, was that we both enjoyed family life, were close to our parents and had siblings we cared for. This was enough of a link for us to enjoy a laugh together, and was perhaps why we had more of a connection than either of us had with Dave or Mike. A few moments later he returned above deck and watchfully lit up. We shared the cigarette, like two silly kids who'd just found a butt on the top deck of a bus. This was what I liked about Matthew – without being irresponsible, he occasionally threw caution to the wind.

There was no sign of the fog clearing or the wind shifting but David's plotting of our course through this grey soup was a sound one. He and Gerry together gauged and worked the tides correctly. *Grimalkin* made her way over the ground, slowly criss-crossing westwards towards Land's End. As dawn broke around 5.30am, we could detect an airborne smell like freshly mown grass or compost – odd but recognisable to any experienced sailor. It was the smell of silage drifting from the fields off the West Country coastline. We knew the difference between dawn and sunrise, of course. Dawn was the time when the sun, still below the horizon, provided sufficient light for objects to become distinguishable. Sunrise was the moment when the leading edge of the sun appeared above the horizon. But there was insufficient light to distinguish anything at all. Not even the horizon itself was discernible. There was only blurred vision.

'Hey, Nick, watch out,' Matt said suddenly, pointing ahead. 'There's something over there . . . a lobster pot maybe?'

Looking to windward I saw he was right. Hardly distinguishable in the mist, there were in fact quite a few. 'Well spotted. I'm going to bear away a touch,' I said, making a small adjustment to the course.

It was not only other boats we had to beware of in these conditions. A mile or even two miles offshore, it was not uncommon in deep water to see long lines of lobster pots.

At the end of our watch, Matt pencilled information into *Grimalkin*'s log. We had covered around 26 miles over the water, a pitiful distance. The mood on board was seriously dampened – we needed some wind, a boost of some sort.

Exhausted, I went below, downed a mouthful of breakfast and climbed into the bliss of my bunk, still warm from its previous occupant. I overheard Matt talking to his dad.

'It's Monday the thirteenth already . . . can you believe it? Where does the time go?'

Yes, even in these strange, sluggish conditions, time does fly by. It was my last thought as I drifted off.

It seemed like I had been asleep only moments when I was wakened by my name being called loudly from the deck – it was Matthew. I opened my eyes and knew immediately that things were changing – for the better.

'There's a breeze beginning to fill in out here.'

It was 11.15am. I was still sleepy but the excitement in Matthew's voice fired me up. I wanted to see what was happening. I stepped up onto the deck and quickly saw that the oily, undulating pond-like surface had at last given up its smoothness to a longer, slightly rippled effect. Matt was right; the sea breeze had finally filled in. This felt different to the light, shifty winds of the previous days. It was fresher, more assured – as if it was here to stay.

The full crew was now working the boat, revelling in the ever-freshening breeze. At around 1pm we passed the Wolf Rock lighthouse – number 12 on my list. Several had been passed while I slept. The mist was slowly lifting and we were beginning to spot bigger boats. David listened to the 1.55pm BBC shipping forecast for the Fastnet area. It told him that the winds would be south-westerly, force 4 to 5, locally force 6 to 7, veering in direction westerly with occasional rain and showers. After the wind had changed direction and increased slightly, David set a course for the Fastnet Rock and awaited the next forecast from the BBC, due at 5.50pm.

By 2.30pm the winds had settled enough in strength and direction for Matthew to rig the spinnaker. That done, *Grimalkin* accelerated like a racehorse down the back straight, creating a great, arcing quarter wave that would have graced a yacht twice her length. She had settled beautifully in on her new course, her speed almost doubling. God, this felt good: fresh breeze, fresh boat. The increasing wind and the raising of the spinnaker seemed to lift everybody's spirits – now there was verve and vitality on board. Our worries regarding lack of water and food supplies disappeared with the flukey weather.

By 3pm we were flying along doing a constant 8 knots, and over the next hour this rose to 10 or 12. Terrific, absolutely glorious – *Grimalkin* at her very best, performing wonderfully. It seemed that the theory about August weather had proved correct. It was a paradox. Whatever weather system was behind, above or, as it now seemed, ahead of us, it was creating unusual effects. The sea's surface took on an unusual contour as if it had been pushed, shoved along by a long, large fetch of a wind. *Grimalkin* picked up her skirts and flew.

By the time my watch finished at 4pm, adrenaline was pumping through my body, and my head was the clearest it had been since the start of the sluggish weather. My right hand and biceps were aching from pumping the spinnaker's sheet but I knew a couple of hours' rest would settle that. Before I went below I looked round me, taking it all in, imagining what it must have been like for the crews on the very first Fastnet Race, back in 1925. In the distance, about half a mile away, were some bigger yachts – still no sign of our nemesis, *Green Dragon*, though; maybe she was ahead. There was no point in thinking about this now. I was tired and there was still a long way to go in this great race.

I climbed into one of the blue canvas bunks – mine for the next four hours. I peered out of the cabin window. Even though the Perspex of the window was blue-tinted, the sea beyond looked as if it had turned a deeper, darker shade of grey-green, as if under pressure. Pondering the diversity of the weather, excited but exhausted, my thoughts turned to the first sighting of the Fastnet and then the rounding of it. If the wind kept up this would happen during my next watch period, beginning at midnight. Then my thoughts began to fade and much-needed sleep intervened.

Five

Ochre Sky

I was disturbed from a deep sleep by the increased volume of seawater passing by outside just inches from my head, and a series of loud winching noises that reverberated through the fibreglass cockpit floor above me. I was surprised, if not a little irritated, to see that it was only 5.30pm – I had been asleep less than an hour. As I sat up, I became aware that *Grimalkin* had taken on a new angle, a different motion in the water. The cabin was empty; the whole crew were on deck. This could mean only one thing: they were making a sail change. Despite my lack of sleep I jumped off my moving bunk and quickly dressed. I had to get back on deck and see what was going on.

From the third step of the companionway ladder I could see *Grimalkin*'s mainsail and genoa – they looked superb, brilliant white, contrasting beautifully with the darker colours of the sea and skyline. A rush of adrenaline surged through my body. Moving up the ladder I felt stronger, gustier winds surrounding me, then I saw greyish clouds scudding across the sky. There was also a greatly increased chop in the water – some of the waves must have been up at around 20 feet. But most noticeable of all was *Grimalkin's* speed, which must have increased by at least 4 or 5 knots in the short time that I had been below, asleep. I was fired up about the prospect of getting out of the last vestige of lee provided by the English mainland and beginning to sail deep into the Irish Sea.

I stepped out from the companionway and into the cockpit. Gerry was at the helm.

'Jesus . . . she's going like a train,' I called over to him.

Clearly exhilarated, Gerry smiled back. 'It's incredible . . . just bloody incredible . . . it's only a few short hours since we had no wind at all. If this keeps up a course record could be set . . . mark my words.'

It was then that I noticed the combination of colours in the sky – reds, oranges and ochres, weird but exquisite, unlike anything I had seen before. The reds reminded me of colours I'd seen in a Rothko oil painting. I joined Matt, Mike and Dave on the windward rail looking intently to the west, all of us transfixed by the beauty of this skyline. With sunset not due until around 8.30pm, I was baffled by the colour scheme this deep orange sun created in the sky so early in the day.

'What an amazing combination of colours,' I said. 'I don't think I've ever seen anything like it.'

We were all agreed. None of us had ever seen anything that could touch this. I regretted not having a camera. How could I describe this in words to anyone back home?

I took a moment to check what kind of position we were now in. Yachts that had been to windward of us had gone. The only boats I could see, two or three larger ones from class four, were slightly ahead, holding the same course as *Grimalkin*.

The vista before and around us was clean, vibrant and open. More than anything it was obvious we were the only class-five boat in the vicinity. I couldn't help smiling to myself at the thought of us leading our class. As *Grimalkin* surfed, planed through the water, she looked neat and fresh, her gleaming white topsides and sky-blue deck paint reflecting light as if she'd just been scrubbed, both hull and deck.

Mike spoke. 'The horizon . . . it seems like it's changing all the time . . .'

I had to agree. The horizon was looking stranger, more uneven, almost ruffling itself up by the minute. I was mesmerised. I wondered if I was experiencing some kind of optical illusion, so I turned away and looked back, several times – but it wasn't an illusion. Rapidly, in front of our eyes, it was becoming more and more distorted, the weird colours of the sky reflecting off the clouds. Abstract and irregular, refracting beams of strangely coloured light onto the sea's odd, undulated surface.

Matthew began to voice what we were probably all thinking. 'I wonder what it means . . . more wind or less? What do you guys think?'

Nobody ventured an opinion because nobody knew. There were any number of possible theories, from old wives' tales to sailing lore – red sky at night, shepherd's delight; yellow skies bring out sea devils. Pa used to tell me that a dramatic sky like this was 'a wolf in sheep's clothing'. Was this sky a sign of bad weather? Or was it just one of those stunning Fastnet sunsets that Dick Langton had told me so much about?

Despite the thrill the fantastic turnaround in the weather had given us, a level of anxiety was also growing among some of the crew. Another thing I had noticed but didn't voice was that all the gulls had disappeared – there was no longer a bird in sight.

David came up from the cabin and began discussing a course change with Gerry, then he too looked up.

'That's a pretty odd-looking sky.'

'What do you think, David?' Dave's anxiety was clearly showing through.

'There's a forecast due in ten minutes,' David replied calmly. 'If there's anything untoward up, we'll know about it soon enough.' He smiled. 'I'm sure it's just a beautiful sunset we're witnessing . . . enjoy it, guys.' He went back down below.

I didn't want to leave this extraordinary sight, but I knew I ought to try to get some more sleep. I descended the companionway ladder. David was back at his navigation table with the radio tuned in, ready for the 5.50pm BBC shipping forecast. I climbed into my bunk and began thinking again about rounding the rock, the Fastnet. This time, though, my thoughts were somewhat distracted by the colour spectrum I had just witnessed in the sky.

The BBC forecast was of winds from a mainly southerly direction, force 4, force 6, increasing to force 8, changing direction to north-westerly later. This forecast did indeed indicate nothing untoward. These wind strengths weren't something to be worried about; we'd all coped with force 8 on numerous occasions before. I closed my eyes.

A short time later I heard Gerry come down into the cabin. Dave had taken over the helm from Gerry to allow

him to cook up a stew his wife Margaret had made for us –
a treat we were promised as Monday's main meal. He was
completely soaked, having been at the helm for the last few
wind-driven hours. He winked at me, taking off his dripping
wet lifejacket and harness.

'Don't get too cosy, Nick. It's getting pretty rough out
there.'

The swaying motion on board had become so strong he
was forced to use the webbing galley strap round his hips to
maintain balance, but this didn't stop him from telling a few
jokes as he went about his cooking, mostly about our newly
elected Prime Minister, Margaret Thatcher, and the handbag
she always seemed to carry that looked like it could – and
would – be used to concuss anyone who opposed her. Gerry
knew how to lighten the mood. I even heard a chuckle coming
from David's direction.

As *Grimalkin* rose to a swell, some cans of food fell off
the galley's shelf and hit the cabin sole with a crack, rolling
across and knocking David's feet. Retrieving them, I jammed
them, securely, back into their place.

The result of Gerry's labours smelt delicious. I got up
and helped him pass the thick plastic mugs of stew round the
boat. It tasted as good as it smelt. I was off watch so I did
the washing-up. Like Gerry, I had to brace myself against the
galley lockers to do so. Mike, also off watch, was asleep in
the bunk opposite. Tired and well fed, I climbed back up into
my bunk and closed my eyes.

At around 7.30pm I was woken by a good deal of
increased movement above my head. The on-watch crew –
Matt, Gerry and Dave – were clearly moving from the
weather rail into the relative shelter of the cockpit. I was

tired and I needed to get some kind of decent rest in before my midnight watch, but such was the motion of the boat I found it difficult to get back to sleep. I looked to the opposite bunk and saw that Mike was also awake. With conditions like this below, it was not surprising the crew above had moved to the cockpit. David was still at the navigation table, poring over charts, checking our course and listening to the radio.

'How are we doing?' I asked.

He looked up. 'We're just passing the Bishop Rock lighthouse. We're doing good, really good . . . but with these winds I bet everyone is.'

Bishop Rock lighthouse? We *were* doing well – this was number 16, the last lighthouse before we reached our midpoint destination, Fastnet Rock.

Just then, Dave leaned in through the companionway. 'Sleeping peacefully, are we?'

I was about to make an irritable retort when David raised his eyebrows at me. 'Come on, Nick, he's young.'

David was right – I was just tired. Again I closed my eyes, and rocked my body with the motion of the boat, trying to entice some sleep. It didn't work, but at least I was more relaxed and resting. Over the next half an hour, lying in my bunk, I noticed that weather conditions were changing at an almost astonishing rate.

Mike, in his bunk, must have noticed too. 'There's some gale blowing out there.'

David nodded. 'It's certainly building.'

I could tell by David's tone that he was puzzled. The next official shipping forecast from the BBC, for all areas, was not due until after midnight, so David tuned in and out of stations until he finally found a forecast for our area. It was in French, but we were familiar with French broadcasts, having relied on them before, and we understood most of what was being relayed. The calm, clear voice anticipated winds of between force 8 and force 10.

Mike immediately sat up in his bunk. 'Oh my God, did I hear that right?'

David concurred, turning up the set's volume to its highest point. The forecaster repeated this warning conclusively – force 10 winds in the Fastnet and Lundy area, the very area we were sailing into. With the volume turned right up, the crew above deck picked it up too.

'What the hell is going on?' shouted Gerry from the cockpit.

All six of us knew, as did every sailor on this race, the deadly difference between a gale-force 8 and a storm-force 10 wind. Force 8 was a bad headache, no more – force 10 was a brain haemorrhage. The winds, and particularly the wave heights, would be multiplied by two, perhaps even more. These were not the conditions for any small yacht to sail into. Matt and Gerry clambered down into the cabin, leaving Dave at the helm. This new information brought with it an increased level of confusion and apprehension on board – everyone began talking at once.

'OK . . . OK, EVERYBODY!' yelled David across the noise. 'We need information and quickly . . . and for that I need silence.'

He got it. Three nerve-racking, silent minutes passed before we overheard a French boat calling Start Point Radio. This was against the rules of the race, but in light of the news we had just heard, not surprising. The boat's French-accented skipper asked the coastguards to confirm that the BBC's 17.50 forecast was correct. We waited for the response, nobody uttering a word. Finally, the coastguards confirmed that the 17.50 BBC forecast had been the correct one. A wave of relief went through the cabin – thank God, our race was not over.

'Should we maybe think about a course change . . . as a precaution?' said Mike to David.

This suggestion was most likely anxiety-based but it was a valid one, and David answered carefully. He reassured us with his conviction in the BBC forecast and his faith in ours and *Grimalkin*'s ability to cope with the anticipated conditions. He also pointed out, quite rightly, that there was no reason to think about turning round or seeking the nearest port, as any course change or abandonment of the race by our fellow competitors would have been apparent by the reappearance of the larger classes of boats. We would easily have seen them returning in the dim early-evening light.

After the windless inactivity of the last couple of days, David did not have to try hard to sell these reassurances. A renewed sense of exuberance, excitement and anticipation on board motivated us all, and reminded us of greater things to come. As far as I could see, there was absolutely no disagreement or friction among the crew – we all backed our skipper's decision unreservedly. With that, David instructed us to get ourselves and *Grimalkin* fully prepared for the night's leg. Our predicted course was to be long and uninterrupted, out into the Irish Sea, towards the rock. Without need of further encouragement, the whole crew, including David, got togged up, layering up to protect ourselves against the cold, wet and windy conditions that had been forecast.

On deck I noticed the sun had disappeared entirely, leaving not a trace of the wonderful colour display we had seen earlier. The sky was filling with dark, fast-moving clouds that were closing in on *Grimalkin*, as if a curtain was being pulled round us, a zip closing it.

It looked and felt strange – like it was not quite day and not quite night – like we were stuck somewhere in the middle, uncomfortably so. It was something like an early-morning eclipse of the sun I had witnessed some years before. That day had been dull, the sun concealed by low, dark cloud. When the moon eclipsed the sun, we were left with an unnatural-looking light, as though it were artificial. I wanted to say something to the others but time was of the essence – *Grimalkin* had to be prepared, and quickly.

Knowing we were in for a substantial blow, things needed to be made secure, tidy and shipshape. All loose, unused halyards were tightened, made fast. The kicking strap, the vang, which held the main boom down, flattening the mainsail, was winched, sweated in, tensioned as hard as we could get it. The spinnaker and jockey poles were checked, clipped and lashed. Working together, we got *Grimalkin* ready for the worsening conditions. Ready as any boat in the race could have been. By about 8.30pm we were done. David turned on the navigation lights – red and green at the bow, white at the masthead and stern. At the same time he checked the batteries of the separate, emergency navigation lights.

Mike and I knew our midnight watch was going to be long, wet and tiring, so we decided to try to get a couple of hours' sleep in. We removed only our oilskin tops, leaving our seaboots on, in case we were called. David was back down below too, at the navigation table. I wanted to talk to him, discuss the race, but I knew he was concentrating hard on the charts. I tried to stay still but I couldn't. There was no chance of sleep.

Just after 9pm I got up again and got fully dressed, this time putting on an additional waterproof jacket over my orange oilskins. I heard *Grimalkin*, slightly free, a couple of points off the wind, at speed. Her bows plunging into seas, no longer surging over them, she was now forcing her way through the increased swell. Often her lee bow slapped onto a crest, making her yaw, the noise of it echoing up in her forepeak. As I moved across the cabin I was forced to grab onto the navigation table for support, knocking into David.

'Clip on out there, Nick. It's building far faster than expected.'

David's expression told me that he was concerned by the speed with which conditions were worsening. I looked up through the half-open companionway hatch and saw seawater cascading into the cockpit. The cockpit was self draining but my crewmates were completely drenched. As I climbed the companionway ladder I heard a spooky sound – odd, almost like an animal screech. I realised it was the number-three headsail's starboard sheet stretching, straining. It was now darker, and freezing; gusting wind whipped round my protected ears. I blinked and tried to focus, tried to adjust to the dark after the relative brightness of the cabin. I clipped my safety harness to the stout U-bolt before climbing the final four steps out onto the deck and into the cockpit. Sitting down safely with Dave, Gerry and Matt, I got a full view of the conditions – what a transformation. The pace of change was incredible. Some waves were now at about 35 feet, and along with their increased height they appeared to have a different pattern – they were longer, steeper.

'Jesus, she's really cracking along,' I shouted over to Matt on the helm. 'How's the wind direction . . . is it changing?'

'Yeah, all the time,' he yelled back. 'It keeps heading us.'

As if to illustrate the point, *Grimalkin* heeled to a heavy, strong gust. Matt reacted by pushing the tiller away from him, heading up into the gust. This took the pressure off the sails, feathering, depowering them. Like an aircraft's wing stalling as a result of too steep a climb, *Grimalkin* responded and settled to a more even angle of heel, dumping a sizeable wave on her foredeck as she did so. Once she was steady, Matt, his face vibrant, shouted more information to me.

'It's happening more and more often, I can't use the extension – too strong.' He was sitting securely inboard on the cockpit seat, the wooden tiller gripped by both hands, the long metal extension unused. 'The wind hasn't even peaked yet – we're making great time. This could be our year, Nick.'

It certainly looked like it from here. If these winds kept up, there was every chance this could be our year. Matt then told me they had shortened sail because of the increasing, unsteady wind strength. While I was below they had put two slab reefs in the mainsail. They had also changed headsails, down to the number-two, then the number-three jib; this made the boat safer in the current wind.

I looked over at the combined speedometer/anemometer dial, adjacent to the compass. The white needle that read wind speed was swinging wildly, registering between 30 and 35 knots of wind, the top end of a force 6, near on force 7. This was good, really good.

I knew that we were likely to experience up to a force 8 in the next hour or two. I also now knew for sure that with these wind strengths it would be during my midnight to 4am watch that we would round the rock. And I knew that the plotted course we were sailing into, where the influence of the Gulf Stream was strong, had one of the highest tidal ranges in the world.

David poked his hooded head above deck and clipped himself on. Standing in the companionway he shouted over to Gerry, 'Have you ever seen winds build this quickly?'

Gerry shook his head. David was right – it had been only 15 minutes or so since I had come up on deck and I, too, had seen the weather change. The waves, more powerful and squall-driven, were now up to at least 40 feet.

'I'll spell you, Matt. Take over for a bit – hold on.' Unclipping and reclipping himself, David took the tiller from Matthew's grip. Looking back and forth from the compass dial to the speedometer/ anemometer dial, I watched him as with his quick brain he immediately computed the wind speed and direction. I saw him mouth the word '*merde*' and saw the glance he shot Gerry – a glance that said it all. He was not happy. This escalation of the weather was beyond comprehension, even David's.

'Course held OK?' David said to Matthew. He was keeping relative composure in his voice.

Matt nodded. 'It's seriously blowing ... thirty-five knots, eh? Much more and I'll think about another reef in the main. Maybe even down to the storm jib?'

David agreed. 'Matt, Mike . . . let's make it a safe and quick change.'

The smallest sail *Grimalkin* possessed, her storm jib, was

prepared and hoisted, replacing the number three, which was bundled through the forehatch. This took about 15 minutes. By the end of it everyone was knackered, but immediately the smaller sail was sheeted in, *Grimalkin* seemed to utter a sigh of relief. The relief was short-lived, however. There was no respite in the wind or seas. Both were increasing in strength, height and frequency.

It was now 9.35pm, more than two hours before my watch with Mike. From the port side of the cockpit, I watched white-crested waves regularly flood the foredeck, and listened to the thudding and thumping against the bows and on the deck. Behind us the seas were bigger, individual waves stacked high, their heights building at an extraordinary rate. The wind speed had increased. The anemometer needle, whirling round, now showed force 8.

'Do you think it's peaking?' said Mike to David.

'It should be.'

We were getting repeatedly drenched with freezing-cold, salty water. Our tightly drawn hoods didn't help much. Spray blowing viciously in our faces made it difficult to see. The sky was darker than dark; the full moon masked and invisible. There was an occasional glimpse of low, fast-moving clouds. Most noticeable were the ever-increasing gusts of wind – they built up inexorably, gust upon gust, increasing the noise level around us.

Grimalkin, our solid, loyal workhorse, continued to press her way through the worsening seas. I watched David, with Matthew at his side. Both looked from masthead to compass, masthead to anemometer. I glanced down at the anemometer needle. Shit, it was 45, sometimes touching 50 knots. This was the top end of force 8 and 9 approaching force 10. It was happening in the space of minutes.

The compass was swinging wildly now. Each time *Grimalkin* reached the top of one of the huge seas, the compass's card dampened and it stopped swinging. It showed David a course of 330 degrees, but the course kept changing, determined by the gusting wind and seas.

'Take over the helm, Gerry,' yelled David. 'I have to try and check our position, check for a forecast . . . try and find out what the hell's going on here.' The last plot David had taken was at around 5.15pm.

It was a struggle but David managed to transfer the tiller to Gerry, who looked at the compass, getting his bearings. David made his way towards the cabin. The wind was so ferocious he could barely keep upright. He trod on our feet, knocked into our knees and then stumbled, falling forward – luckily grabbing the lip of the coach-roof hatch, halting a bad fall. He paused on the companionway ladder, cupped his hands round his mouth and shouted: 'Inflate your jackets. Thumbs up, everyone.'

I released the yellow inflation tube from the left collar of my lifejacket, blew into it, then put my right thumb in the air, indicating to David I had done it. The others did the same.

Illuminated in the companionway by the dim cabin light, David gave further instructions. 'Right, the mainsail has to come off.'

We were in a full-blown, volatile storm. David wanted a clear deck, and a clear cabin-top for ease of movement and communication. He also wanted the on-watch helmsman to have a clear view ahead, currently obscured by the mainsail and its boom.

David went below and we set about removing the mainsail – not easy in conditions like these. Matt clipped onto the windward jackstay and, after looking back at us, no smile, crawled forward to the mast to gather in the now flogging sail. Spray bounced off its leach as waves swept the foredeck. I saw a sail batten fly out of its pocket, missing Mike's head by inches. Crouched over the coach-roof-mounted winch, Mike took the halyard's tension by putting two turns round the winch and wrapping the halyard round his open fist – I released the clutch handle. With the mainsail's halyard now freed, Matt pulled and yanked on its boltrope like a man possessed, inching the sail down the mast.

As I worked with Matt and Mike, I was leaning forward in the cockpit. All of us continually faltered in the face of the elements. Even with our harnesses clipped on and our life-jackets fully inflated, we were exposed and vulnerable. Finally, the mainsail was off, tightly flaked, wrapped to the boom. The boom was securely lashed to the deck and control lines made fast. We retreated to the relative safety of the cockpit.

From that point on we saw only ourselves, the boat and the weather. As we sat there, waiting for news from our skipper, one thing was for sure: the atmosphere on this boat had changed. Dave was aft of me, close by. I saw the whites of his eyes against the dark of his oilskin hood. He caught my glance.

'Do you think this lot will blow itself out soon, Nick?'

It was an earnest question, and I had no idea of the answer. It was now very clear to me that this sometimes irri-tating but nonetheless likeable young man was understan-dably frightened. I nodded, reassuringly. 'It should do, soon, all right.'

But my instincts told me otherwise. I mulled over the disparate forecasts we'd heard, in particular the BBC's at

68

5.50pm. I had listened to many, many BBC shipping forecasts and had always accepted what was said, good as gospel.
Tonight, though, was different. The forecasters had not seen
the ochre sky. If they had, would they have revised the forecast? Pulling up the left sleeve of my oilskin, I pressed the
button of my LCD watch, illuminating its face: 10.15pm.
Time was flying.

David regained the deck, struggled into the cockpit and
told us that he had not been able to get any more information, from the radio or the VHF, about the weather situation,
nor had he been able to update his last plot. He remained
calm but he looked shaken.

'OK . . . we're going to close up below and all stay in the
cockpit.'

The washboards were put in place and the sliding
companionway hatch closed tight so no water could find its
way below. Everything was as secure as we could possibly
make it, both below and above deck. The six of us now
huddled together in the open cockpit. We were headed for
the unforgiving Irish Sea, all nigh-on ten thousand square
miles of it. Were any boat to founder, I thought, lifeboats
would come from both coasts, from Waterford, maybe Cork,
Baltimore on the Irish side, from Penzance, Newquay on the
Cornish side, St Mary's in the Scillies – they could come,
sure. But would they find?

That damn multicoloured sunset, that ochre sky – that
had been bad news, beautiful but malign. David had based
his judgement on the BBC shipping forecast, as I was sure
our fellow competitors also had. The French forecast of force
10 gales that David had overheard, the one we had been told
to ignore, must have been correct.

'Try heaving-to,' David shouted to Gerry.

This was a common tactic and the obvious next step in a heavy storm. It meant setting the boat on a predetermined course into the oncoming sea, unmanned apart from one crewmember on watch – almost the equivalent of autopilot. This would be achieved by first determining the safest course, then lashing the tiller securely in order for that course to be maintained. The idea was that the yacht could ride out the storm safely. It would also allow the crew to get some much-needed rest and food, while they waited for the wind and weather to subside.

We tried this tactic two, three, four times, but *Grimalkin* was having none of it, simply refusing to stay where she was put. Gerry tried hard, very hard, we all did, but the seas were too steep. She slid down the faces of waves I'd never seen the like of before. The wind was gusting so hard that we kept risking a broach on a wave top, being turned side on to the wind and the sea, which would leave the hull vulnerable. And a serious broach could lead to a knockdown or capsize.

David was, as we all were, nonplussed over *Grimalkin*'s refusal to heave-to. What other course of action could he take? Heaving-to in big boats or boats with long keels was easier; I had done it many times before to ride out storms. But as I looked at the conditions that surrounded us, I began to think that no boat, of any length or keel shape, could have ridden this out.

We were caught in the middle of a phenomenal weather pattern, something none of us had experienced before. And we were now far out in the western approaches. It would be fatal to simply turn round on a reciprocal course – the seas were too steep. Somehow, somewhere, somebody had got this forecast desperately wrong. We were left with no option but to tough the night out. We had already sailed into the eye of this unforeseen storm.

Grimalkin had reached the point of no return.

Six

Off the Scale

It was 11.25pm and there was no sign of the storm subsiding. In fact, the barometer was falling, which meant only one thing – there was worse to come. *Grimalkin* was already fighting her way through mammoth walls of water; how could she cope with anything greater than this?

Gerry was still at the helm. I could just about see him through the mayhem between us. He was sawing away as best he could, the tiller almost thrust from his grasp as he directed *Grimalkin* uphill through monstrous waves. Each time the boat mounted then crested a wave, he prepared for the smashing of her bows into the trough at the bottom. He hung on grimly; it looked as if his freezing hands were hurting badly.

A loud, gunfire-like noise sounded – all eyes scoured the decks for the source. It turned out to be nothing more than the storm jib and its sheet being whipped against the starboard shrouds. Unnerved but relieved, all eyes went back on watch. I noticed suddenly that we were sailing far too close into the wind. So must the others, because at once everyone started yelling.

'To the RIGHT, Gerry . . . PULL THE HELM UP!'

With all the commotion, Gerry had had a momentary lapse in concentration. Almost before we knew it, *Grimalkin*'s bows became extremely vulnerable, leaving us fully exposed to the extreme fury of oncoming wind and waves, almost throwing the boat aback. Had we been taken aback, we would have pivoted on the peak, the highest, most powerful and dangerous part of the wave. As it was, we barely escaped capsizing.

David understood that the level of effort Gerry had spent keeping *Grimalkin* on track had taken its toll. His ability to concentrate on his task had gone; his momentary lapse had put us all in danger. David at once took over, instructing Gerry to go below to try and get warm, get dry and feed himself. Gerry was done in – exhausted. He looked as if he might throw up. Mike and Dave slid the coach-roof hatch forward and removed the two vertical washboards for Gerry to go below. I didn't fancy his chances down there as I watched him descend the companionway ladder, half sliding into the chaos below deck. Even over the deafening racket above, loud noises could be heard coming from down below. Cans of food were flying around at head height. David shouted for me to take over the helm. Making sure I was secure – clipped to a strongpoint on the boat – I made my way across the cockpit, falling against the legs of Mike, Dave and Matt.

Once I was sitting where Gerry had sat, I knew why he could no longer continue. All that I had witnessed from the forward end of the cockpit was now magnified beyond belief. Perched up here at the helm, right back aft, God knows how far above the true surface of the sea – 40 feet, maybe more – the sight was breathtaking. The seas appeared higher than twice the length of *Grimalkin* at times.

David passed me the wooden tiller and as I took control of the boat at first I felt excitement. But this feeling swiftly turned to one of horror, then fear. I saw and felt the power and magnitude of these black, storm-ridden seas with their white-capped peaks. The strength of the winds was now fully apparent – they blew from every direction, leaving me bodily dishevelled and mentally bewildered. Almost at once, I was thinking the thoughts and looking the looks that I had seen on the faces of Matt and David at the helm an hour or so before, particularly the quizzical, rhetorical look that our skipper David had given me.

Keeping *Grimalkin* pointed into the wind was proving gruelling, near impossible. She fought the waves as best she could, but it would take only the smallest lapse in concentration at the peak of one of the waves to send her aback – as Gerry had almost done. It felt as if the storm jib was overpowering her. The storm jib, *Grimalkin*'s smallest foresail, was tiny in area and made out of the strongest sailcloth, but on this course, with these seas and in this wind strength, it was still far too big. If we weren't to be completely overwhelmed, wiped out by this storm, it had to come off.

As if sensing my thoughts, David yelled, through cupped hands, to the crew: 'We have to get the storm jib down.'

After a disjointed discussion, which I could barely hear, about who was going to do what, David remained in the cockpit while Matt, Mike and Dave started preparing themselves. Eventually it was Matt who ventured up onto the violently bucking foredeck to see the storm jib gathered in. I was glad of this decision – his surefootedness had already been proven up there an hour or so earlier. From where I was sitting, all I could see of him was his silhouetted profile, white seawater spray crashing against his back. Ever so carefully he clipped himself on at the mast, then slowly knelt. Keeping a continuous watch for rogue waves, he began to gather in the soaking wet, flogging sail.

All the while David looked on, willing his son to hold firm.

Matt was finally finished; Dave and Mike leaned forward and lowered the halyard. Then all three of them tied the storm jib securely to the guardrails and stanchions of the foredeck so it could not blow free and tangle itself round *Grimalkin*'s shuddering mast. I saw relief, even a brief glimmer of pride, as David helped his son back down. Everyone, including Gerry – who was now back on deck having eaten and changed – huddled back into the relative safety of the cockpit.

We were all drained by the relentless slamming and pounding, and once more the respite we fought for was agonisingly short-lived. The effect of *Grimalkin* being bare-poled – having no sails up whatsoever – quickly became apparent. It was not good. There was no way, absolutely no way that she was going to keep her bows into the wind and point into the direction of the ever-increasing wind and waves. This was a shock for David, for us all. This was dreadful news; it couldn't have been worse. If she had done as we expected and remained pointing into the wind and seas, then we would have had time to tie the tiller and could then have followed one of the prescribed, well-known and well-practised methods of riding out heavy weather. This attempt had failed utterly. We were being totally overwhelmed.

The seas were now like bloody great blocks of flats but twice as wide – it was a manic, surreal, alien environment. From my heightened position at the helm, I looked over the crew's heads, down into the waves. While searching for a flat spot to aim for, it became more and more obvious to me that *Grimalkin* was in danger of being pitch-poled. Her bow, plunging into the face of a wave, risked being overtaken by the stern, which would cause her to cartwheel through the water. We would then be thrown forwards and downwards by gravity, and brought up short by the tension of our harness lines. This is one of the worst possible consequences of downwind sailing. Now, here, upwind, sailing under bare poles in heavy weather, we were in the same danger.

I could see what the others could not – and it occurred to me that we might have a chance if we streamed every spare sheet, guy and warp out behind us. Then by bearing off we could turn the boat round and run with the seas, the wind and waves behind us. This procedure, again, was a well-known and prescribed tactic against heavy wind and seas, used as an alternative when heaving to was not an option. The idea was that the trailed lines – two lines of 150 metres, from the rear of *Grimalkin* – would induce some drag, slowing the boat down. Trailing lines also had the effect of breaking up the patterns of waves behind the stern of the boat, thus breaking wave crests – the most dangerous part of a wave – prematurely. This lessened the probability of a huge wave crest dumping itself onto the stern or deck of the boat. The last thing *Grimalkin* wanted now were huge waves breaking over her stern and us, her crew.

I told David my idea. After observing the situation from my position, he concurred – we had to try something. Doing this would mean a course change, but that didn't matter. Steering away from our destination did not make resuming the race impossible – anything was possible at sea. There was no reluctance from my crewmates over this decision to change tactics and run before the gargantuan seas. We were concentrating on the here and now. But I'm sure that everyone on board knew that our race was done. Our Fastnet was over.

While we prepared for the next move, I glimpsed worried expressions beneath oilskin hoods. I stayed on the tiller, while the rest of the crew opened all of *Grimalkin*'s cockpit lockers, locating every possible length of suitable rope or line, including mooring warps. Then everyone, with cold hands, fumbled with reef knots, sheepshanks and bowlines, making up two separate lengths of warp to tow. Once done, David prepared the crew so that when I swung *Grimalkin* round, with the sea, they could deploy the lines over the side without them twisting and further endangering the boat.

Before attempting this precarious turn through the wind, I had to get my timing in sync with the seas – the forces generated by these waves were immense. If my timing was out, *Grimalkin* would capsize. I was deeply afraid. Sitting on the floor of the cockpit, knees bent with both feet planted against the cockpit's side, gave me extra leverage on the tiller. I carefully timed *Grimalkin*'s movement between the troughs and peaks, then, judging what I deemed to be the safest time to turn, I signalled to David that I was ready to go.

Never before had I exerted as much pressure on a tiller – at one point I was sure it would snap – but gradually *Grimalkin* responded to the angle of her rudder and I felt her begin to swing. Midway through the turn she heeled at an extraordinary angle and her pitch changed – taken by surprise, I nearly had the tiller yanked from my arms. I craned my neck round to the seas and saw my crewmates, Gerry,

Matt, Mike and Dave, streaming the warps under David's watchful eye and sweeping gestures. As *Grimalkin*'s bows dipped into a trough, I centred the shuddering, vibrating tiller to complete our 180-degree turn. Almost everything had gone to plan, the warps were successfully streamed and *Grimalkin* was roughly on the course we anticipated; most noticeable was the lessening of the cacophony around our ears. The pressure was off somewhat – or so we thought.

Mere seconds after *Grimalkin* completed her turn, the wind noise returned with a vengeance and the deadly helter-skelter ride began. Travelling now at a far greater speed, we had even less control. As the first wave smacked beneath her I was nearly ousted from the cockpit. My hands clamped on the tiller, I pulled myself back up and sat as far into the cockpit seat as I could. We were now travelling 'downhill' – being blown along with the wind, rather than against it; with the seas rather than against or into them – away from our supposed destination, the Fastnet lighthouse. It was a bit like putting your foot fully down on the accelerator pedal of a sports car while travelling down a very steep hill. This down-wind route we had chosen was proving hazardous and it became obvious that *Grimalkin* could no longer be helmed by just one person. I motioned this to David – promptly, he instructed my on-watch partner, Mike, to join me on the helm. We now jointly guided her at ludicrous speeds and dangerous angles down the faces of massive waves. Even though we were no more than an arm's length apart, we had difficulty communicating. Our crewmates helped, pointing out bigger waves chasing us from behind. The view ahead was of row after row of white-crested ridges.

We squinted ahead, lip-reading the shouts of the others

as we tried to guide *Grimalkin* through, over, into, and some-times under walls of water. As well as the wind-borne spray, *Grimalkin* was creating her own enormous wake: sheets of water raced up her topsides, many feet above us, as she accel-erated at what seemed to be the velocity of a 30-foot waterski. To add to our worsening situation, the lines we had streamed did not have the anticipated effect. While they helped to slow the boat – the crests of the waves behind us were broken by them – phosphorescent spray was flying off them, with the rollers beneath the crests continuing to overwhelm us. Even worse, the chance of *Grimalkin* pitch-poling, cartwheeling through the water, was now even more likely. This tactic was not designed for such immense seas, but how could we have known?

The main priority for Mike and me now on the helm was to prevent *Grimalkin* from either pitch-poling at the bottom of a trough or broaching on the wave's top, its peak. As we sat, scared stiff, picking our course through these black iceberg-sized seas, it took all of our effort, concentration and physical strength to keep *Grimalkin* upright. We pushed and pulled the tiller with cold aching arms and blistered hands, guiding the boat into the next black abyss. Matt, Gerry and Dave sat opposite us in the cockpit, yelling or pointing when a bigger than usual wave came thundering up behind the boat.

We had all endured broaches and even knockdowns before. It is common, while racing, for small, medium or large boats to broach in strong winds. Knockdowns – known as B1 and B2 – are more violent than any broach, but both happen rarely. A B1 knockdown levels a boat at a 90-degree angle – in the blink of an eye – and there she stays until she manages to right herself. It is lethal, striking out of the blue with many times the power of a controllable broach. Like whiplash, it cannot be stopped. If you are lucky enough and remain with the boat during a B1, you end up either crumpled in a corner of the cockpit, usually with a crewmate on top of you, or on the side deck, clinging to a stanchion or guardrail. If unlucky, you travel over the stanchions and guardrails, landing in the sea with only your harness and lifejacket retaining and supporting you. Once the boat rights herself, you have to drag yourself back on board by the rope of your safety harness.

If the thought of a B1 was bad, the idea of B2 knock-down, here in the bloody anger of the Irish Sea, turned my already cold blood to ice. Everything happens as in a B1, but a B2 knockdown is more extreme, more violent, and follows through to a 180-degree capsize – at which point the boat stays there, inverted. Crew are trapped in or under the boat, either in the cabin or in the cockpit, or thrown clear of the hull where they are in danger of being dragged along and then forced under the surface if their harness ropes are still attached. An extra hazard is the mast snapping under the force of the water, leaving a lethally sharp weapon attached to the boat, risking further injury to crew trapped under-water. A yacht can be righted from capsize, either by the force of wind and waves or by the crew climbing onto the upturned hull and exerting force on her keel to right her. At its worst a B2 knockdown causes a yacht to sink, usually resulting in loss of life.

The spine-chilling thought of a B1 or even a B2 knock-down stayed with me as Mike and I, hands tight on the tiller, roared our way through the darkness. As the waves got bigger, our fears became greater. No unnecessary movements were made by anyone. I saw Gerry sheltering forward in the cockpit – he was beginning to look absolutely done in. David sat closest to us in the cockpit, hanging onto his pitching boat, helping and guiding us wherever he could. Shouting, only half heard, he offered to take over from either of us at the helm, but Mike and I held doggedly on. We seemed to be glued to the tiller. We were still working as a crew as best we could, but we could barely even see or hear one another.

As I peered with my salt-sore eyes into the madness ahead, I thought I saw navigation lights in the near distance. Such was my state of exhaustion that perhaps I was imagining this. I had not seen a thing for hours – why now? I searched the seas around me for confirmation, not wanting to create more alarm unnecessarily. The terrifying thought of two yachts of similar size making impact at a combined speed of roughly 28 miles an hour . . . But yes, once again, then twice, to our left, I caught glimpses of red, white or green glows. Jesus, there were other people out here too, trying to cope with these conditions, and they were close to us, too close. I nudged Mike.

'Look . . . nav lights . . . can you see?'

It took a while but then Mike confirmed that yes, he could see them too. We alerted the rest of the crew, frantically pointing in the direction where we had seen them. Although unnerving, this also cleared my head and focused my concentration more intently on the noisy waste of ploughed-up sea ahead of us. All we could do as a crew, under these conditions, was keep a watch, which to the best of our abilities we were doing.

Surprised by a rare lull I glanced at my watch – it was just after 1.30am. I looked at the anemometer at the same time: the wind speed was now between 60 and 65 knots. If the anemometer was reading correctly, then 65 knots of wind roughly translated to 75 miles per hour, a Beaufort scale of force 12. The Beaufort scale does not go any higher than 12. Force 12 going downwind under bare poles in southern ocean-sized seas – unreal.

As if sensing my terror, Mike also clocked the dial and saw the wind speed. He looked at me – at that moment there was no need for words, shouted or otherwise. We just looked at one another, an open-mouthed, almost hopeless look, both telegraphing, 'Where the hell do we go from here?'

This storm was bigger than any of us or any race. *Grimalkin* and her crew were being crushed by this heavy-weight bruiser. We were all suffering from the body blows, the knockdown punches. Each time *Grimalkin* was pitched into a monster wave, we were violently flung about, thrown against a combination of wood, metal, fibreglass and each other – our heads, arms, hands, legs, chins, elbows, knees – virtually every part of our bodies hurt.

Nobody could have prepared us for this. There were no rules, no boundaries to this fight, for a fight it now was – we were fighting for our lives.

Seven

Dark Alleys

By 2.45am on Tuesday, 14 August, the seas were indescribable. Over the last hour or so, *Grimalkin* and all six of us in her had been like a cork in rapids, just about keeping our heads above the boiling water. I did not know how much more I could take at the helm. Mike and I still grimly shared the tiller, negotiating wave after wave, each totally out of sync with the next. We were travelling at what seemed like three times the speed *Grimalkin*'s hull was designed for. The whole boat vibrated violently, particularly the rudder, its bearings and the tiller. Somehow, so far, we had been shown a path, swerving in and out of the endless dark alleys around us as our crewmates screamed warnings to us.

'Behind you . . . to port . . . look . . . LOOK!' Suddenly Matt and Dave were shouting and gesticulating manically with, if it were possible, an even greater sense of fear and urgency in their voices.

Mike and I looked behind us, slightly to port. An unusually large, unsynchronised wave was poised above us, its curling lip about 10 feet above our heads. At this time we were surfing along at a terrifying angle down the face of a breaker – as we bottomed out in the trough, we had no choice but to go with it.

'HANG ON!'

Gripping the tiller tightly, readying myself for the roar coming over my left shoulder, I heard Mike bellow to no one in particular: 'Jesus Christ!'

The wave roared under us and lifted *Grimalkin*'s stern up. It wrenched the tiller from our hands and rendered the rudder useless. *Grimalkin* was out of control – the wave's mass completely overtook us. I felt the straps of my harness tighten, and a huge gaping pit seemed to open in my stomach. As we began to tip over to a 45-degree angle, my harness tether jarred under pressure at its fullest extent. My attempts to cling to something, anything, failed. I was sucked from my seat and thrown through the air. Thoughts – quick and immediate, like electric shocks – shot through my brain. Was this it? Was *Grimalkin* going to hold on, or this time be pitchpoled or knocked down? While in the air I caught sight of the foredeck and the mast toppling into the sea and staying there. I was both spectator and participant. Yes, this was it, a knockdown. Gravity then took over and I was forced downwards at speed.

A terrifying, thundering, rolling racket penetrated my eardrums. In spite of this unearthly noise I could still hear the pain-filled screams of my fellow crewmates as they, helpless like me, collapsed, tumbled and free-fell. I landed with a thud, squashed up against a stanchion with cold sea engulfing me. Stunned and hurt, the breath knocked out of me, I understood my harness line had brought me to a body-blow standstill, just short of the water. I sucked air in hard, but coughed and choked on freezing seawater. Checking I still possessed my legs, my arms, my hands and feet, I held onto the stanchion I had collided with for my life.

We must have suffered our first B1 knockdown. My head throbbed and my teeth chattered uncontrollably. I looked around and saw nobody. Where in God's name were the others? Then I saw someone to my left, slightly behind me. Through the rain and spray I struggled to see who it was. Was it Matt?

'Matt, MATT, ARE YOU OK?'

A deep voice roared back at me. It wasn't Matthew, it was Mike. Even in this chaos I recognised his voice. I now saw him only feet away – he looked as disorientated and as distressed as me. I heard another voice yelling from slightly further away.

'DAVID here ... Gerry's with me ... ANYBODY ELSE THERE?'

Mike and I responded, then kept a keen ear out for the others.

'MATT, DAVE ... MATTHEW!' David yelled again.

I could hear the panic rising in his voice. About 30 excruciating seconds passed before we heard, in the distance, the voices of our other two crewmates. Thank God – all six of us accounted for. Now we just had to hang on while *Grimalkin* righted herself and hope that all the crew either stayed on or, if thrown off, made it back.

Although it felt far longer, in reality it was only two, maybe three minutes before the boat righted herself. Once upright, she shook herself free of the mass of water around her. Gripping onto the guardrails and each other, Mike and

I dragged ourselves upwards, almost throwing ourselves into the relative safety of the cockpit. As I slumped there, catching my breath, totally shaken, I saw a jumble of bodies do much the same, Gerry being dragged along by David and Matt.

'Come on, Nick, COME ON. We have to get back to the helm . . . this is way out of control,' shouted Mike.

Grimalkin's tiller was unmanned, allowing her to be swept along at merciless speed. I glimpsed the foam-topped line-up of waves stacked behind us, grabbed a line and clawed my way towards the back of the cockpit. In the scramble I became tangled up in my harness line. Eventually I freed myself and then, on my stomach, crawled through the gap underneath the mainsheet traveller. Jesus, my head hurt. I had hit it on the underside of the traveller. Now, finally upright, I saw that Mike was opposite me again. Somehow he had found his way back too. We grabbed at the thrashing tiller with our four hands and managed to bear *Grimalkin* away again, away from the eye of the wind.

Although four hands were better than two, we struggled to keep the bow back on course downhill. I watched as from above us another wall of water came crashing down. I looked at the compasses – there was a compass to each side of the companionway entrance; the one on the right was beside the anemometer. Their lights had dimmed, which probably meant the battery had been thrown out of its box. But *Grimalkin* was once again under a control of sorts from her two bruised, drenched, bewildered helmsmen.

I saw that Matt, David, Gerry and Dave were safe with us in the cockpit. Thank Christ – nobody had been washed overboard. We had all either been retained within the boat by her guardrails or been brought up short at the end of our lifelines. This last wave had unleashed so much energy – as if it were alive and we were the target of its inexplicable fury. Not knowing what would happen next or when it would happen, we had no choice but to keep going. But from where I sat and from what I could see, it was apparent that this knockdown was merely going to be the first of many.

And so it proved to be. As *Grimalkin* hurtled through the darkness, this was an experience the whole crew went through time and time again. Each knockdown sent all six of us hurtling through the air then crash-landing on the boat or, worse, in the water – whichever way, we were either awash or completely immersed in bitterly cold sea.

Grimalkin behaved marvellously – each time righting herself within minutes of a 90-degree B1 capsize. On several occasions, she teetered on the brink of a B2 – a full 180-degree capsize – but she managed to hold her own. But the conditions were still, unbelievably, worsening, and I think we all knew it was only a matter of time before the worst happened, perhaps during a momentary lapse of concentration, a wrong call or an incorrectly judged rogue wave. All we could do was to concentrate hard on the roaring obstacle course behind and in front of us.

I had seen enough over the last couple of hours to understand that these seas were capable of anything. I had never heard of, read about or experienced anything like this. Weary, soaked through, dispirited, Mike and I still gripped the tiller, and just as we caught one acutely angled, steep wave, we made a misjudgement of timing. This misjudgement slowed us too quickly. I had pushed instead of pulled the tiller, and we shot into the back of the wave in front. *Grimalkin*'s fore-deck – from her bow right back to the mast – was forced underwater. The back of the next wave threatened to push us completely under.

As *Grimalkin* stopped dead, from somewhere I heard a scream, and then another. The force that threw all six of us out into the water was so violent that I heard almost nothing but screams – and above them all, my own. Miraculously *Grimalkin* righted herself and we clawed our way back up our six-foot-long safety-harness lines onto the deck and towards the cockpit, grabbing whatever we could to aid us – stanchions, each other, winches, anything. All six of us were back on board, stunned. Numb with cold, we set about clearing the warps and ropes that had been trailing behind us and which were now a jumbled mess in the cockpit. David manned the tiller while the rest of us, carefully and slowly, threw the lines back astern. Once done, David shouted at the top of his voice for Dave to join him at the helm. I watched the two of them as they peered ahead through the rain, spray and spume, desperately trying to orientate themselves to the crazy, unpredictable rhythm of the heaving mass of boiling black liquid.

Mike and I were back in the cockpit, exhausted. I huddled up against Mike to try and gain some warmth. Matt and Gerry sat opposite, also huddled together. I looked at my watch – it was 5am and still dark. Not a sign of daylight, and even more worryingly not a sign of this force-12 storm relenting. All four of us concentrated on the seas around us, trying to indicate to David and Dave, at the helm, the direction of the next onslaught. I tried to stay alert but found myself becoming transfixed by the surreal beauty of these slow-moving mountains. I thought of Pa's Japanese stamp. Had he heard about the storm? Oh God, Ma would be worried, they both would. In my dreamlike state I saw Matt shouting, then screaming at me. I stared back, seeing him but not reacting to him.

'For God's sake, Nick . . . HOLD ON.' Mike had grabbed me and shaken me hard.

Too late – one of these slow-moving mountains of water speeded up and poured down onto *Grimalkin*, throwing us all upwards before smashing us back into the cockpit in a heap. Quick, jerky, violent. I landed on top of Gerry – poor guy, his whole body seized up with pain. I rolled off him before helping him up, back up onto the cockpit seat.

'Sorry, mate. Are you OK?' I knew he couldn't hear me over the noise, but it made me feel better. With these conditions it was impossible to prevent collision in the confines of the cockpit, but I knew I had to concentrate harder to try to prevent a serious injury.

Once more *Grimalkin* steadied herself, and each of us braced ourselves for the next onslaught.

'CHECK THE HARNESS LINES,' screamed David from the helm, barely visible or audible through the wind and spray.

With numb hands, Matthew, Mike and I scrambled through the rope tails on the floor of the cockpit: one, two, three, four, five and six. We checked the lines thoroughly for snags.

'ALL FINE, NO SNAGS, ALL ATTACHED.'

We were still interacting with one another, but communication was reduced to stilted, shouted words and minimal gestures. Only what was necessary. None of us ate; none of us wanted to. I thought of the odd ochre sky we had seen. Christ, how many hours ago was that? We were now a seriously weakened crew. I prayed for daylight, feeling sure it would give us back some conviction, and a renewed ability to deal with this storm.

Eight

Before Light, After Dawn

At 5.30am the first traces of light slowly appeared. But the dawn brought with it a new and unexpected shock – the fear on each other's faces that had been unseen in the dark. My teeth chattered from the bitter wind and the cold; everyone's faces were pale and their lips quivered. Anxiety gripped me. For the first time it struck me – we might not survive this.

Nothing could have prepared us for the horror of our surroundings. The noise was cacophonous; dawn had turned the volume up. The low light magnified the heights of the waves. Menacing and unpredictable, these monstrous white-topped bodies of water swept everything aside. I said nothing; nobody did. I just sat there and thought: what on earth have I got myself into? With daylight now almost established, it was clear to me that my prayers had not been answered. There was no new conviction among the crew and no new reserves. Not one of us had ever experienced anything like these conditions. There were no smiles between us, just looks of uncertainty and disbelief.

I began to wonder how everyone else was faring in this

storm. I thought about the guys I'd waved to on the marina before we left Hamble – were they somewhere around us in this deafening sea? Where was our nemesis, *Green Dragon*, and the French class-five boats we'd been duelling with soon after the start? Were they here too? Was this weather affecting all the three-hundred-strong fleet in the same way, or was this storm localised? I wondered if they were opting for different tactics. I wondered what the great Eric Tabarly would have done last night. Would he have done the same? He would have run with the seas – of course – but his *Pen Duick*, longer and faster, would have coped better with the peaks and troughs to which *Grimalkin* had succumbed, both last night and this morning. All these questions were rhetorical, irrelevant; just a distraction from the cold boiling hell around us.

Dawn also revealed how entirely out of control *Grimalkin* was, sheering off downwind, running and surfing at unbelievable speeds beyond the control of David and Dave at the helm. Where the hell was this storm taking us? We could end up anywhere in these conditions – shoal waters, the shoreline, crashing into rocks. We were running into dangerous waters where the English Channel joins the Irish Sea. We could be headed directly for the Scilly Isles, the Seven Stones or even southern Ireland – God knows, we certainly didn't. It felt as if we were on an involuntary suicide mission, being carried along by these 40–50-foot waves. With things happening so quickly and noisily around me, I found it increasingly difficult to do anything other than stay clipped on in the cockpit and watch for rogue waves. I wondered how much longer *Grimalkin* could survive after the battering she had already taken.

I looked across at Gerry, sitting on the other side of the cockpit. He looked completely exhausted – my deepest worry was for him. He was showing marked signs of deterioration and his reactions were noticeably slower than I was used to from him; like David, his mind was usually quick. His fingers were white and wrinkled, as were all of ours, but his knuckle joints were swollen. I feared now that his arthritis had got the better of him. Had he had time, or even remembered, to take his medication since this maelstrom had begun? He was shivering uncontrollably and his face was paler than anyone else's – I was sure he was not far from becoming danger-ously hypothermic. I now stared over at Matt – for the first time he really looked his age. Jesus, this guy was only a kid. His tough, confident veneer had gone – he looked absolutely terrified. He was slumped in the cockpit, his eyes fixed on Mike, who was struggling to shift Gerry's dead weight into a more comfortable position. I wondered why Matt didn't help – why was he just staring at them? It was then that I realised I was doing exactly the same – just staring. I wanted to help, I wanted to stand up and help lift Gerry back to some sort of comfort, but I couldn't.

Everyone was done in from negotiating our way round these monster waves. It was as though we were all too scared to say anything, as if acknowledging our greatest fear would make it more likely. 'There may be no way out of this.' I could see the terror in Mike's face and I remembered the night before—

'Hold on, I'm bearing off . . . HOLD ON, HOLD ON!'

My manic train of thought had been interrupted by Dave roaring at us from the helm. All of us in the cockpit braced ourselves – holding on yet again for dear life. *Grimalkin* dipped her bows and her stern rose so violently that I shot across the cockpit at speed and was then lifted up high. This knockdown was without doubt the most violent one yet. As I was hurled through the air I looked down and could see, as if in slow motion, the rest of the crew below me being thrown in the same manner, but not at the same height. This was truly petrifying. I was being propelled over them all – I could see them but I couldn't make myself heard because of the howling wind. *Grimalkin* ploughed into the trough of the wave and I was once again catapulted into the ferocious seas.

The water was so cold that the breath was forced out of me. My safety harness tightened round my chest as I was towed along at terrifying speed. The rush of freezing seawater undid the fastenings of my oilskin top and found its way down through the opening at the neck. The inner, thermal layers of clothing, including my socks, soaked up water; I was being dragged down like a sack of cement. I became uncoordinated; instructions sent from my brain seemed not to get through, a creeping torpor dulled my senses. The intense cold of the sea made me want to inhale; this involuntary reflex choked me. I knew that if I swallowed much more of this black liquid, one thing would lead to another – more swallowing, more choking, then drowning. I began to panic. My leg, the left one, was hurting like hell. I knew straight away that I was badly injured as this was the first time I had felt any sensation in this leg since my brain haemorrhage eight years earlier. But I had no time to think about this now – simply grabbing enough oxygen to keep me conscious was all I could cope with. I had to somehow calm down, get a grip. I twisted my head round and saw the outlines of David and Matt just above me, aboard the boat. Thank

God. They were leaning over the guardrails, yelling, roaring at me. I yelled back at them.

'My leg . . . MY LEG.'

I have no idea whether they heard me. Their arms were stretched out to me. I reached my right arm up but the speed and the motion of the boat kept dragging me away from them. I made several attempts to lever myself those few crucial inches up my safety-harness tether but could not do it – instead, each attempt left me weakened. I fixed my eyes on David, who bellowed frenzied shouts of encouragement.

'COME ON, NICK. PULL YOURSELF UP . . . COME ON, NICK . . . YOU CAN DO IT.'

Both my hands were raw and bleeding – I had to let go, be dragged helplessly along by the boat. From my position in the water, three or four feet below, all I could see were my crewmates, yelling ferociously down at me. Why the hell weren't they doing anything?

'FOR CHRISSAKE . . . GET ME OUT OF HERE!' I shouted back, to no one in particular.

Anger welled up inside me. It gave me a much-needed adrenaline boost. I grabbed my safety-harness tether and yanked myself up, managing to get my injured left leg onto *Grimalkin*'s toe rail, but she was travelling at such speed my leg didn't stay there long – I was forced back into the freezing water. On my second attempt, I swivelled round with my back to the seas, the flow of water supporting my damaged leg. I reached up and finally felt a firm grip on my right arm. I had no idea who it was but I clung on. Between them, waiting for the right moment, they pulled me over the guardrails and onto the deck.

Slumped over, I coughed and vomited endless amounts

of water. Crouched there, on my hands and knees, water dribbling out of my mouth, the anger I had felt towards my crewmates was instantly replaced by gratitude. As Matt and David helped me back into the cockpit, I began to comprehend that I had been saved from drowning. Huddled back in the safety of the cockpit I looked up at them both, father and son – they had just saved my life. Still coughing and spluttering, I gasped, 'Thanks.'

I attempted to express further gratitude but the words were lost in the roaring wind. David put a firm arm on my shoulder – I knew he was trying to tell me that everything was fine. Breathing hard, I looked down at my left leg, fully expecting to see blood and perhaps my femur protruding through my oilskin trousers, but no, nothing. I couldn't understand – it had hurt so much. I carefully moved it back and forth: nothing, no feeling, no sensation. Had I imagined the pain? I moved it again, this time a little further – I seized up in agony. I wanted to explain to David, to everyone, that I normally had no feeling in this leg and how amazing it was to feel anything, even severe pain, but I was beyond exhaustion. With Mike's help I placed the injured leg into a more comfortable position.

I was on the starboard side, and looked round at Gerry, sat to port – he was by now impassive, apparently oblivious to what was going on; it was probably better this way. I looked at Mike, who was scared, and then at Dave, who was helming, doing his best, but he was frozen, almost beat. David was knackered too – I could sense that he had begun to wonder what the hell to do next. The immersion in the sea had left me colder, more scared than I had ever felt before. There was nowhere to hide – not in this cockpit, not on this boat. This couldn't go on; we couldn't take much more of this.

Matt, Gerry, Mike, Dave and me – all five of us looked to David, our skipper. Decisions had to be made.

'We're going to make a Mayday call for rescue. Matthew, come with me.'

A silent wave of relief went through us all. Matthew and David both unclipped their safety harnesses. David's decision was a prudent one, given our circumstances. Up until now it had been considered too great a risk to go below into the cabin; that area of the boat was untenable in a storm of this magnitude. But in the rapidly deteriorating conditions, this became a risk that had to be taken.

David and Matt struggled against the storm towards the cabin. Matt reached the closed cabin first and slid the horizontal hatch forward. He then removed the two wooden washboards that prevented seawater from getting in.

I sat wedged in the cockpit with Mike and Gerry and could just about see down below. Amid the mess and debris in the cabin, I saw David attempting to make contact through the handset. Matt was leaning over him trying to steady them both against the storm. David used the VHF radio to contact *Morningtown* – the Royal Ocean Racing Club observation boat for the race. *Morningtown* then transferred David's call to Land's End Radio to verify our position. I could not hear precisely what David was saying but I knew that giving our exact position was going to be difficult – we had not had a decent position plot since the previous evening. We all waited in anticipation – then finally David shouted up to us. 'THEY'RE COMING . . . rescue is on the way . . . *Morningtown* is sending a helicopter.'

David now turned to Matthew.

'FLARES . . . quick, get them.'

97

Matt grabbed the flare container from beneath the navigation table and passed it up the companionway ladder. Mike struggled forward and grabbed the container. I could see Matt's face plainly now – he was elated. For the first time in hours we experienced hope; contact with *Morningtown* had given us all a morale boost. Someone, some authority, now knew of our predicament.

Mike opened the container, took a parachute flare and crouched to port, cowering as far forward as the cockpit allowed. It was immediately clear he was having difficulty operating it. In normal circumstances Mike would have been able to let off one of these parachute flares within seconds. After an agonising wait, two rocket flares went off at odd trajectories – neither of them vertical. The ideal trajectory would have been angled into the wind so that the flares drifted back over us at about a 200-foot zenith. One went into the waves, the other flew off at an odd angle. We watched as their smoke wafted pathetically over the boat. Who would see the flares? How close was *Morningtown* or a helicopter to us? How close was anything, for that matter?

Tempers quickly escalated. We knew we had to get at least one flare vertical for any chance of making our position clear to oncoming rescue. Matt roared angrily up from the cabin.

'COME ON, GUYS ... GET ON WITH IT!'

These yells did nothing but hinder Mike's efforts, his soaking hands fumbling and losing grip on the long slippery tube of another parachute flare. Just then a wave smashed on the foredeck, completely enveloping Mike in spray. Pandemonium broke loose as we all started blaming each other. In the midst of this, I heard David's voice.

'COME ON, NICK ... give it a go ... HELP HIM, FOR GODSAKE.'

I grabbed a flare and attempted to operate the firing mechanism of the parachute. My hands were trembling with the cold and the flare continually slipped from my grip – I could do no better than Mike.

Just at that moment there was an almighty bellow from Dave at the helm.

'HOLD ON ... HOLD ON ... we're bearing off!'

Grimalkin's stern began to lift. Dave's shouted words became indistinct as I looked up and saw a rogue wave towering above us. The situation had turned so chaotic that we had all dropped our guard. I yelled down into the cabin, 'Hold on ... HOLD ON.' Again it was too late. The colossal wave pitched *Grimalkin*'s stern up at such a crazy angle that the boat rolled forward, leaving David and Matt helpless. They were flung round the cabin along with the other flying objects in the boat's churning interior.

I was thrown upwards but this time I landed back in the cockpit. My relief was short-lived when Gerry's full weight came crashing down on top of me. My face was crushed against the cockpit floor, impressing a diamond-pattern on my cheek; my ribs and chest hurt. Again everything speeded up into fast jerky movements. With Mike's help I struggled from underneath Gerry and we shifted him upright. We checked and saw that Dave had managed to hold on at the helm. Mike and I now exchanged the same sort of look we had God knows how many hours ago when we were both at the helm.

'Jesus Christ, David and Matt.'

The rain and spray prevented us from seeing into the

cabin so we attempted to climb out of the cockpit, but the strength of the gale forced us back. We began yelling down into the cabin, 'DAVID . . . MATTHEW . . . DAVID!'

We waited for some sign, a shout for help – something, anything. But there was nothing, not even a whimper. Mike tried again to crawl out of the cockpit towards the cabin entrance, but was forced to retreat. The elements were in control; we had no choice but to wait for some kind of lull. We found ourselves staring at each other, shit scared. Then, through the howling wind, we heard Matthew's terrified voice.

'HELP ME . . . I NEED HELP DOWN HERE.'

We both pushed forward against the oncoming gale, this time refusing to give in. Matt finally came into view – holding his father in his arms. He was distraught, his eyes wide with fear and his face pallid and drawn.

'He's injured . . . DAD IS INJURED.'

Despite the appalling visibility we could see that David's head was gashed – blood pumped from a gaping wound. Matt by now had David propped up against the companionway ladder, his free hand pressed against his father's head wound, desperately attempting to stop the flow of blood.

Mike grabbed hold of David and hollered at Matt, 'THE FIRST-AID KIT.'

Matt reached across with one hand, grabbed the red plastic box from its fixed position on a shelf and tore off the lid. I crouched down, looking directly at the back of David's bare head. The gash was about two and a half inches long, easily visible through his thinning hair – if he was not so cold the loss of blood would have been even greater. In normal circumstances this wound would not have been life threatening, but David's circumstances and our predicament were by no means normal.

My own injuries, even Gerry's, seemed of little consequence compared to David's. Matt grabbed some plastic skin from the first-aid kit and protected the wound as best he could. He handed me the spray and I did as well as I could with it though the can kept slipping through my soaking, shaking hands. Matt then pulled David's balaclava back up on his head and his oilskin hood up over that, to afford him some protection.

Somehow, with *Grimalkin* still pitching and rolling, Matt swivelled round, struggling against the boat's gyrations, and with his father's full weight in his arms he gained a toehold on the companionway ladder. With our help, he guided David's booted feet up the ladder's steps and we managed to get David out from the nightmare below and into the cockpit.

It was then that I caught a proper look below deck. The cabin was unrecognisable – it was submerged: not much, perhaps only nine inches, but enough to allow the floorboards to float free. There were cans of food, saucepans, cutlery, crockery, batteries, wooden boards, personal gear and other, heavy general detritus, as well as light stuff such as pencils, all flying round inside the boat at great speed. Everything was wrecked – the engine, its housing and the chart table. It was a miracle the first-aid box had remained wedged on its shelf.

Mike leaned over me and he, too, had a good look – he shook his head in shock. We slid the cabin hatch shut.

Grimalkin continued downwind, at a frantic, helpless rate. We were all freezing, wet, exhausted and terrified. Matt, white with fear and distress, had his arms protectively round his father, who appeared to be slipping in and out of consciousness.

'QUICK . . . TRY ANOTHER FLARE,' shouted Dave from the helm.

Grimalkin's regulation RORC flare pack contained four parachute flares, three of which had been wasted. Mike grabbed some hand flares. After some fumbling, they went off, one after the other. These hand flares were less effective, less visible, but easier to ignite. There was no cheering as they went off, no celebration. Mike then threw the two buoyant orange ring-pull smoke canisters over the side, one after the other. In desperation, he ripped open the yellow sachets of sea marker dye, dropping them over the side.

'This is the last one . . . should I let it off?' yelled Mike.

Matt, Dave and I simultaneously roared yes.

The last flare went off. It glowed bright for a couple of minutes, sparks falling harmlessly onto the deck as he held it aloft in his right hand. Then it was gone. That was it – all used. Although we could not reasonably expect an immediate response, it was still maddening to have no acknowledgement of our signals of distress. Mike became agitated.

'How long should we wait?'

Matt and I shrugged. Our lack of response made Mike even more agitated.

'We have to prepare the life raft.'

From the helm Dave, although barely audible, yelled in agreement. I was horrified. The rule of thumb – the unwritten law – for any sailor is 'never leave the boat', not unless she is sinking. *Grimalkin* was the biggest, safest life raft we had. Her fibreglass, cold and hard as it was, was much better than any soft, inflated rubber raft. For me this was not an option, not yet anyway. I looked at Matt, who again said nothing – he was more preoccupied with his father. I felt I had to answer for the two of us.

'No way.'

Mike seemed to lose it at this point.

'One more knockdown and that's it, we're done for . . . this boat could go down at any second . . . WE HAVE TO GET OFF THIS BOAT.'

'NO WAY . . . we're NOT leaving the boat, not unless she's going down.'

I was furious. We had to keep giving *Grimalkin* a chance. She'd performed miracles so far. Gut feeling told me that David and Gerry would never agree to leave the boat, were they in any state to contribute to the debate. From the helm Dave joined in, shouting over his agreement with Mike. I turned to Matt for support.

'Tell them, Matthew . . . it would be crazy.'

Matt looked at his dad, who was clearly incoherent. Matt had always followed his father's decisions to the letter. Now, holding his badly injured father in his arms, Matt looked raw and scared. He spoke softly to his father.

'Dad, what shall we do? Should we prepare the life raft?'

David nodded in semi-conscious agreement. Avoiding eye contact with me, Matt now nodded to Mike. I could not believe it – it had all gone beyond my control in a matter of seconds – less. Matt was now with Mike, and Dave nodded from behind the mainsheet traveller.

Up until this crucial point, David had followed the right course of action and had acted with all caution. Now, semi-conscious and delirious, he had clearly become overwhelmed. I thought of what Pa had told me once, a few years previously – that you do not become a survivor until you have been rescued. In these conditions, these surreal conditions, I thought that yes, with us pulling together, it would be possible to survive. I tried to reason with Matt.

'It would be suicide to leave, Matt . . . help is on the way.'

Matthew, almost skipper by default, in a crisis, now appeared to be a bewildered young man. In adversity, it looked as if Matt would take a snap decision – not the considered one his father would take.

'COME ON, MATTHEW . . . Just think about it. What would David do?' Suppressing my anger, I pleaded with him.

'DAD NEEDS HELP . . . I HAVE TO GET HIM OFF THE BOAT,' Matt yelled in reply.

Mike spoke up. 'OK, we have to prepare the life raft.'

Matthew nodded.

Jesus Christ, how the hell did this happen? I was angry with Mike. I was sure that once the life raft was prepared, he would opt for abandoning ship. Serious hostility set in – both of us refusing to give in. Meanwhile, the seas continued their unrelenting attack.

It was then that I heard an unfamiliar noise. I looked around. Now that it was a little lighter, the clouds, almost unseen in the dark, seemed to be lower, more sinister; there was no definition between sea and sky. What did have definition, however, were the noises. They were blanketed by the clouds, which made them all the more strange.

'LISTEN . . . LISTEN . . . can you hear it?'

Everyone listened, looking upwards. We couldn't see a thing but we knew what it was. It was the noise of jet engines – an RAF Nimrod search aircraft was circling somewhere above us.

Matt was suddenly ecstatic – he looked to his dad. 'They saw the flares, Dad . . . they've spotted us.'

Human nature, instinct, soon had all of us believing that we had been spotted and we were nigh on rescued already.

Mike jumped up. 'THE LIFE RAFT HAS TO BE READY!'

But everything was moving too quickly. If the engine noise was, say, a Nimrod or any other SAR aircraft, all they do is search and find. The rescue comes from elsewhere, from mainland, shore-based helicopters. Signals have to be sent, and then received. I thought of last night, when I had glimpsed other navigation lights in the dark. There must be other boats out here too, close to us, in the same fix as us. How far down the list of casualties were we? We had heard the engines but not seen anything because of the low cloud. How could we know they had seen us?

'Get real, will you,' I said to Mike. 'Look at the seas. They're huge, look. Once the raft's launched there's no going back. It's a parachute – only one chance, no back-up.'

With that, everyone started shouting, yelling at each other. It was impossible to make sense of anything. All I knew was that no one agreed with me. I tried again, but my voice was lost to the wind, and my argument was lost to the majority opinion. They had already decided on their next move. David, Gerry and me, all incapacitated in one way or another, were excluded from the decision. I knew, too, that with my injured leg, and as much as I believed that *Grimalkin* was our only real hope of survival, I would have no chance if left on board on my own. This was what I was faced with – I had to go with them on the life raft if they decided so.

So with David's tacit, semi-conscious agreement, *Grimalkin*'s cockpit floor was lifted – made possible by everyone raising their legs – to reveal the six-person life raft. The raft, sitting there, inert, almost had a sign on it saying, 'Use me.' But Pa's words were embedded in my brain, 'Never leave the boat.' Even as I was hearing his words I was helping with the raft's preparation, checking its tethered bowline. How could I argue with them? With every passing moment, *Grimalkin* was close to foundering or capsizing again. With everyone's eyes full of terror – how the hell could I argue?

The life raft was now prepared but still securely fixed to a strong attachment point, bolted right through the cockpit floor.

We waited, for God only knew what. I began to wonder if what I had gleaned from Pa, Dick Langton and many other, respected sailing friends, all professional, was right. I began to wonder if 'never leave the boat' was the way forward. If they were here now, with us, in this cockpit, would they put into practice what they had been preaching to me over the years?

Then, within the blink of an eye, unseen by any of us, a huge wall of water, far bigger than any other wave we had encountered so far, advanced on us. I felt *Grimalkin* lifting, being thrust upwards. This overwhelming, half-obscured, unforeseen rogue wave was iridescent at its top – what little light there was radiated through its curling lip. This is what I remember about it: its lip, its high curling lip on top of its crest, that seemed to be hanging in wait, even while the wave itself was moving at speed. It was as if the constituent parts had minds of their own – each piece with its own destructive agenda.

As I watched this wave hovering above us, something crashed violently against the back of my head – something solid and cold, forcing my head downwards and forwards into a grey, quickly fading pit. It came so fast there was no time to think, no time to react. I was immediately disorientated,

Sunday service with Pa, Ma and Simon. Pa's hand is resting on my shoulder.

Pa at Hamble Quay waiting to take me on my first sail in *Fred* (1959).

Less than a year later I was sailing *Fred* on the river by myself.

All togged out in new sailing gear for the beginning of the 1968 racing season.

Above Getting ready to crew a Merlin Rocket in March 1971. This photo was taken just a week before my brain haemorrhage.

Right In the spring of 1972 I was back to my beloved Hamble River – not yet fully recovered but ready to try my first sail with Mark.

Back racing again –
rushing towards Hamble
Quay (1977).

Left Enjoying a break on one of my
many deliveries (1978).

Grimalkin earlier in the 1979
season during a Solent
Points Race.

11th August 1979. Another Fastnet start in Cowes Roads off the Isle of Wight, but this time I was more than an onlooker – I was finally taking part.

This photo of *Grimalkin* was taken just one hour before our Fastnet 1979 start. While waiting, we put in some practice tacks as David carefully sussed out our Class V competition.

The Fastnet Lighthouse – this, the most southerly point of Ireland, was the turning point of our race. On August 12th 1979 *Grimalkin* was headed towards this infamous rock along with 302 other yachts, all completely oblivious as to what lay ahead. When the killer storm struck during the night of August 13th it disabled the entire fleet.

My first Fastnet start with Pa – this was the breathtaking sight that inspired me to one day take part in this great race.

overwhelmed, all train of thought gone, all senses blocked. Everything moved from light to dark, as if someone was turning a rheostat in my head, dimming the light. I tried to fight the closing of my eyes; I tried to see the indistinct bodies, I guess those of my crewmates, miming silent noise in front of me. The intoxicating sea seemed to want me. I felt the cold of the cascading water all around me and through this water-scape found I was looking directly at the red dial of *Grimalkin*'s anemometer, the white needle spinning clockwise, wildly out of control.

I yelled, but nobody heard me. I was losing the battle for my consciousness. Everything was fading to freezing cold black. My eyes were forced closed to a black hole silence.

Nine

Muddled Mind

I could feel my head being slammed against something hard – over and over. My ears rang loudly, painfully, with the noise of hissing, like static. It was like being in a whirlpool. Not quite fully conscious yet, I slowly opened my eyes. Within seconds I experienced a terrifying surge of fear – I was under-water – in dark, murky, turbulent waters. My body was being dragged along by my safety harness, still attached to *Grimalkin*. How long had I been in the water? I tried to move but couldn't – my legs were completely tangled up in rope, restricting any movement. Suddenly my inflated lifejacket ejected me to the surface, long enough for me to gasp in some air. I was dragged underwater again – hands above my head, I felt the cold air. Once again I was ejected to the surface – and this time I managed to keep my head above water.

I could now see that *Grimalkin* was upright. The seas around her were still raging – huge, terrifying and relent-less in their ferocity. They towered above me – towered way, way above *Grimalkin*. I felt tiny, minuscule. I tried to stop my teeth chattering but it was impossible. It seemed that no sooner had I inhaled a lungful of air than I swallowed twice the amount of seawater. This nightmare had not ended, nowhere near it. I was overcome with a sort of nausea, and an ataxia, in which my muscles were unable to move. I closed my eyes to block it all out. I just wanted to take a breath and then let the elements do the rest, let them take me away from this. Strangely, I found myself drifting into an almost peaceful, dream-like state. It was then that I heard a voice.

'Get a grip.'

I was completely unnerved by this voice in my head. My mind started racing again. Perhaps this is what happens when you are close to death. No, not this – I had been near death once before and this never happened. No, it's supposed to be peaceful, you drift towards a light, or float above yourself or something like that. Jesus Christ, I didn't know. I just wanted the voice to go away but it seemed to follow me, staying in my head, getting louder and louder. It now became familiar, very familiar.

'Pull yourself together, man.'

I realised it sounded like Pa.

'You heard me, Nicholas. Pull yourself together. You've come through worse than this.'

It was Pa – he was the only person to call me Nicholas, to address me by my full name. To everyone else I was plain old Nick. This was the jolt, the spur, hearing my dad's voice in my head. Sod the pain, forget the numbness in all your fingers, in your toes, do something, Ward. You're your father's son, make him proud, answer him, get a grip.

I had to find help, and quickly. 'DAVID, MATTHEW, GERRY . . . IT'S NICK . . . HELP. GET ME OUT OF HERE. I NEED HELP!'

Where the hell was everyone? My safety harness and lifejacket were so tight round my chest that I began hyperventilating. I had to do something positive, something active – keep my circulation going, keep breathing, stop the panic, try to breathe normally. During a lull I managed to take a few deep breaths. Now that I had a little more control, I reached up and grabbed at the base of a broken stanchion on the deck of the boat. Another deep breath and I managed to raise myself slightly. It was then obvious that *Grimalkin* had been dismasted. With one numb, freezing hand now gripped round the stanchion, I fought to untangle the writhing, snake-like lines that imprisoned me. Looking up at the oncoming walls of waves, I realised that if I judged the timing of the next upward surge I might be able to pull myself back aboard *Grimalkin*. Grabbing my safety harness, I waited for the next wave to lift me, then with my right hand still firmly gripping the stanchion, I let go of the harness with my other hand, grasped the starboard primary sheet winch and used it to yank my waterlogged body fully on board.

I lay slumped on the deck, breathless, panting, physically drained and sick, for a few long minutes, then the same question began to race through my mind again. Where the hell were the others? I had to calm down, to think, to try to remember. My train of thought became a little clearer. David, our skipper, had been injured. Yes, I could remember David lapsing in and out of consciousness. Gerry was also out of it. I vaguely recalled much shouting and screaming. In my dulled, muddled state of mind, it dawned on me that my crewmates, all of them, might have drowned. The last I could remember was receiving an almighty blow to the back of my head, then nothing. What had hit me? I didn't know. I desperately wanted to replay those last few seconds before I had lapsed into nothingness.

Suddenly I became overwhelmed with panic and started to shout again. 'DAVID, MATTHEW, GERRY . . . IT'S NICK . . . WHERE THE HELL ARE YOU?'

I kept shouting for what seemed like an age, but the shouted, screamed names of my crewmates were simply taken away by the wind. I knew I had to get to the shelter of the cockpit. I tried to stand up by leaning into the gale, but I was immediately knocked forward by a massive gust. I felt a jarring pain in my chest as I hit the floor of the cockpit well, three feet below. On my knees now, winded, I pulled myself up on the starboard-side deck.

Grimalkin was still lurching heavily on the huge seas, crashing up and down. I was astounded by the strength of this gale. In the water I had been sheltered compared to this onslaught. I huddled back down into the relative safety of the cockpit and heaved much-needed air into my lungs. My legs dangled into the void of the storage well where the life raft was housed. As I stared down into this void, a cold fright came over me. The life raft had gone. It had gone! Wet and cold, I started to shake uncontrollably at the implication of this – the dawning, frightening reality of what the empty well might mean. Had the life raft been lost during a capsize? Or had the others panicked, then launched it? Yes, maybe they had gone for help. No, this wasn't possible. They would never have left me in this precarious situation – injured, in-capacitated – not in these deadly conditions. They would have got me into the life raft somehow, taken me with them. Despairing, I cried their names into the wind until I was too exhausted to continue.

Not knowing what else to do, I stared downwards in disbelief. All the thoughts and fears I had experienced in the water replayed themselves in my head. I was terrified of standing up again but I had to check for signs. I lifted my head above the cockpit. I had trouble keeping my eyes open with the spray, which was like horizontal rain, but I managed to scan the area round the boat. No orange canopy, no life raft. No sign of anything, nothing.

I ducked back down into the cockpit; things started to come back to me. That's right, yes, we were preparing everything for the worst. Images, confused and blurred, came into my pulsing brain and, slowly, my thoughts pieced themselves together. I was in the cockpit with Matt, Mike, also David. Mike was letting some flares off; I remembered the sound, the fizzing of the phosphor, magnesium ... he was crouching down and had difficulty with the parachute flares. Of course, yes, the flares, and the life raft. The last I remember the life raft was securely tied and bolted to the floor, so it couldn't have been displaced during a capsize. It was then that I took in the sight of a couple of blue safety harnesses, their safety hooks still attached to strong-points. They'd been abandoned. Then I saw two more – one of them looked as if it had been cut. What the hell was going on? Panicking, my heart racing, I called out names again, at first feebly, then louder, until I was screaming.

'DAVID, MATTHEW, GERRY . . . DAVID!'

Had my crewmates abandoned me? No way, not our skipper, David. He would never have allowed it – he would never have left a crewmember on his beleaguered boat, dead or alive. A horrifying image suddenly flashed through my head. The image of, oh my God, David, our injured skipper, being swept away from *Grimalkin* and then sucked under by a massive wave. Was that really what I had seen? I knew that he had been safely attached to the boat, like everyone else, but this vision, this image of David being swept away felt powerfully real. I then had a blurred flashback of Gerry and me lying in the cockpit tangled in ropes while voices shouted around us. I must have had brief moments of consciousness after the blow to my head – for I now knew for certain that I had witnessed David's disappearance.

But where were the others? Where was the life raft? My lifejacket had a yellow plastic whistle tucked under its inflated collar. I fumbled around, withdrew it and blew it as hard as I could until I had no further breath. There was no reply. Confounded, I sat back down, my teeth chattering again uncontrollably. As I stared down into the empty well, dark thoughts of being abandoned passed through my mind. I began to recall remnants of an argument. I tried to piece it together. Yes, there had been an argument. Should we leave *Grimalkin* on the life raft or stay and wait for rescue? I knew I had been against the life raft option. But had they used it after David was swept away? They wouldn't have left me alone on *Grimalkin*, they couldn't have. But the cut harness line. Who had cut it, and why?

Nothing made sense; I began to doubt myself. I had to look for more signs, signs of life – signs of anything. I stood up. I fell down. I stood again, more determined, and clawed my way on to the side deck. The massive, roaring waves were growling at me, still coming from all angles, all directions. On my hands and knees I searched all around, as much as the onslaught would allow. I noticed something in the water alongside the boat. Something red. And then I saw what looked like a head, a mop of red hair. Hell, it was Gerry.

'GERRY! GERRY! GERRY!'

There was no reply. Gerry was floating there alongside the boat, supported by his lifejacket, still attached to the boat by his harness. I inched my way across the deck and traced the line of his harness. I realised that he was clipped to the same strongpoint as me. How on earth had I missed him in the water? He must have been almost alongside me. Who cared now, there he was. But was he still alive? Either way I had to get him back on board. I had to think and think hard. I picked up a length of rope, and grabbed Gerry's harness lifeline to get him closer to me. I looped his line round the alloy genoa cleat, sited beneath the starboard primary winch. Then, by half kneeling, half crouching on the deck and by leaning out over the side of the boat, I managed to thread the loop of rope through the straps of his life harness. Gerry was absolutely waterlogged. He weighed a ton as, like me, he was wearing full wet-weather gear. Slowly, painfully, I started half pulling, half winching him aboard. My legs felt like lead, my head was throbbing, my eyes were salt sore. I felt like giving up.

'No, you won't. Pull yourself together, man!'

God, I was talking to myself again, or was it Pa? Whoever it was, was helping me, greatly. As I yanked Gerry upwards towards the deck I was geed up by hearing what I thought was a moan. He'd better not be dead, he had to be alive – Gerry had to be alive. I was now talking to myself, shouting, encouraging myself. I needed to get the encouragement, the strength from somewhere.

'Look, Gerry's there, he's almost within reach. Now get him aboard and he can help you. Gerry can help with the boat – you can't do it on your own!'

A huge wave banged loudly and forcefully against *Grimalkin*'s port quarter. I watched as the rope slipped from the winch drum – Gerry was back in the water. My manic behaviour turned to rage.

'COME ON, GERRY, HELP ME! Damn you, Gerry! I'm doing my best here. I NEED YOUR HELP!'

My gloves were of no use so I pulled them off. I saw that my hands were white, swollen and bleeding – I felt no pain, though; they were frozen numb. Once again I looped the line clockwise round the winch. I timed my pulling with the rhythm of the swells. Over my right shoulder, the swells looked like green-tinged mountains, malignant with white peaks. I was pitting myself against them, and they were against me; it was personal.

It took all of my strength to pull Gerry's dead weight onto the deck. Once done, I fell back into the cockpit, shattered. My sense of achievement in getting Gerry back aboard was soon dashed – a monster wave lifted *Grimalkin* and Gerry rolled into the cockpit on top of me. He was now pinning me down into the well, which was awash with seawater, only a few inches deep but enough to drown in. Gerry was so heavy, so wet, I couldn't move. That's how we stayed for a while, me breathless, my crewmate lying seemingly inanimate, face down on top of me. I felt no breath coming from Gerry's mouth, which was pressed up against my face. His face was pale, and there was a massive abrasion across the left side of his forehead.

I could only take short breaths of air between the submerging of my nose and mouth in the water sloshing around in the cockpit. This was not really the way I wanted to die; to be found, pinned down, drowned, beneath my dead crewmate. Would we even be found at all? And if we were, what would they do with us, where would we go? Where would we be taken? With Gerry an inch from my nose, I began to recite the Lord's Prayer. After this, 'Desiderata' came in my head, taught to me by my mother.

> 'Go placidly amid the noise and haste,
> And remember what peace there may be in silence.
> As far as possible without surrender
> Be on good terms with all persons.
> Speak your truth quietly and clearly,
> And listen to others,
> Even the dull and ignorant:
> They too have their story.'

Another bloody great white-topped mother of a wave crashed into the boat's stern and filled the cockpit well with water. The noise was deafening. Once again I had to fight for breath. 'Desiderata', I recalled, means 'something to be desired'. Well, I, we, me and Gerry bloody desired something, and I was going to get it.

The struggle to get out from underneath Gerry was monumental. First I had to unclip his harness line and get my painful left leg out from under him. Then I squeezed the rest of myself out using my fingers to gain purchase. Finally clear of him I stood up, shakily. Another huge wave knocked me off balance and I fell back, crashing into Gerry's chest. As I did so, I heard him moan, the same sort of moan I thought I'd heard when he was still in the water. I immediately began talking to him, gently now.

'Gerry, it's me, Nick. Can you hear me? Do something, anything; let me know you've heard me, for God's sake.'

Gerry remained still, he needed help. He was lying contorted in the cockpit. I had somehow to get him flat, on his back. The only flattish surface that could take Gerry's full length was the side deck. I dragged him upwards and onto the starboard side deck. Seriously weakened by this manoeuvre, I took some deep breaths and waited a few moments for my head to clear. I then cleared Gerry's airways – his throat and mouth – with my fingers before I put my lips to his. They were very cold, far colder than mine. I gave him mouth-to-mouth. He stank of vomit and snot; his mouth was caked with the stuff – not nice but I didn't care. Every breath I took meant getting a buffeting from the gales. My mouth was sore and Gerry's stubble was like sandpaper. Somehow I combined this artificial respiration with pummelling his chest – relentlessly thumping his hard sternum. After what seemed like an age, Gerry coughed and spluttered and began to show signs of life. He vomited a great deal of water but at last he breathed on his own.

I'd asked for help, for strength, and got it. Somehow I had revived my crewmate, but now what?

Ten

Footprints in the Sand

Gerry was still lying on the starboard side deck. Waves crashed down on top of us. I did not know what to do with him, where to place him to recover. Ideally he needed to be somewhere safe, somewhere dry. This was impossible, given our situation, exposed and vulnerable, so I just knelt up in the cockpit, my head ducking the waves, to be near him.

Now that he, Gerry, my crewmate, was alive, no longer inanimate, no longer just a waterlogged body lying inert in the well of the boat, but someone who could work alongside me to get us out of this hellhole, I felt a lot better. I was able to think more clearly, more rationally, to tap the same line of thought that had got me through difficult times in the past to where I was today, whatever the date was. The thirteenth of August, I thought. No, it was the fourteenth – it must be. Last night, yesterday, was Monday. It was Tuesday morning, the fourteenth of August.

Gerry's position was precarious; his head supported by the starboard genoa winch. His feet, only one of them now booted, the other covered by a grey thermal sock, were tucked against the starboard spinnaker winch. The only thing keeping Gerry from rolling into the well or even over the side was the tension on his safety line, which I had tied off on the cleat, sited under the winch. He was moving quite weirdly, not in time with *Grimalkin*, for she was still crashing her way to nowhere. I pulled my hood tighter. I remembered the mitts in my pocket and put them back on; they were soaking wet, but they would dry, I hoped.

Gerry's eyes were rolling. He was gurgling and moaning softly, his moans just about audible. Gerry was trying to talk. I didn't really know what to do. I thought coldly, clinically, taking it in stages. Finding Gerry had been the first stage, getting him aboard had been the second stage, getting water out of him and air back into him had been the third stage. OK, so I'd achieved those, but what next?

I knew that I had to get him to a state of consciousness, get him aware, get him to sit, get him to help me, help the boat – but how? I knew that Gerry needed more than me; he needed medical help. He looked done in, bruised and battered. He was suffering, shivering, his face was pale – no, not pale, ashen. The combined effects of the weather, the gale and the seas had all conspired to smash his body; the immersion in the cold sea had brought on hypothermia. This man, my crewmate, about whom I knew little but wanted to know more, was lapsing in and out of consciousness, occasionally moaning, trying to talk. I needed to know more, ask more. Compared to my crewmate I was in relatively good shape.

I started to think back a few years to some of my own most difficult, troubled times, the times when I had had to tap into my own reserves, my own then young psyche.

'Gerry, you can do this . . . you have to stay with me!' I shouted at him. I needed him, damn it.

I found myself telling him about the brain haemorrhage I had suffered eight years earlier, when I was fifteen years old. I told him about being on my back, bedridden, for months. I thought that if he could hear me this might help him, motivate him; it might spur him on or, even better, annoy him back into a state of full consciousness.

'I counted the holes in the hospital ceiling tiles to keep myself sane, conscious and awake,' I told him. Then I told him about my dreams of sailing again, and other dreams, and how I'd realised some – this bloody race was one of them. I told him about willing the fingers of my left hand to move again and about the pain of having to learn to walk once more. Compared to all that, this was easy, well perhaps not easy but at least here, on board, where we could move and breathe, we could – would – have a go. I had survived then, on the surgeon's table, and we, Gerry and I, would survive now on board *Grimalkin*.

But Gerry had to recover. He had to help me repair the boat, pump it out. Stupidly, I thought of an inane question I really wanted to ask him: Why on earth had he, Gerry, bought a green Puffa jacket instead of a dark blue one, like the rest of the crew wore? I was getting angry again; angry that I didn't have the full story of what had happened to me and Gerry. I was angry with myself and angry with Gerry for having been injured, although why I was angry, I was not quite sure. Yes, I was afraid, very afraid. Yes, I was cold, bitterly so, but I could cope with that. Physically, I was badly bruised and battered, but as I crouched in the cockpit sheltering from the wind, looking at Gerry, I told myself that I was absolutely, utterly determined not to be beaten by myself, not today, not here, not alone.

Gerry was deadly pale. Panicked, I felt for a pulse – there was none. I leant low over Gerry's mouth, sheltering him from the gale with my back, and tried to feel his breath on my cheek. There was no sign of breath. Christ almighty, not again. I drew myself up, tightening my tether round the same cleat as Gerry's to steady myself. I leant over him to once more blow into his mouth. I saw his chest rise and fall, and blew again. I braced my arms, and with right hand over left I pushed hard down on his chest.

'One thousand, two thousand, three thousand, four thousand, five thousand. COME ON, GERRY.'

I pinched his nose to blow again. I did this for what seemed like ages, eons, but it must have been only minutes. My brow was throbbing, pulsing.

'You're not going to go, you bastard,' I yelled at him. 'You're not going anywhere. Stay with me, I want to ask you about your green Puffa, let me find out more about you . . . please, Gerry. Help me to help you.'

I shook his body, trying to encourage life back into him. I began to reassure him that help was on its way, even though I doubted that it was. I added that the others, Matthew and David – 'Remember David, Gerry? You know that David, our friend, our skipper, would never leave you, us, stranded here, alone, hurt' – would try their best. I felt like a con man trying to shoot a line, a bit of a fraud, but it might work. It might reach him. Gerry might respond to it.

There was a gaze, a look that Gerry gave me then. He revived and appeared to breathe for himself. He coughed, stuttered and tried to say something. I leant closer, my right ear close to his mouth. This was important, I knew it. I had to hear what he was trying to say, what he was trying to get out. Finally, over the noise, I deciphered a word – love. Christ, just say it, Gerry, please say it. Some more incoherent mumbles and I heard the name Margaret. Gerry took one further breath, deep as his water-filled lungs would allow. This time I heard the words of a man who knew he was dying, and it took all his effort to get them out.

'If ever you see Margaret again tell her I love her.'

Some more coughing, some muffled inaudible stuttering, and that was it. I began to pummel his chest again, one hand over the other. I tried in vain to thump some life back into him, but with no result. Gerry was gone.

His eyes were red and open. I took off my mitt and closed them, then kissed his forehead and said a prayer, the Lord's Prayer. Then I said goodbye, sobbing selfishly, sobbing for myself. This sort of thing only happened in books, on the screen, in battle, not to me, not to Gerry. We were ordinary people. This couldn't happen to me, to us! But it just had. How could this be?

I had prayed, I had beseeched for help, for strength, and I'd got it, and somehow revived my crewmate. Now what? If I'd been shattered before, I was doubly so now. My stomach was knotted. I clung onto Gerry and sobbed like a child. I was physically and emotionally shipwrecked. I slumped down into the cockpit, down into the water-filled well and wept; I was sorry for Gerry and sorry for myself.

My cold brain once again began to race, play tricks on me. I now began to think about the repercussions of Gerry's passing. If I got through this, if I saw Margaret again, what on earth was I going to say? Obviously, I would pass on what

Gerry had asked me to, but what else could I possibly say? Impossible, I couldn't think that far ahead.

My thoughts drifted back to prayer. No, it wasn't prayer – this time it was more of contemplation. I thought of something that my godmother, Myrtle, had given to me around the time of my confirmation, more than ten years ago. It was an illustrated postcard with some lines on it. A poem maybe, I wasn't sure. It was about a man who was walking along the beach with the Lord. I tried hard, really hard to piece together the words. I became obsessed, as if remembering it correctly might somehow help to save my life. At first my thoughts were disjointed. Then, as my memories of the card from years before became clearer, the words began to assemble themselves in the right order. I recalled that the man became upset, even distraught that in times of difficulty he could see only one set of footprints in the sand; he thought that during these times the Lord must have abandoned him. Eventually fluent, I cried the last couple of lines above the noise of the chaos around me:

> "Why, when I needed you most, have you not been
> there for me Lord?"
> The Lord replied,
> "The years when you have seen only one set of
> footprints, my child, is when I carried you."

Substantial and appropriate, tears came easily. I felt better for saying it, but only slightly sodding better. Words, however well written, however well said, are only words; comforting, but still just words. Written words could not save lives, not my life, or Gerry's.

My mouth was sore, swollen by saltwater, dry. I was alone, and paranoia was creeping over me. I poked my head above the cockpit coaming and looked astern. There were no footprints at all, there was no bloody sand, there wasn't even a horizon, or a sky, just cold grey nothingness rising up behind.

If ever I needed friends, crewmates, Gerry, I needed them, him, now. At that moment, a wave lifted the boat's stern, swept me off my feet and threw me backwards, up in the air, past Gerry's body. I landed on my back, head first, onto the horizontal lip of the companionway, the entrance to *Grimalkin*'s cabin. It took me a while to recover my senses but when I did I swivelled my head round and peered into the dark of the boat's interior. What a god-awful mess.

Eleven

Blood-tinged Red Roses

I turned onto my stomach and lay there, face down, staring into the depths of the dark cabin. Behind me the waves thumped violently into *Grimalkin*'s stern: bang, bang, bang. A bitch of a rain-squall pitched the seas into added anger, accelerating the crests. Above me, thick black clouds hurled solid, ice-cold lumps of liquid at my face. This storm defied every meteorological term, defied every law of gravity; it quite simply defied everything I had been taught over the years.

Through squinting, sore eyes, I caught a glimpse of another mountainous wave thundering towards *Grimalkin* like a prowling beast. I stretched my neck upwards to find the top of this monstrous body of water, but I couldn't, it was too high. I had seen waves of similar formation in north Biscay the previous year. Its shape was similar, but that was all – the noise this one created, the size of it, was something else. This wall of water must have been 60 or 70 feet high and as wide as Waterloo station, with steam-like foam hissing and venting from its tumbling sides.

As the crest of the wave lifted the stern, I felt its power.

Its noise, its vicious signature, gathered me up like a watery-gloved claw. *Grimalkin*'s angle steepened, she gathered momentum and I plunged down, pathetically, frantically snatching at sodden rope tails, mooring cleats, debris – everything slipped from my grasp. She was now almost vertical. A stanchion appeared – reaching out, I missed it by inches. I felt like I'd lost my footing on a crumbling cliff edge. Now airborne, both prisoners of this wave, Gerry and I were flung round the cockpit – our heads, limbs and trunks collided violently.

Grimalkin, now fully vertical, was on the brink of pitch-poling, exactly what Mike and I had spent most of the night trying to avoid. Her hull was swept up by an avalanche of high-speed madness. From between Gerry's flailing legs I saw the foredeck. It was submerged. *Grimalkin*'s stern was above me, tumbling clockwise. She was cartwheeling. It was instant, sneaky, slippery and finger-snapping quick, quick as a flash.

Now her bow was in one wave, her stern in the next trough. Gerry and I hung in mid-air, nothing beneath us. I clung to my harness tether. The boat's stern overtook her bow and I felt myself corkscrew. I was showered by spume, unable to see anything. I had to wait for the boat to catch up with herself and settle, all the time knowing there would be a painful price to pay. With a thud I was slammed straight back into the cockpit on top of Gerry. Despite the pain, the choking and the vomiting, I thanked God that it was Gerry and not the sea that had broken my fall. I watched the floor of the cockpit slowly right itself and wondered just how this ballsy 30-foot yacht had recovered herself yet again from these glacier-sized waves, from these torrents of abuse.

I clung onto the slippery sides of the cockpit, tasting, smelling, seeing and hearing the intoxicating madness going on around what was now my boat. More than ever, my life hung on the malicious whim of the next wave. As *Grimalkin* tumbled down yet another trough, Gerry's elbow walloped me, bang in the centre of my right cheek.

'Jesus Christ, Gerry . . . BACK OFF!'

Oblivious to me, to pain, to everything, Gerry crashed into me time after time. There he was – a silent, lifeless shadow stalking me. I feared the unpredictable actions of his body, knowing that during a large swell I had no control over them. As I worried about the consequences of this ongoing battering and wondered how much more I could take, a thought went through my mind. It would be easy to unclip Gerry and let the sea do the rest – rid me of this added and unnecessary worry. In a mad, breaking-news-type message that interrupted all other ideas, lightning-quick flashes relayed information to me about the unlucky dead, about how they hindered a ship's progress, about corpses bringing bad luck.

But then I caught a view of his battered face, his prominent, bloodied nose, and his lips now grey but still familiar. No way could I do that – no one could have done that to a friend, a crewmate. I dismissed the idea immediately. What was I thinking of? It was a ludicrous, nasty, selfish thought. But pursuing the idea in a more reasoned, rational manner, I thought maybe I could move his body into the cabin. It would take some effort but it could be done. I could drag him to the companionway entrance and then lower him down with a line. But then what would happen? I began to visualise Gerry being tossed about in the debris-filled cabin.

Shuddering, I abandoned the idea – his body would be slashed to bits in no time and blood-red water would be left swishing around the bilges beneath. Gerry had to stay with me in the cockpit, and one way or another we would have to try and avoid a serious collision.

I looked up to the skies and then around me. The seas under the low clouds could hardly be described as seas any longer – they were vicious, fast-moving, unearthly matter. Higher than *Grimalkin*'s length, they were powerful and brutal enough to toss her around as if she were a matchbox. I was a matchstick man, in a matchbox boat, at the mercy of the elements.

'What should I do next?' The cold, grey matter between my freezing ears kept asking the question. If *Grimalkin* rolled or capsized again, I would not survive, that I knew for sure. With no crewmates left and in my deteriorating physical condition, there was no point in trying to control the boat. This storm would beat me down – that, too, I knew for certain. I had a sudden macabre desire to try to revive Gerry again. I checked his neck and wrists – there was no pulse. He was bitterly cold to touch.

Only one option remained open to me, if I was not to be bullied to death by this storm – to risk going below into the cabin, however dangerous, and see if anything was working down there. I needed to make contact with some kind of rescue. But just how insane a risk was this?

I reached out and clung onto the cabin entrance to steady myself. I checked my harness tether, its attachment, then grabbed the mainsheet traveller. I waited for a let-up in the violence around me.

'One ... two ... three ... four ...' Like a referee counting out a boxer's knockout blow. I made it to ten, four, maybe five times, before the lull finally came.

Still anticipating the peaks and troughs, I clutched the bridge deck, the raised approach to *Grimalkin*'s cabin. My grip held firm. At last, some headway. As I deliberated my next move, I heard an alarmingly loud scraping noise from beneath the boat – unfamiliar and foreign, it unnerved me completely. What the hell was it? I held my grip and warily scanned the area.

Finally, through the thick weather, I saw the exact cause: the mast was still attached to the boat and was being dragged through the water. Bloody brilliant! On top of the mast was the three-foot whip antenna, and with that still attached there was a slim chance of the VHF working – a lifeline to contact. I had to think fast, regain my focus and make a decision. As I ran my eyes over the length of the mast – the words risk and survival tearing through my mind – I saw that it was broken in what looked like two places. This was not good, but if there was no break in the coaxial cable and the aerial's connection, or in the wired terminal and the plug, it might still have power. My decision was made. I had got this far and despite physical risk I was going down there.

I glanced back down into the cabin. I noticed its smell for the first time: oily, acrid. I saw scum floating on the surface of the water, a surface that surged violently back and forth, up and down. Beneath me, I could feel the seas building to a new attack. An image flashed into my mind – blood pumping from David Sheahan's gaping wound, followed by an image of him being swept away, drowning, unheard.

However violently I shook my head, I could not erase this image from it. My resolve had weakened. I stared down into the depths of *Grimalkin*'s ravaged cabin.

'Go on, chicken . . . you can do it.'

Then a stream of voices, all my own, arguing.

'You can't risk your life down there.'

'You have to. How else are you going to survive?'

'You're a coward.'

From nowhere, a monster wave reared its ugly head. I was caught out, unprepared. I fought frantically for balance, for grip – none was possible. The wave knocked the legs from beneath me and tossed me about like a rag doll before smashing me face down into the cockpit – back on top of Gerry, back where I had started. Blood spurted from my nose and seeped through my sodden gloves. I could barely lift my head with the pain, but worst of all I knew I had blown everything. At the last minute I had fluffed it.

Bodily battered, I could do nothing but stay slumped in the cockpit alongside Gerry. His face was next to mine. I noticed a thin trail of blood running from his mouth, staining the bitterly cold water in the cockpit-well pink. Or was it my own? Dead flesh. Poor Gerry; beyond prayer but still not at peace. I gazed at the man, not the flesh. More than his friendship I had needed his survival; instead I had experienced a death. I had heard the dying words of a friend. Death had been in my arms; I had tasted it. And I was likely to suffer a similar fate – with the difference that no one, not a soul, would hear my last words. I shook uncontrollably, and heard myself crying into the wind.

All the while, *Grimalkin* continued to buck and kick like an out-of-control bronco, unbothered by the fact that she no longer had a helmsman or that five of her crew had perished or abandoned her. I slumped further into the well, frozen, dispirited, waiting – waiting for what? I was so cold that I'd stopped shivering; my teeth had stopped chattering too. Although my brain was dulled, I knew well the symptoms and sequence of hypothermia. When the body begins using up all reserves, it stops chattering, stops shivering and begins shutting down. I began writhing, rocking in time, as far as I could, with the boat's violent, unpredictable motion.

Waves crashed onto *Grimalkin*'s decks; streams of water poured into the cockpit and joined the surging reservoir down below. I wanted peace now, with no pain. I found myself hypnotised by a stream of water directly in my eyeline. I had arrived at a point of oblivion. The noise around me began to grow silent; the smell drifting up from the cabin diminished, replaced by something different, something more familiar – the smell of nicotine and flowers. I closed my eyes and felt peaceful. I was going to a safer place, a place of refuge that offered comfort, warmth and security.

I was flat out on my hospital bed, at 15 years of age. Ma was sitting on a chair beside me, reading some racing results from *Yachting & Boating Weekly*. Then that familiar tang of untipped Senior Service cigarettes – great stuff, Pa was coming. I tried to sit up, but of course I couldn't. Although weeks had passed I hadn't got used to this yet – being paralysed.

'Hello, old man, how are you today?'

Pa stood over me with a bunch of red roses in one hand and the stub of a Senior Service in the other.

'I thought these might cheer you up a bit. Here, take a smell.'

Pa leaned forward and held the red roses close to my face. They smelt good, like apples I thought. For a moment I savoured their scent. As Pa pulled away, I felt something

131

cold on my left arm. I stared down and saw that a droplet
of water had fallen from the rose stems onto my skin. Pa
and I exchanged a glance. Pa instinctively understood that
something new had happened – that I had experienced some
kind of sensation, at last. He pressed the alarm button next
to the bed.

'Nurse, NURSE! Please . . . quick!'

Ma jumped to her feet. Pa kept calling until one, two,
then three nurses ran to my bedside. Surrounded by so many
concerned faces I became overwhelmed. An unwanted loud
noise began to fill my ears, as loud as a turbine, all-pervading
and annoying. I felt myself being pushed forcefully away – as
if being pushed back into the mattress where I lay. Away from
Ma, away from Pa, away from all that I found warm and
secure. I wanted to stretch out my arms and hold onto them,
but I was being sucked down into a murky, wet, freezing place.
Their faces began to fade, then there was nothing. All was still
– eerily so, chillingly so. Moments passed before I was abruptly
catapulted upwards and thrust forward out of the water,
cracking my forehead on the lip of the cockpit lid.

This was a brutal awakening. I was drenched and
freezing once again, but coming to now, I had a greater
recognition of myself, as if potent smelling salts had been
wafted beneath my nose. I felt different. A new, deep-rooted,
mind-changing conviction engulfed me. That moment, eight
years earlier, had been inspirational – it had given me
strength, a lifeline to recovery.

My parents were told back then that as a result of the
life-saving cut the surgeons had been forced to make, the left
side of my body was paralysed and it was unlikely I would
ever walk again. It was Pa who gave me this news. I clearly

remember him and Ma sitting either side of my bed, desperately trying to retain some kind of composure. I realised that they were trying to come to terms with this news, but for myself I felt nothing, no reaction whatsoever. The thought of not being able to walk again was not something I would contemplate. I simply refused to accept it as an option. Maybe it was youthful naivety or maybe delayed shock – I have no idea. But it was the best reaction I could have had, because in the weeks that followed I was determined to prove them wrong. No walking? Worse still, no sailing? That's what I lived for. I'd rather have died than not walk, not sail again.

Back to the present, back on *Grimalkin*, in this cockpit, this hellhole, with Gerry beside me, the effect was equally inspirational. My teeth were beginning to chatter, my body was shivering again. Life was forcing its way back into my frozen, exhausted body. The loud turbine noises I had heard still rang in my ears – increasingly loud, increasingly close. Instantly I felt a wave of relief – they were the very same high-pitched noises we had all heard circling above us before *Grimalkin*'s final capsize. I looked at Gerry, jumped up and started yelling with joy.

'It's back, Gerry, the Nimrod is back! They're coming to get us!'

With black clouds still low I could see nothing. Panic set in. I had to be sure the Nimrod could see me. My first rational thought was to somehow make contact with it, let them know we were here. The flares – shit, the flares. I remembered they had all been used. But it was dark then, and we were in total pandemonium – one flare could have fallen aside, got trapped or wedged in a crevice. I ploughed through the endless lines of sodden rope that surrounded me. I found nothing. I now began wondering if there was maybe an undischarged flare beneath Gerry. I forced my hands under his back but couldn't shift his dead weight. Fraught, I shouted at his bloodied face.

'Come on, Gerry, MOVE, for God's sake . . . get the hell up.'

Gerry didn't move; the turbine noises were still above us. My desperation turned to anger. I locked my arms beneath his armpits and managed to roll him aside. No flares. Shit. A jolt of the boat knocked me backwards, sending a searing pain straight through my shoulder. As water filled the cockpit it lifted Gerry, making him float towards me; that was weird, too weird – I closed my eyes tight. *Grimalkin* steadied herself. I opened my eyes. Nothing had changed, but like a startled rabbit, that jolt had made me reorder my thoughts.

OK, so the flares were all gone, that was blatantly clear, as blatant as the engine noises circling above us. I needed another means of contact. What else could I do? I had to communicate with the rescue services, be they the RAF, the Navy, the RORC, the Coastguard or the RNLI. The Nimrod just above us could at least give our position to someone else. I could risk going below but time was against me and the Nimrod could be gone before I even got there.

Then, like a bolt out of the blue, I remembered the Callbuoy, a piece of emergency equipment, a waterproof, removable transmitter that was stowed in the cockpit locker. How the hell had I not thought of it earlier? We hadn't used it last night because the main VHF set, in the cabin below, had been far more powerful – it had more channels, more frequencies, greater range and was connected to the boat's supply. The Callbuoy had limited battery life and was only used as back-up in a last resort. Well, I was in that last-resort situation, and back-up was exactly what I needed.

Down on my knees, I pulled open the cockpit locker – the Callbuoy wasn't in its stowage position. I scrambled through the locker's contents but could see nothing. It was bright orange so it would have stood out. Frantically, I ripped out what I could get hold of: sail ties, winch handles, race instructions, stowed fenders, water filler-cap keys – everything but what I wanted. My mind began thinking the same stomach-churning thoughts as when I'd discovered the cut harness line. Had the others taken the Callbuoy, my only other means of contact with the outside world? It made sense, if they had left on the life raft.

Or had the set fallen out, maybe drifted off somewhere? No, this wasn't possible; the cockpit locker had been firmly closed. Head first now, I almost climbed inside the confined space – and there it was, the Callbuoy, under bilge water, tangled in the Morse gear and throttle cables. I grabbed it and extracted myself from the locker. I could still hear the Nimrod circling above, but how much longer would it stay there? I raised the aerial and deployed its earth over the side. The set crackled static. I began to shout into the transmitter.

'MAYDAY, MAYDAY, OVER. Yacht *Grimalkin* dismasted – two crewmen, I repeat, two crewmen. OVER.'

I waited for a response. None came.

'MAYDAY, MAYDAY.'

I paused. One, two – deep breath – hands trembling as I gripped tightly onto the Callbuoy.

'YACHT *GRIMALKIN* – SAIL NUMBER KILO, FIVE, SIX, THREE, SEVEN. OVER.'

The noise of crackling static was beginning to fade out.

This was not at all what I'd expected – why hadn't it lasted longer? I checked the earth line; it was OK. I checked its connection to the set; it was OK too. I checked the transmit button and again it looked OK. All this time the crackling noise was growing fainter. Afraid of opening the set for fear of making things worse, I kept checking the rubber 'panic' button, its transmit switch. My right thumb ached from the pressure as I tried in vain to reactivate the set. Then, like the fizzing sound of wet sparklers, as if creeping up my arm, the crackling faded to silence. The Callbuoy was defunct, of no further use. I flung it into the water-logged cockpit and watched it float off. Utterly distraught that I had received no response from the outside world, I looked down at Gerry.

'What the hell are you doing there?' I yelled angrily. All the while, I could hear that damned Nimrod noise just above me. 'Help me, for God's sake. Jesus Christ almighty, I can't do everything.'

Then I began to talk to him more calmly. 'Do you think we got through, Gerry?' Not thinking about it or expecting a response, I just carried on talking. 'It's still there, isn't it? You can still hear it, can't you?'

Instantly Gerry was the greatest of sounding boards. It seemed right, somehow – not normal, but right. The clarity I gained from consulting with him was so steadying, so re-assuring. I certainly wasn't about to stop. My thoughts were vivid and sharp. I had to keep my mind active – any thoughts were better than none – any speech better than the wind-filled roar. Shaking, I had a compulsion to risk going below once more and make that mayday call from the main VHF. I conferred with Gerry.

'Should I go down below? You were down there last night . . . it was working then, wasn't it?'

All I could hear was that enticing Nimrod noise above me. My only means of contact with it, however slim, lay below deck. With this thought of one last, desperate chance, the decision was made. I waited for the next lull, then gave Gerry a nod of reassurance.

'Right, Gerry, you stay up where the Nimrod can see you. I'll go below.'

Standing upright was difficult with unsteady legs and I accidentally trod on Gerry's chest with my full weight.

'Sorry, Gerry . . . sorry.'

There was no moan, no complaint from him. I stumbled across the cockpit from the helm to the companionway and placed my hands firmly on each side of the boat's cabin entrance. This time things were going to be done on my terms. Cautiously, I unclipped my harness and swung myself over the sill. With my legs dangling over the void, I saw the companionway ladder was gone. Shit, it had been wrenched from its mountings. I had no choice but to use the companionway sides to take my weight. As I lowered myself, slowly, painfully, into *Grimalkin*'s cabin, my boots filled with cold seawater. It sounded like a fast-flowing but log-jammed river down here – wreckage was banging and crashing from side to side. Avoiding serious injury was going to be my biggest problem. By the time my boots touched the floor I was in water and debris above the knees.

I took a good look around. I'd never seen a boat so water-logged. How the hell had she not sunk already, pitching around with what looked and felt like a couple of tons of the stuff? A small blue plastic bucket floated by and my instinct was to pick it up and start bailing. I had to stop myself – I had to keep firmly focused on the job at hand.

Nothing looked familiar down here. The engine housing had come completely apart; the navigation table was off its hinges; the VHF had been wrenched off its bracket. My eyes quickly followed the telephone-like cable to the set's handset – there it was, submerged. There was no hope of it working. Even so, I clutched the forward bulkhead, heaved myself through the mass of freezing sea and grabbed it, my thumb poised, ready to depress the switch. I pressed – nothing happened – I pressed again, over and over, till my thumb stiffened with cramp. The handset was completely screwed, useless. As I tampered with it, a loud scraping noise along the outside of the boat was an insensitive reminder of the fallen mast carrying the defunct antenna – my last hope of contact. I smashed the handset against the bulkhead of the ravaged cabin and let out an almighty roar, above the howling gale, above the tormenting scraping noise of the fallen mast. I thought I could hear the screams of my crewmates in response – it was some job to convince myself that this was just my imagination.

Just beneath me I felt the seas shorten and steepen – an absolute bitch of a gust swept up the swell. *Grimalkin* tilted harshly, slamming down on her starboard side – a cold, green sea forced its way through the shattered port light above me, filling my nose, mouth and ears. I stood there, cold, stiff, trying to regain my senses, and then realised, to my horror, that I could no longer hear the jet engines. Shocked by the absence of the screaming turbine noises, I yelled up to Gerry:

'Is it still there?'

I pulled down my hood, narrowed my eyes and strained to hear.

'Can you hear it?' I yelled to Gerry again. I was maddened and confused. 'Come on, GERRY – pull your hood down! OPEN YOUR EARS AND LISTEN.'

I shook my head from side to side, trying to unblock my ears, but with the noise of the boiling seas around me nothing was distinguishable. I had to get back on deck and find out what the hell was going on. Breathing hard, desperately trying to identify some kind of engine sounds, I dragged myself upwards and out through the companionway, snagging my trousers on the jagged, torn metal ladder. Freezing liquid shot into my oilskins up to the base of my spine. I panicked as the coldness penetrated my body.

Leaning against the companionway I frantically scanned the low skies. As I jumped up into the cockpit an anger swelled up inside my head, thumping loudly at my brow, as I grasped that the noise of engines had disappeared entirely. The dead man sharing this cockpit with me inspired my wrath. It was an indecent, incandescent wrath – it spawned in me the desire to shout, swear and rant.

'What the hell are you doing? I told you to keep watch . . . why the hell didn't you warn me the Nimrod was going?'

I shouted obscenity after obscenity at my deceased friend. Profane things, things I would never normally have dreamt of saying, of even thinking. I felt an outlandish desire to inflict bodily pain. I purged myself, purged that wrath, directly at Gerry. It was an expression – not an acceptance – of gut-wrenching loneliness. Was that my last hope of rescue gone?

The swell I had felt below in the cabin was escalating. Ceaseless seas like corrugated iron were stacked up behind us, row upon row, as if awaiting their turn. I picked one out, choosing the most deformed monster from this cliff-face of madness. I stared at it, mad, enraged. I kept staring. I focused on this one huge moving mass, waiting for it.

Grimalkin lifted sharply. The horizon was nearly vertical but this time I made no effort to save myself. All instinct for survival had abandoned me. I stood in the cockpit with Gerry at my feet, taunting the wave to get me. As the horizon disappeared I implored this malevolent beast to knock me out cold, kill me.

'Come on, you bastard, come on . . .'

The beast towered above me. Then a fleeting image – Pa, Ma, my family, my friends – my life, still unlived. My gut twisted, I stopped shouting. A rational, balanced, simple thought came into my head.

'No, no . . . I don't want to die. Not yet.'

My about-turn had come late. The beast pounced, throwing Gerry and me upwards out of the cockpit, its force pulling, pushing, hurtling us through its body in whatever direction it chose. Eyes closed tight, I waited for my fate to be delivered. I landed, felt my legs being pulled through the icy water. Opening my eyes I saw I had been saved by the deck but was being dragged towards the sea. Inches from my head, I spotted a winch drum – reached out my right hand, grabbed it and held on. This was it, life or death, right here, right now on the edge of this boat. As *Grimalkin* dragged herself upright again, shaking off gallons of water, I used every last ounce of strength to heave myself on board, into the cockpit and to safety. I clipped on, out of such stupid, senseless, self-inflicted danger.

This latest barrage left Gerry upside down in a posture only a tethered corpse could manage. Inanimate and white-faced, he looked bizarre and sad. I felt embarrassment, guilt, at my verbal attack on him. None of this was his fault – we'd been left, maybe even abandoned, alone together. Finding it difficult to be gentle with him, I manhandled his body into a less ungainly position, as dignified as the seas allowed. I needed him now more than ever, just as I knew he needed me.

Overwhelmed by what lay ahead, I felt alone, isolated – shockingly so, and this feeling was compounded by Gerry's dumb presence. I had to get my sounding board back, get my clarity back – I had to get him back on side. We had to talk.

Twelve

Dead or Alive?

Every sinew, every muscle, each and every tendon in my body hurt, excruciatingly so. I could see no real signs of any change in the ferocity of the storm – the noise, the drenching, went on and on, beating me down, forcing me to cower down in the well. I needed a breather, some respite to gather my thoughts, regain some strength – get some clarity back into my thumping head. My foremost worry was the amount of water we were carrying. Having seen it for myself, I knew that just one more violent combination of wind and wave, together with the surging mass of water below, could lead to us sinking.

Maybe I could venture out of the cockpit and onto the deck to see how far the waterline had changed outside the boat – see how immediate the danger of foundering was.

On my knees, I reached out and grabbed a stanchion and slowly, cautiously, gripping tightly, I craned my head forward into the gale. I couldn't see anything, the rain – the hail – bounced off the deck, creating a stinging, impenetrable obstacle. Glass-like lumps, bounced off the deck and the cabin windows, were hurled against my face. I reached out further and with all my strength gripped the next stanchion – the guardrail wire painfully cut into my gut but I could just about see the water level. I quickly realised that what I could see was not the true surface, the actual waterline. The spume created by the swells and the hailstones smashing up against the hull prevented me seeing this.

Somewhat frustrated, I stretched yet further to the next stanchion, three feet or more along the deck. I could just about reach it but the raised genoa track prevented me from getting a sure footing. This was all getting gravely tricky. Holding on grimly, leaning hard against my harness, I gripped the next stanchion and looked over. My suspicions were confirmed. As below decks, *Grimalkin*'s waterline was around two feet higher. She now lay so low in the water that only a small portion of her exterior could be seen – her dark-blue handwritten name barely visible. I needed no further evidence to recognise that this boat could go down, founder at any time. One rogue wave and we were gone. Utterly shocked by this and the vision of her half-lost name, I loosened my grip and slipped as *Grimalkin* plunged down into a trough. I was hurled upwards, then thrust heavily downwards onto the guardrail, my chest taking the brunt. For an instant I teetered on the brink of plunging head first over the side. Inches from tumbling overboard I had managed to grip the horizontal guardrail wires either side of my body. Heart pounding, on all fours, going through the same procedure in reverse, I retreated into the safety of the cockpit – once more thanking God and my harness for saving me.

Half sitting, half kneeling, I unclipped my harness and rubbed my chest – it ached beyond any soothing. *Grimalkin* tilted sharply, tipping me bodily into Gerry. Head thumping, I hurriedly clipped on again.

I wanted to get back down in the cabin and start bailing, but the risks were still immense. At any moment a violent surge in the storm could result in injury. My primary worry was the free-floating floorboards, which could smash into me, breaking one or both of my legs, perhaps leaving me unable to get back on deck. Any injury at this point, no matter how small, would severely weaken my chances of survival.

It seemed that everything I attempted to do was thwarted by a barrier; every way I turned there was an obstruction. I knew, only too well, how all this stuff should work – Callbuoys and their like – but fixing it, using it, was impossible. Nothing wanted to work for me. *Grimalkin*'s once willing, once inspiring hull was now just a sodden container for two sodden bodies.

'What the hell are we supposed to do now, Gerry?'

Glancing down at my watch I saw it too was cracked and broken, and had stopped. Like so much else around me, my trusted timepiece had fallen victim to the battering. It was strange that I hadn't noticed its malfunction earlier, but then time, an integral part of any race, had become irrelevant – like the race itself. I remembered then that Gerry had a watch – yes, of course he did – we all did. I sat up and took his wrist, gently pulling up his oilskin sleeve. Through the condensation I studied the face – trying to figure out where the hands were. As far as I could see it read twenty minutes to two – surely not? Could so much time have passed? I leaned forward to study the face more closely and realised that, like mine, his watch had stopped, the hands stuck at nine minutes past seven – probably around the time I had lost consciousness. I looked at Gerry's hand in mine. His gnarled finger joints seemed to have been squeezed with a pipe wrench before being frozen. They were blue in colour, squashed, tight and slightly bloodied. At that moment I glimpsed an empty harness next to Gerry, still clipped to its strongpoint. The sight of this abandoned harness left me feeling very uneasy.

'It just doesn't add up,' I murmured softly.

What exactly did take place at nine minutes past seven? What were the circumstances on *Grimalkin* at that time, the circumstances that led to Gerry and me being left alone in the Irish Sea during a storm of this magnitude?

Crouched in the weather-beaten cockpit with Gerry, my head still swirling from the many blows I'd sustained, I nonetheless coldly and unemotionally began to picture the worst-possible scenario. Could Matt, Mike and Dave have been swept away from the boat to their deaths? While this was the most logical explanation, it didn't make sense. What about the abandoned harnesses? Why had they taken them off? Even more bizarre, why was there a cut line? If they had gone overboard, I would have found one, perhaps two of them clipped on alongside the boat, like Gerry, dead or alive.

My thoughts began to go haywire. Even that last image I had of David being swept away confused me. How could he have been swept away while still clipped onto the boat? Unless, God forbid, it was his harness line that was cut. But who would have cut it, and why? Taking a few deep breaths, I tried to concentrate. All of my assumptions now led me to think that something else had occurred, another event had happened on the boat or to the boat.

What if that last image I had of the huge wall of water

had led to a B2 knockdown? There was strong evidence of this: the mast had broken, which was usual in a full 180-degree capsize. While this made sense, nothing I could bring to mind would explain the disappearance of my three remaining crewmates, the cut and abandoned harnesses and the missing life raft. Could the life raft have blown away while Matt, Dave and Mike were trying to transfer Gerry and me into it? I began to picture Gerry and me alongside the boat, in the water. But I couldn't quite get my head around this either – one of the crew would have seen us. And if so, why wouldn't they have pulled us out of the water? I began to remember the arguing – the loud, heated voices, my own words strongly advocating that we stay on the boat. Perhaps my crewmates saw me as an obstruction, an inconvenience to their proposed course of action. Even this didn't really make sense – what of Gerry? Why didn't they take him? Maybe they saw us both as liabilities.

With my mind jumping from one scenario to another, my heart began to race and my breath to shorten. As I replaced Gerry's contorted, swollen hand on his chest, a new anger welled up inside me. My brain was cold, numbed, but it was still working – for me, for Gerry and for *Grimalkin*. What the hell had gone on? Nothing made sense. I knew for certain David was dead, but what of the others? Where the hell were my three crewmates?

The anger, generated by the thought of Gerry and me being left behind, turned to guilt as I considered the possibility of my three crewmates drowning. But I needed anger in order to survive; guilt would surely finish me off.

'No, damn it and damn them too.'

They were all damned as far as I was concerned –

damned by Gerry, too; I was sure of it. I cursed all three of them on behalf of myself and Gerry. Expletives filled the wet air around us.

I felt motivated once more. I looked up – the clouds were still well formed, a palette of dark greys and blacks that was at once beautiful and evil. There was no sun. I searched for signs of light but the clouds were low and angry and the greyness blocked everything out. It wasn't even possible to judge the sun's height. I guessed it was around eleven in the morning but I had no real idea. As I watched the formations of movement and colour above me, I noticed that occasionally, very occasionally, *Grimalkin*'s movement was different, less vehement. The weather, although still atrocious, appeared slightly less threatening. It was very subtle and I began to wonder if I was imagining it. Was it a trick?

Meticulously studying the conditions around me, both on and off the boat, I noticed that the severed mast had a positive braking effect on *Grimalkin*, and realised that this may have prevented a total capsize in the hours Gerry and I had been alone. Gradually, after watching all this for a time – it could have been ten minutes, it could have been an hour – I gained a sort of confidence that there might be hope for us. We had hung on so far, as had *Grimalkin*. Even half full of water, she had persevered, refused to give in – submission was not part of this boat's being. I felt now she was protecting me, me and Gerry – doggedly. She was awesome, bloody miraculous. I grabbed hold of Gerry.

'Can you feel the pressure change? The weather is turning, Gerry . . . I'm sure of it.'

This confidence in the apparent moderation of sea, motion, wind and weather prompted me into thinking about

147

my next move. I knew certain things: I needed my medication and, Christ, I was thirsty, hungry. Hours and hours had passed since I had eaten or drunk anything. I knew that the body could go without food for days, but water was far more important, vital. Fresh water, I needed that – my mouth was dry, salty-dry, and needed hydrating. But still my most pressing worry at this point was the water level inside the boat. Water, food, medication – all irrelevant if the boat went down.

Could I risk it now and go below? I was searching Gerry's face for a sign of what I should do, when a childhood memory flashed – like a ticker-tape message – in front of my eyes. It was something Pa had said to me when I was nine years old. He was on his knees, weeding the back garden.

'If you're going through hell – keep going,' Pa said, borrowing from Churchill. He found some aspects of gardening a chore.

I was looking at Gerry, but thinking of Pa. That's what Pa had said, and I knew if I was to survive this very real hell – the hell around me as well as the hell in my head – I had to keep going. That half-glanced blue bucket – seen floating among the debris of the cabin – I could and would bail the boat with that, no matter that it was small. Moving towards the companionway, I rubbed Gerry's leg with my left hand, for me as much as for him.

'Right, Gerry . . . I'm going below again. OK?'

There was work to be done.

Thirteen

Softly, Softly, Catchee Monkey

My boots had barely touched the cabin floor and I was immersed in freezing water to well above my knees.

I called up to Gerry. 'Jesus, you think it's cold up there . . . try it down here, mate.'

My words were strangely muted in the cabin – probably because of all the water. As I predicted, avoiding lethal debris – floating floorboards, shattered fittings and other items, some randomly airborne – proved difficult. I reached for a bunk pole and looped my safety harness round it. I kept it short for stability, but with enough length for me to reach out to about a three-foot range.

Odd noises came from both within and outside the cabin. It was hard to know what was coming from where and what each noise meant. Powerful waves were still smashing their way into and under *Grimalkin*'s hull, trying to tip her over, and the debris-filled water on the inside continued to surge back and forth. The reverberations from outside made me feel nauseous. But if I was to progress in my task, I would have to adjust myself to this new environment, accept that crashing and banging were the features of my new abode.

First, I needed to establish the quickest means of escape. It was obvious: the companionway. The only other exit was the forehatch and under these conditions it was unreachable. My next task was to find and secure the blue bucket – unsurprisingly it wasn't where I had last seen it. Treading cautiously like a tethered animal, I rummaged through the mountains of debris for something blue. The boat lurched with an unexpected swell. I gripped the headlining above me and waited for it to pass. A galley locker door swung open – J-cloths and a can of Bilgex floated out into the rising bilge water. On the hunt once more I noticed David's single-handed dividers, their two pointed ends embedded into the headlining above the navigation table. This was a dangerous habitat.

To my right I spotted something blue wedged between the hanging locker and a shelf – the bucket. I reached out for it but the floating floorboards trapped my feet and I fell, face first, into the filthy freezing water. I gagged. I had swallowed some; it tasted foul, and smelt worse. Still gagging, I reached out again and found the handle. I yanked till the little blue bugger freed itself, then I pulled myself back upright.

'Yes . . . yes . . . yes!' I whooped with joy. Something was going my way at last. Two fingers to the giant – I'd got it, it was mine.

'I got it, Gerry, I got it . . . I GOT THE FRIGGING BUCKET!'

I now possessed an asset, a means to an end. I emptied its contents and tied it to the broken companionway ladder. My thoughts turned to the next priority – nourishment. I was thirsty, so damn thirsty . . . I was drawn towards the galley sink. Another massive wave prised its way beneath the hull, forcing me to wait. Finally the swell passed. I moved towards the sink pump, reached it, grabbed the handle and pushed – nothing. I pushed again, this time with more force – what little liquid came out was salty and contaminated. The non-return valve must have sucked in some rubbish. Willing it to work I gave it a couple more pumps but it jammed completely. This was pointless anyway. The main tanks had clearly ruptured at some point, probably during a knockdown, and emptied themselves into the heaving mass of water around.

So, no easy access to fresh water via the sink, but I knew there were tanks of water somewhere in the cabin. David had installed two extra 5-gallon tanks of drinking water, specially for the race. They were more robust, so less likely to have punctured. Like everything else, they weren't anywhere near where they should have been.

I began to scour the debris around me. I was surprised I couldn't see them – they were too huge to miss. Then it struck me – if they hadn't been ruptured, would they be floating? No way – their weight wouldn't allow it. Retching at the mere thought of it, I got down on my hands and knees to dredge through the bilge. I noticed excrement floating on the surface. The toilet had been pumped dry, but the pipe between hull and bowl had regurgitated its contents. I kept moving, keeping my mouth firmly closed. Torrents of water surged around me, permeating my clothing. It was vile, fetid. I forced myself to stay down, trying not to think about what was seeping down the neck of my oilskin.

Agitated at my failure to find the tanks, I was about to vent my frustration up to Gerry when I saw the reason staring right at me – the cabin entrance. Of course, with both washboards no longer in place, the tanks had most likely been flung out of the boat during a B1 or B2 knock-down, and were probably sitting on the bed of the Irish Sea, hundreds of feet beneath us. It was time to give up this pointless scavenge. I felt *Grimalkin*'s stern begin to lift, severely – I had to get back to my stronghold, the bunk pole. Moved along by the torrents of water that journeyed in bulk from one end of the cabin to the other, I nonetheless managed to hold on to the bunk pole and regain my balance. As I waited for the boat to level herself, a can of pineapple chunks rolled down the water slide towards me. This was the most bizarre, unexpected thing – a gift of liquid and food in one. The juice would slake my thirst and the chunks would quell the bile, stop the griping. The label peeled away in my hand, and it occurred to me I had no knife, no opener. Another hand and knee trawl through the cabin? No, that would be hopeless.

Head spinning with utter frustration, I was about to toss the can up into the bows when I remembered David's single-handed dividers embedded in the headlining – their points would at least access me some liquid. Stumbling towards them, I grabbed and pulled with all my might but I could not dislodge them by even one millimetre. They had forced their way deep into this hard, solid surface.

I was maddened, panicked. I also knew I was being sidetracked by my search for liquid. The rising water level had to be tackled, sooner rather than later. My body could keep going without fluids for a while yet. For how long, I didn't know. But for the moment I had to accept that my thirst was not immediately life-threatening, whereas

Grimalkin's foundering was. It was time to push on – get my priorities right.

I decided to scrap all thoughts of looking for my medication – there was no point at all. The Tupperware box in which they were sealed was long gone from its safe haven near my flooded bunk. Twenty-four hours must have passed since my last 30mg tablet; normally I'd have taken it twice daily. This was the first time I'd ever missed taking it since the diagnosis of my epilepsy. I knew that fitting or convulsing down here could lead to serious injury, to drowning. Talking myself down from a state of near panic, I reminded myself that so did every other option, and with that I prepared to bail.

With a piece of splintered wood, I scratched a mark on the forward bulkhead to give me the current water level. The boat's continuous seesaw movement made it impossible to determine the real level but I had to have a reference point, something to encourage me. I unhooked my bucket and started to bail. The most effective way was to throw the water up out of the companionway entrance, where I was positioned, and into the cockpit, which was self-draining. On occasion the motion of the boat allowed me to throw water right over the side. Getting into a rhythm was difficult at first. Apart from the continual swaying in the cabin, my clothing felt tight and cumbersome, heavy as lead from the immersions and constant drenching, but without it I would already be dead. Despite the discomfort and restriction, something was telling me to keep going, and I soon settled into bailing with a will.

For a while, maybe half an hour or so, I went at bucket-chucking non-stop. Having something to do – a task with an aim, ridding *Grimalkin* of water, bailing her dry – lifted my spirits and my self-esteem. For the first time in hours I had a chance of achieving something. No longer a passenger hanging on for grim death, I felt elated, in control. This blue bucket was a joyous possession.

While bailing, I also became really deeply immersed in conversations with Gerry, which ranged from football to Formula One. I also updated him with what I was encountering below in the cabin – in particular, relaying any difficulty with an ample supply of expletives. Eventually, all too soon, I was out of breath. I was light-headed, and began to faint and confused – my brain and body were reacting too slowly in this volatile domain. Without some kind of breather I risked passing out. I decided to go up into the cockpit and check the weather.

I sat on the edge of the cockpit taking deep, slow breaths. God, this was so surreal – me and Gerry trapped on this tiny, low-lying yacht surrounded by tower-block swells. If only this storm would blow out as quickly as it had peaked. A foamy spray doused me, cut my face, chilled me to the marrow. With nothing else to do, I carefully studied the sea's movement and frequency. A monumental swell still ran, but I was sure that only every fifth or sixth wave was taller than its neighbours – rather than every second or third, as it had been the last time I'd looked.

'Looks like it's eased off more . . . there might be some hope for us yet, hey, Gerry?'

Even so, this was still a dangerous, possibly fatal place to be. I had to get bailing again.

Back below I counted ten buckets out, then stopped for balance and breath. I was slowing down. I tried to ignore the creeping exhaustion and ploughed on, pushing myself harder

After I realised that rescue had finally come I sat there waiting – with Gerry, dead, at my feet. The sea conditions had moderated but *Grimalkin*'s deck was still rising and falling around 20 feet according to Peter Harrison, the Royal Navy winchman. Danbuoy and lines trail astern.

Tuesday 14th August 1979: *Tai Fat* rides out the storm before spotting *Fragola's* flare and discovering *Grimalkin* wallowing in the waves. The sea's brutality had gone, but misery remained.

Christian's Mayday from *Tai Fat* brings a Royal Navy Sea King helicopter swooping towards me. I am hearing rock music in my head and thanking God for being spotted. I am telling Gerry his ordeal is nearly over.

Grimalkin sits low in the water, hidden in the troughs. The seas are still confused and it is very cold. Another night at sea with *Grimalkin* and I was sure of death.

Gerry is finally lifted off the yacht.

The sheer size of the seas can be gauged here. The wind had dropped to Force 7, but with the seas still running at 25–30 ft, I couldn't help but think that, along with Gerry, the other crewmembers had perished... I was described as catatonic.

Glénans Sailing School's *Fragola*, taken from *Tai Fat*. *Fragola* fired a parachute flare, then stood by during my rescue. Sightings of her were obscured by the huge swells.

Being winched to safety by Peter Harrison, I later found out that I was the last person to be taken alive from the sea during the Fastnet disaster.

Waterford in Ireland – September 1979. This was the first sight that Matthew and I had of *Grimalkin* after getting off the bus. I was surprised at how emotional I felt on seeing her.

When I walked around to the port side I was shocked to see her name was all but gone.

Above left This is the starboard side looking forward showing the compass and speedometer. Despite a tidy up by the salvage crew, debris still littered *Grimalkin*'s decks – even the bunk poles were laid across them. The bent stanchions were probably caused when she was dismasted.

Above right Port side view looking forward.

Above left This photo of the starboard side shows a large crack in the cabin side. I hadn't noticed this during the storm, and I knew that it must have caused considerable leakage into *Grimalkin*.

Above right This was the port quarter berth where I rested between bouts of bailing. The freezing water rising inside the cabin continually drenched me as *Grimalkin* was thrown around by the Force 10 gale going on outside.

Above left My first steps into the cabin brought a familiar, all too unpleasant reminder of my time alone with Gerry – the overpowering smell of diesel oil. Then I saw the shattered navigation table with the VHF radio from which David and Matthew had made our Mayday call for rescue.

Above right Right up in the bows amongst the debris I spotted the small blue bucket I had used to bail the boat for hours before my rescue.

The cockpit looking aft. This is the view I had whilst bailing. The empty winch on the left of the photo is the one I used to pull myself and then Gerry, barely alive, out of the water. Although *Grimalkin*'s cockpit was self-draining, the water didn't drain out because she was floating so low in the water. The life raft well in the centre of the cockpit is empty.

Top The lines and ropes we had streamed behind *Grimalkin* during the storm in an effort to slow down her breakneck speed were strewn all over the deck.

Above The galley sink, filled with cans and jars of food. These were flung from their shelves during the storm and became deadly projectiles.

My original gear: this lifejacket and harness saved my life.

15th July 2005: Sinéad and I aboard *Grimalkin*. It was shortly after this that we decided to collaborate on writing this book.

I am at my happiest trimming. Keith Grainger (*Grimalkin*'s co-owner) is standing and Jerry Smith is helming *Grimalkin* on the 55-mile Round the Island Race, in June 2007. It was wonderful feeling *Grimalkin* roaring along.

Weymouth, June 2007. My hero, Commander Peter 'Harry' Harrison, who plucked me from *Grimalkin*.

– until the pain of every intake of breath was cutting through my chest so sharply I had to stop. Slumped over, I caught my breath and let the spasms slowly lessen.

With my hand still locked round the handle of blue bucket, I checked my marker. The water level was the same. But I managed to convince myself that I was making an impact, because while the water level may not have gone down, neither had it gone up. My bailing was keeping it at bay, and for the moment that was good enough for me.

Trying to get a rhythm back, I started singing 'Ten Green Bottles' – it worked.

'Come on, mate . . . join in,' I shouted up.

I kept on singing by myself – from ten down to one over and over, then, for a bit of nonsense, from one back up to ten. For some reason I found this funny. I started teasing Gerry for not joining in.

'I can sing it the usual way if it makes it easier for you, mate, eh?'

But eventually I had to pause. My head was aching as badly as it did after a convulsion. It was a deep, nauseous, migraine-like headache that made my eyes throb. The primary cause was dehydration, added to by the many head-on collisions I had sustained out in the cockpit. My weaker left hand, which was hypersensitive to the cold at the best of times, was deadened. I knew I was wearing out fast and should at least try to pace myself, but I was driven by a fear that if I stopped, everything would get worse. Trying to alleviate the throbbing in my head and the salty dehydration in my throat and mouth, I splashed my head and lips with the cold water to refresh myself. The effect was the opposite. The brown, murky water fouled my mouth and throat with a taste so vile

I gagged, coughed, retched, then gagged again – over and over till I could barely stand, let alone bail.

To add to a worsening situation, *Grimalkin* lifted with a swell. With no chance of securing myself, my legs collapsed under me and I hit my head on the cooker.

Unclipped and dazed, I now drifted free through the cabin. A lone sock floated past me, inches from my nose – I knew it was my skipper's. Overwhelmed by the sight of his sock, I retched again, not from the fetid liquid this time, but from the knowledge that unless there had been some kind of miracle, I would never see David again. He was such a good man – he didn't deserve to die like that. How did all this happen? This had started out as a race, well planned, well prepared for. How had it gone so horribly wrong? I thought about David's wife Gay, poor woman – so young – too young to be widowed. She was expecting a family holiday with her husband, not this. I sincerely hoped, prayed now that Matt had survived – somehow. To lose a son as well as a husband would be too much for anybody to cope with.

Overcome with exhaustion, emotion and dehydration, I clambered onto the port quarter berth and slumped on my side. Water kept lapping against the soaking bunk but I didn't care. I wanted to shout up to Gerry, tell him I was resting – but I had no energy, it would have to wait. Cold air and spray blew in through the companionway, but I became oblivious to it. I simply could not imagine ever being able to get back up again.

I kept my eyes open. I was afraid of falling asleep. I examined the effects of the storm on *Grimalkin*'s interior – the damage was beyond belief. Her beautifully cared for surfaces, her lockers, her headlining and interior fittings looked as if something demonic had attacked them with knife in one hand and hammer in the other. Everything was precision-trashed.

My legs began to cramp painfully so I stretched out my back as far as my inflated lifejacket allowed and stared at the headlining above me – a less disturbing view. I breathed deeply. While my body seemed to have stalled, my mind was off at double the speed, worrying, thinking, panicking about what to do next. Bail, rest or keep watch? My left arm and hand were painfully numb. I removed the glove of this hand and began touching my fingers in turn against my thumb: forefinger, middle finger, third finger, then little finger – a coordination exercise I had learned in hospital. While I watched my bloodied, blistered hand trying to flex its swollen knuckles, I thought: I have to stay active. I have to keep my circulation going.

I wanted to talk to Gerry, tell him how important it was for me to keep active, how I had to get back to bailing, but I had sudden fear that saying this out loud would only make more real the physical difficulty I was now experiencing. So I said nothing; I just kept at my fingers, trying to flex them.

'Come on then, get on with it,' said a voice, not my own.

For a brief moment I thought it was Gerry. Then I realised it was Pa. No doubt whatsoever. He was back. Savouring the instant security and warmth I felt on hearing this, I closed my eyes.

I saw my hand again. This time it looked different – no hard, blistered or bloodied skin, but smooth palmed, if slightly wasted. It was a hand that hadn't been near salt water, a jib sheet or a winch for weeks. I tried to lift one finger, but the effort required was too much. It sort of twitched, and I gave up. Then there was another hand – longer, tanned, with slightly nicotine-stained fingers. It took my left hand, palm facing upwards, and massaged it.

'Softly, softly, catchee monkey, Nicholas,' said Pa.

That's what he used to say to me when things became too much – when the physical obstacles overwhelmed. Comforted, encouraged, I continued trying to move my hand – cold numb finger on thumb, finger on thumb, very slowly, slightly awkward. The movement began, little by little, to improve – I saw that a rhythm was returning. Yes, yes.

'Where there's a will there's a way, son.'

Pa again. My rhythm, my coordination was returning, and with it a resolve. Still lying on the bunk, I turned onto my side and looked round the cabin again, as if ready to confront the bedlam. With my head clearer, I knew that to maintain my stamina it was essential to bail and rest in equal measures. I needed to devise a system to match my physical capacity.

I decided to bail for one hour then rest for half an hour. I would have to guess the time by counting – maybe breaths, or bucketfuls of water. This would be a real-life time-and-motion study. While lying there, mulling this over, refining my plans, I noticed something rather familiar drifting out from beneath the navigation table. Floating in the murk was a small brown plastic bottle – seeing its white label I knew instantly what it was.

'My medication . . . my bleedin' medication, Gerry!' I was overjoyed.

In an excited, adrenaline-filled state I pulled myself up and reached out for it, missing it by millimetres. Reaching further this time, I clasped the bottle firmly. Got you! Fumbling, trembling uncontrollably, I clicked off its white top to see nothing but a smidgen of white mush floating in the contaminated water. Nothing had survived this maelstrom intact, even a childproof tablet container. I began to panic again – finding this brown plastic bottle was an all too vivid reminder that I was without medication and liable to fit at any given time. Knocked back, I wished to God I had never set eyes on the damn thing. This was a setback; it just made it harder to maintain a positive frame of mind. As I stared into the floating debris, nauseated by the smell and sight of it, I spotted something bobbing up and down just beneath the surface. It looked like a green and white origami paper yacht – a carton of long-life milk!

Without further thought of fitting, convulsing or gagging, I cast aside the little brown bottle and grabbed the carton. Full and intact – it had somehow survived the assault. Biting off the waxy corner, forgetting about the muck in which it had been floating, I put the carton to my sore, dry mouth and drank deep. Never before had I felt so much satisfaction from anything   I savoured every drop.

Drinking this nectar brought back a trip I had taken with Ma the summer before, to see my brother Peter in Japan. We visited the Kiyomizudera water temple at Kyoto, and drank cold, clear water from tin cups riveted to wooden poles. As I drank I remembered Yuko, Peter's wife, telling me that to drink from this waterfall would assure me a long life. Now, more than ever, I hoped she was right. All too quickly the contents were gone, so I split open the carton and licked the silver lining.

Finding this milk had been totally serendipitous. It had to be a sign. Everything that had happened before finding that one, simple, everyday item had been chaotic, exhausting, a test of my will. Then this cardboard carton, filled with nectar, had floated in out of nowhere. Someone was on my side. What or who I didn't know, I didn't care. But it lifted my spirits. This was physical, and spiritual, help, and I was determined to prove to myself that this was merely the first sign of our salvation. The tide was turning; our luck was changing.

Fourteen

Unmarked Time

With my energy levels back up, I felt upbeat, positive – it enabled me to think straight, straighter than I had been able to for a while. I wanted to get on with things – get my new bailing system under way and get water out and off this boat as fast as I could. I fastened my harness, grabbed the blue bucket and began bailing and counting again – this time louder. As I got my rhythm back, I thought about those six weeks in Japan and remembered that Yuko had taught me how to count to ten, so I started to fill and empty the buckets in halting Japanese – *ichi, ni, san, yon, go, roku, nana, hachi, kyu, ju.*

The first bit went well, better than I had anticipated. I have no idea how long I carried on for – probably far less than my allotted time of an hour – but long enough for me to get my confidence back and ensure that some progress, some impact had been made. I rested on the port quarter berth and decided how to divide the time up. First was recovery: breathing deep, regaining composure and energy. Then I would relax and rest till my next bailing session. This part of

161

my plan proved more difficult to implement. Feeling more alert, more aware than on my last rest period, the splashing water round my body and near my face quickly irritated me. I decided to move up into the cockpit. Once up there and clipped in, I realised that this was probably a better, more sensible place to rest. Although bitterly cold, I could regularly scan the seas and skies for rescue, and talking to Gerry would keep me alert.

In the cockpit, though, I found it hard to relax. Sitting there doing nothing made me jittery, anxious to get on with it – I forced myself to go below and back to work. Again, I fixed my harness and got a good rhythm going. I was unable to judge if the water level was going down, but even so I felt compelled to continue bailing, determined to focus on this one thing alone. During this productive period my mind was uninterrupted by worries about anything else on board. My head was concentrated on keeping *Grimalkin* afloat, keeping me alive and Gerry safe.

After a while I could feel my right hand beginning to tremble from gripping the metal handle. I was starting to lose control and most of the water was now coming straight back down on top of me. Something felt wrong. I was experiencing an overwhelming taste and smell – not for the first time today, but this was different. This felt like what is known to epileptics as an aura – early warning of an oncoming fit. To quell it, I needed to rest. Rather than stopping completely, however, I decided to take a breather by going back on deck and doing a scan of the sea and skies.

No sooner had I stuck my head up out of the cabin than I realised I had a problem – the drains of the cockpit had become blocked by debris and sludge and it was rapidly filling up with water. Damn this. All I had been doing for the last while was transferring water from one part of the boat to another. I clipped on in the cockpit and removed the blockage. The water began to drain. Then I noticed that Gerry had slipped in the heightened water level and I had inadvertently been throwing water directly into his face. Poor Gerry.

'Sorry, mate, don't know what I'm at half the time here . . . you OK?'

I propped him up in a better, more comfortable position, tightening his safety harness round him. Standing up in the cockpit, I saw that the seas had moderated a little more. I could swear that the hull was moving up and down less violently. Not much less, though – the waves were still around 30 feet high and the swell carried with it as much force and malevolence as before.

I drew the strings of my balaclava hood closer to afford some more protection. I twisted my head and scanned the greyness that should have been the horizon. No definition, nothing. It would have been encouraging to see something, anything at all, but there was no clarity of vision. It was still bleak out there. I stared into the abyss and began to will something to appear, a seal, porpoise, anything that was animate – anything that might indicate we were near land. Seagulls knew the weather better than any yachtsmen and were most likely holed up under a hedge or some dry stone wall in Newquay, Perranporth or St Ives – retreats on the north Cornish coast. There was nothing airborne around us – apart from spray. Not one solitary living thing in the sky. This was a lonely, sad, mournful place to be.

I was preparing to head back below to my endless bucket emptying when I did finally spot something in the distance.

Whatever it was disappeared behind a curling wave. I was just about to indicate its presence to Gerry when I decided I didn't want to tempt fate. I took the whistle from my life-jacket and waited for the wave to pass. Like a man-overboard drill, I kept my eyes focused on the spot where I was sure I had seen something. I was convinced by now that what I'd glimpsed could be a boat. The wave passed, clearing the view ahead, but nothing came into sight. Frustrated and confused, I scanned the area rigorously. Still nothing. Determined to get a better view, I decided to get up on the cabin roof. This was the highest point now the mast was severed. The safest way to get there in these conditions would be to crawl across the deck and pull myself up. Once there, I could gauge the safest way to get myself upright.

On my hands and knees, I unclipped and reclipped to the deck, then pulled myself along, slowly, carefully. Unexpectedly, *Grimalkin*'s stern was lifted by a surging swell, leaving me hanging. My grip held firm but I found myself looking down into the bottom of a trough – 25 or 30 feet below. Terrified, I retreated, deciding that attempting this manoeuvre in these rolling, unpredictable seas was reckless. I was bound to fall in.

Back in the cockpit I waited, still watching, although I knew too much time had passed now. Was it an illusion, a trick of the light, a mirage? A shiver went through me – my body was succumbing fast to the wind-chill. Finally I concluded that this sighting, real or imagined, had done me no good at all and I would be better off down below. At least when I was bailing, my circulation was being boosted by the activity.

It was hard not to feel deflated as I made my way back

down below. Fastening my harness and unhooking the bucket, I looked at my scratched mark on the bulkhead – studying it closely, I thought levels were up rather than down. Small vortex-like whirlpools kept appearing all around me, adding to my confusion. Did we have holes in the hull? But no, it was just the swirling, circling movement of the sea outside creating the effect. With so much movement it was almost impossible to tell, but for the sake of my sanity I concluded that the water level must be the same. Starting to bail again, I became aware that my body felt more sluggish and tired. With the water lapping up against my freezing shins and knees, I felt so very cold now. The wind may have been bitter up on deck but the water down here was colder. It was bloody cold.

I carried on bailing but found myself dispirited, confused – breathing hard, blood rushing to my pounding head, I found it impossible to be optimistic. The uplifting, energising effects of the long-life milk had diminished and the liquid gone straight through me, filling my bladder. This was no place for niceties, so I went straight ahead and let go. It was good, instant relief. I was wonderfully warm for a moment, then colder than before – smelly too. Filling a bucket with bilge water, I doused myself down. But the coldness shocked and with this my left knee gave way and I head-butted the companionway. I heard the crunch of wood against bone. That was it, I'd had enough – it was time for a break.

Too exhausted to climb up into the cockpit, I undid my harness and clambered onto my soaking, half-submerged bunk. Lying down now I took short, sharp intakes of cold breath while clenching and unclenching my toes in my boots, trying to keep my circulation going. Afraid of falling asleep,

I started to whistle – somewhat disjointedly – the signature tune to *The Thomas Crown Affair*: 'The Windmills of Your Mind'. The music just came into my head. Then I sang it – it felt good. Distracting enough to alleviate my worries a bit. I was no Noel Harrison but I sang my socks off until I was completely breathless.

Lying there, silent now but somewhat heartened, I began to hear eerie noises again, noises that only something afloat and waterlogged could make. To banish them, I allowed the music of my favourite album into my head: Pink Floyd's *Dark Side of the Moon*. Manic but beneficially distracting. I remembered every sound effect from ticking clocks to cash registers, and I sang out the words.

More and more sound effects pounded through my head and in the midst of the chaos I could hear the sound of rotors – helicopter rotors – another sound effect from this same album. My God, if only this joyous sound was real. Tired, out of breath, I had to stop. I had to relax, have some quiet time – ready myself for the next bail. Time passed. How much, I couldn't tell – but I was still lying there in my bunk with water swilling all around. Still exhausted and somewhat light-headed, I finally dragged myself off the bunk to the companionway's entrance.

I looked into the cockpit. Gerry was still there, clipped on – his demeanour dark, still, livid. I climbed into the cockpit, acknowledged him, clipped myself on and looked around. It wasn't exactly a brand new day, but I noticed the first patches of blue among the lighter clouds. What was the time? Where was the sun? I looked at the compasses. One was swinging drunkenly off its pivot; the other showed us pointing north or near on. With all this I guessed it was around 2pm.

Although it was cold, and getting colder, the blueness of the sky, like my singing, had perked me up.

I propped Gerry up, then returned to routine: the cycle of bailing and resting, resting and bailing. I made concerted efforts to keep my brain alert and active. Voice hoarse, throat dry and sore, I shouted up to Gerry about Japan – about the traditional family-run lodgings I'd stayed in while in Osaka with Ma, how neat and beautifully clean it was. I told him that the only slightly disagreeable thing about the *ryokan* was the next-door neighbour's minah bird, which had been trained to swear both in English and Japanese. Quite funny but it had kept Ma awake shouting phrases at three in the morning like 'Bloody English' and 'Leave me alone, piss off, *gijan*'.

I reckoned I was boring Gerry with Japan so I began to sing again. I wanted music that lifted my soul, music that meant something to me, so I allowed the Canadian melancholy of Joni Mitchell, the echoplex complexities with the strong bass and acoustics of John Martyn, to fill my head. If lyrics could be married then Joni's would be my many wives – I loved them, loved her. I belted out all of her classics. Singing helped the buckets of water out through the companionway opening. Some flew back in my face but I went on – bailing and resting as unmarked time passed. I had to do something to prevent me from stopping, lying down, giving up, giving in. Hopelessness was a place of no return.

As the afternoon wore on, the water level inside the hull was no lower – in fact, it was undeniably higher. I felt like the Dutch boy with his finger in the dyke. My surroundings were becoming ever more claustrophobic too. It seemed as if *Grimalkin*'s interior was shrinking, the sides of her hull distorted as water continued flowing up and down her length. And the smell was overpowering. I was increasingly aware that the amount of time I was able to bail before needing to rest was shortening greatly. I wanted to lie down again but lying down meant more discomfort – aching, resting in a wet, pitching stench. I was in another quandary. Stand, sit, bail.

I thought constantly about moisture, thirst. Dehydration was becoming my overriding fear. I became convinced that there had to be something else liquid or at least edible in this swirling mass. To hell with the bailing – I needed fluid. I hooked up the blue bucket and was back on my hands and knees, combing as far as my rope allowed, searching for sustenance. Less than a minute into my hunt I scooped up a silver tin – a 200g can; it had to be Heinz baked beans. I held the can in my shaking right hand. I'd been here once before – food, a source of nutrition and energy, but no means of opening it. Starving, thirsty and desperate, I began to bite at its top – it hurt. Tearing off my gloves I gripped the can tightly in my numb fingers and began to whack it into the broken companionway ladder. Apart from a small dent, the only result was several cuts to my inflamed palms. With the can still firmly in my hand, I moved towards the cooker with the intention of smashing this damn tin open, but instead a huge wave pitched *Grimalkin* downwards. A mass of water in the hull surged forward, sweeping me off my feet as it went. I dropped the can and lost it in the seething mess. On my back now, half floating, my legs flailing, I was forced to wait for another wave to help propel me upright, regain my feet. Picking myself up, drenched, exhausted after the fall, I slumped onto my soaked bunk.

Where else could I go? What else could I do? I needed

a source of energy and had a powerful incentive to look, but I found no reward. The fruitless scavenging through sewage and bilge had left me so wrecked I couldn't imagine being able to move again. My limbs were cold and aching. I looked at my hands. They were white and bloated; the swollen knuckles even looked like Gerry's. Pulling my sodden gloves back on I saw how bloodied my palms were by the self-inflicted cuts. Christ, what was I doing to myself?

I stared blankly up at the headlining, light-headed – praying for help, for dry clothing, for water, for food. I began to wonder whether 'catastrophic' or 'disastrous' was the best way to describe the shattered mess I was lying in. Distressed and upset, thoughts drifted from hunger and pain back to the same ongoing worry. Why had nobody come? The winds had calmed enough and the skies were getting clearer. Why hadn't I heard any more aircraft, seen any ships, any yachts, anything at all? Were they even looking? Had they given up the search? Then it occurred to me, struck me like a thunderbolt – maybe we had been presumed dead.

In my panic, my legs began to stiffen with cramp and spasmodic pain, particularly the left one. Again I found it odd to feel pain in my left leg; I had to assume it was due to the injury I got while in the water. My left side was always more susceptible to cold so maybe these freezing conditions were helping bring the pain on. I didn't know, but at least I was able to move the leg. I tried flexing it within the confined space of my bunk. Huffing and puffing like an old man, I was forced to stop; I had to put up with the pain. I had hit a brick wall. I could do nothing more physically, so I had to work mentally instead: I must think of long life and familiar faces. I brought to mind my two main sailing mentors: Dick

Langton and Eric Tabarly. It didn't help. Even thinking of Pa did nothing to inspire me – just saddened me, frightened me to think I might never see them again.

I needed something more, something that would jolt me, push me on, keep me going. A sharp spasm pulsated through my left leg again. I let out a pained screech. As I did, I remembered a similar pain – self-induced. Pa and Ma had watched my right hand as it firmly gripped a beam. Then, pulling myself up and out of my wheelchair, I finally took my first step. My right hand began to tremble violently and I faltered, falling to the ground in a heap. But it didn't matter – after weeks and weeks of exercise I had willed the wasted muscles to work again.

Back on the ward, I waited impatiently to tell Sister Sampson, a tough but inspiring Scottish nurse, that I had at last taken my first steps. She wrote a quote into my autograph book beside the bed. I thought it was cool – obscure, but cool.

> 'Never measure the height of a mountain until you have reached the top. Then you will see how low it was.'
>
> Dag Hammarskjöld

As I endured the long and difficult road to recovery, I began to identify with its true meaning. Now, on my bunk, still staring at the headlining above me, I wondered exactly how high this mountain was, and how I'd ever reach the top. Just then, a rain squall pounded the deck above, startling me.

Hallelujah! As though answering my prayers, the heavens had opened, releasing liquid – cold, fresh, drinkable liquid.

Untying my harness, I scrambled off my bunk, faster than I had at any time during that day. Heaving my sodden body along as quickly as the bilge water allowed, I grabbed each side of the companionway and pulled myself upwards. To my dismay the downpour stopped as suddenly as it had started. Refusing to be deterred, I tore off my gloves, clasped my palms together, held my face up to the heavens and caught the last few drops. It wasn't enough – my mouth was barely moistened. I scoured the deck for rainwater trapped in a crevice. Turning my glove inside out, I used its fleecy lining as a sponge and soaked up water from halyard bags, winch handle pockets, anywhere I could see it. It tasted foul but less foul than that down below. I got on all fours and licked rain from the deck – every corner, every inch got scoured until I was satisfied I had every drop.

I sat on the deck. It had to be well into the afternoon by now. I'd be lucky to see another shower, judging by the colours and layers of cloud. From the intensity of the light it wouldn't rain like that again until after dark. Thinking of the dark, I checked Gerry and the space around him. Then I spotted some liquid in the cockpit well, by Gerry's foot. On my knees, I scooped it up in my palms. Despite its pale reddish colour, I put the water to my mouth and quickly swallowed. Licking my lips I felt blessed with a second wind. Despite the freezing-cold conditions I was ready to bail once more. A primal need welled within me, an absolute yearning to survive.

I retreated below again, this time in the renewed belief that somebody, somewhere was out there looking for Gerry, me and *Grimalkin*. I began to bail again and finally got a momentum going. I felt warmth spread slowly through my legs. With warmth came determination. The water level was going to go down – it had to.

I bailed faster and faster, careful not to rip the handle off the bucket. Head down, concentrating hard on the bucket and the rhythm of my breaths, counting the minutes, one to sixty, one to sixty, I became fixated. A one man, time-and-motion bucket chain. A floorboard kept banging against the galley side, hindering my rhythm. Annoyed at it impeding my progress, I nudged it aside, then wedged it under the table.

In the midst of all this I heard an unfamiliar sound – but I had heard many unfamiliar sounds all day, none of which had been of any use to me. I stopped bailing and shouted up to Gerry.

'Can you see anything up there?'

I decided it didn't warrant a look, so I carried on. I had to keep going, keep the pace up. Forget about everything and get on with it. What chance had I of getting this water level down if I was distracted by every new noise I heard? In that cauldron-like space, head down, I continued bailing as if someone had hypnotised me. I heard the noise again. Although it was close, I ignored it, just kept going. Then, as if a switch had been thrown in my head, I stopped bailing.

Straining, really concentrating, I finally distinguished this noise from all the others. There was something un-deniably different about the sound – it was definitely not shipboard. I dropped my hood and balaclava. Increasing in volume now, it sounded clearer, more urgent, like a midge getting closer. Christ – it was a single-engined aircraft, it was a piston engine – probably a spotter plane. Dropping the bucket I scrambled to get out of the cabin but fell flat on my face in the water – my harness was still attached to the bunk pole. I swallowed copious amounts of bilge water, but coughing and spluttering I didn't care. I could hear that spotter plane so close now that nothing else mattered. Desperate to get up there, I fumbled with my harness.

'Come on, Nick, for Christ's sake – COME ON!!'

Blood pumped in my brow – I was getting light-headed again. At last freed from my bonds, I lunged at the companion-way. Out on deck I saw it – it was still there, not far off – it looked like a Cessna. Excited, panicked, relieved – quick, my whistle – I started blowing it, at the same time waving my arms and jumping up and down, running, limping along the decks of the boat. Then I stopped, horrified. The bloody thing had not even lowered its height or banked towards us. It just flew on, as if on autopilot. Had I missed it? Or had it missed us? Maybe he didn't spot us in this early evening light? Maybe the pilot was in a sweeping search pattern. Yes, he'd return, lower his height, change direction and see us. Change direction – see us, for God's sake!

'Look, man! Come down, come down,' I implored the receding aircraft. But the plane flew on, as if on a training flight. I looked to Gerry for some kind of explanation. 'That pilot's blind, surely, he must be.'

I was distraught, confounded. So near yet so far. I shook a painful fist at him, at it.

'Look at your bloody radar screen . . . the weather's cleared, open your eyes, man!'

My heart pounded out of control. I stood there open-mouthed, disbelieving. The sight of this spotter plane receding into the horizon knocked me back. In silence, craving comfort, I began to rock with the boat's motion. Eventually, accepting my chance had been lost, I stepped backwards and tripped over Gerry's harness. I felt a wrath rising – I swore at Gerry, berated him again and again. I tried not to but this was beyond my control. I shouted to God, all gods. I was angry, furious with God, creation and religion. He'd created this mess. Why couldn't he get us out of it?

Still seething, I turned my rage on my missing crewmates. I berated them, swore at them, swore about them – called them every name under the sun. Vengefully I questioned them and all their actions. I accused them of abandoning me – Gerry and me – leaving us for dead. The belief gave me the licence, all the justification I needed to judge, condemn, vilify all three of them. Where were they now? Bastards, three self-centred bastards. Wrath, I'd show them wrath.

Fifteen

Falling Forward

I let myself fall headlong into the deepest, hardest, wettest part of the cockpit – its inner well – the lowest part of the deck. My fall was broken by the webbing of a blue harness still clipped to a strongpoint. My ear rested against it, my eyes focused on the label – 'Made in England'. Seeing this harness, cast aside, swishing up and down in the well full of water, brought my deepest fears to the surface. I felt like howling out loud.

Instead, I pulled myself up by this slippery harness into a sitting position. I caught sight of my hunchbacked, swollen-faced crewmate as I did so. My God, Gerry looked awful, shockingly so. Remembering my outburst, I propped him up, clamped my gloved palm over his icy blue hand and apologised. Apologies to Gerry seemed to have become par for the course.

'Sorry, mate, not like me at all, don't know what came over me.'

Sitting back now I caught my breath. I was shivering uncontrollably. I looked around – *Grimalkin* had slowed down considerably since the last time I'd been up here, confirming my earlier fears that her cabin was now more waterlogged. Peering over the side, I saw that she was at a slant, bows down in the water – only the first four handwritten letters, 'Grim', were discernible – she was becoming more overburdened and less stable. I felt sure water was leaking in from some unknown orifice. A wave slopped its way on board, over the deck and into the cockpit. Panicked by this, my first thought was to go below and continue bailing. But if I did, I risked missing another flyover or sea rescue. But to stay up here in the cockpit with Gerry was to allow *Grimalkin* to settle even lower in the water and risk her sinking. I was torn by indecision – my mind raced. Should I go below and bail until I dropped, or drowned? Did my fate lie in a bucket and my own two hands? Or should I sit with my friend waiting for bloody Neptune to engulf me, engulf us both? Maybe God knew – I certainly didn't.

To attempt to process my thoughts in a more rational manner, I began by taking slow, deep breaths, trying to inhale as much air as possible, oxygenating my brain. I felt my pulse slowing, back to a reasonable pace, reasonable under the circumstances. I resumed the sort of clarity that I had lacked over the last half an hour or so. I tried to picture both of my parents and what they might be doing right now. I saw Pa in our garden, tending to his roses. I could hear him, in my head – he was shouting at our cat.

'Get off the roses, you black devil.'

Breathing more easily now, I turned my thoughts to Ma. I pictured her at church. A woman with strong faith and solid values, Ma was a regular churchgoer and spent much of her spare time singing in the choir, helping with fêtes and raising funds. I suddenly felt ashamed for my earlier outburst – my torrent of abuse against God and religion. If she had heard me, what would she have thought? Dear Ma. I couldn't stop feeling guilty over what I had said and thought. And as for my condemnation of my three missing crewmates, all three of whom could now be dead . . .

I felt comforted by thinking of Ma, sure that she would forgive my outburst. I had regained control of sorts over my racing mind. Calmer, I noticed that the cloud base seemed to have lifted a bit more. I stood up and carefully scanned the area. *Grimalkin* was still pointing head to wind but no longer was she thrust into and through the swells. Although still at heights of 25 to 30 feet, the waves were longer and slower. With less of a fight on her hands, she rode them more comfortably, head into the direction of the decreasing wind. It seemed as if the air pressure was rising and the weather was going to improve a bit more. I looked at Gerry and thought: I can't change what has happened to us or to him, but I can make a decision that will affect the here and now.

I discussed our options with him – bailing versus not bailing – in a rational manner, not wishing to hide anything from my crewmate. I pointed out that each option carried with it a huge risk. I told him that neither was a sure thing nor a guarantee of our rescue or survival. In detail I described the pros and cons of both. Below, I could keep trying to chip away, attack the rising bloody level of water. It would keep me active, keep my mind alert, however cold. But I was exhausted, done in – dehydrated too. Hour by hour, I had become progressively weaker, and the energy expended on bailing could be conserved for survival. Or I could stay above, here in the cockpit, and keep watch, but *Grimalkin* might sink. Of course, this could just as easily happen with me down below. This dilemma, one that would most likely seal my fate, was the worst I had ever faced.

The sun began to poke through the clouds. There was no rainbow, but it was uplifting to see beams of sunlight glistening off the surface. Despite the swell, these improving weather conditions and the better all-round visibility they brought convinced me that we had more chance of being spotted and rescued than at any other point that day. With this heartening thought my decision was made. I secured myself into the cockpit, clipping myself on, then armed myself with the foghorn and my whistle. I was fully prepared for being seen and for rescue. Along with occasional blowing and honking I stood up regularly, reporting back to Gerry what I saw around me. In between, I chatted away, trying to keep mentally active.

'Tuesday evenings, eh, Gerry, what would you normally be doing?'

Only a couple of Tuesdays ago I had gone to see Queen at the Gaumont in Southampton. I told Gerry how they had performed 'Bohemian Rhapsody' and how we sat next to Brian May's mum – she had told me that Brian had been classically trained. Freddie Mercury had worn a white, skin-tight, one-piece suit. I told Gerry it was very revealing, and had had a lightning flash, bright orange, embroidered across its front and down his leg. We had seen some lightning last night but strangely there had been no thunder. We continued to talk about music: folk, rock, country and western. I was frustrated because I'd meant to ask Gerry what his favourite music was a few watches ago. So I chose a group for him. I thought Steely Dan were appropriate. This conversation lasted for ages.

Time dragged on; still nothing happened. I began to realise that jumping up and down, sounding the foghorn, waving tired arms and blowing my whistle intermittently was doing no good. It just made me more tired, more desperate. I thought about a book I had bought in Covent Garden's piazza bookshop on my way home from a yacht delivery in 1978: *The Master Mariner* by Nicholas Monsarrat. Set in Drake's era, its central character, a sailor called Matthew Lawe, was condemned to wander the oceans for eternity as punishment for an act of cowardice. With the increasing visibility, all I could see was empty seas. Water-logged, heavy and alone, we were drifting off to God knows where. I was by now not only bodily exhausted but also fed up with talking to Gerry, sick of the sound of my own voice. There's only so much you can say to someone who listens but doesn't respond. This had become tiresome, making me drowsy, less alert.

If you don't care where you are, then you're not lost. I cared. I was lost. Staring at the empty sea, it was easy to visualise things: boats, ships, lifeboats, other forms of rescue intermittently darting out from behind the rolling swells. This was making me paranoid. It was torture. I had to stop it.

But I was even more scared of stopping thinking in case I drifted off, fell asleep. I needed a new device to keep me alert and banish the disquiet at the same time – something simple. I began picturing the lighthouses along Cornwall's southern coast and testing my knowledge on Gerry. I reeled them off, going east, up channel to Hurst Point and the

Needles over and over, until I got bored with that. Then I began reciting my family's telephone numbers, including my brother's in Hong Kong. After telephone numbers, my family's birth dates. I'd always wondered why October was so popular. Then each sign of the zodiac rolled off my tongue. I kept missing Aries out and having to go back and start again. I recited the list again and again until I got it right. Then I went through them backwards. I tested Gerry, tested myself – same thing, but who cared? It kept me awake.

Planet names were next: Mercury, Venus, Earth, Mars, Jupiter, Saturn, Uranus, Neptune and Pluto. I tried to remember their moons' names as well, and how close each planet was to the sun. Was the sun a planet or a star? Which planet was warmest, coldest, nicest even? I had a hankering for Pluto. By this time things were getting a little out of hand – I was obsessing over my lists.

The absence of the physical movement I'd become accustomed to while bailing was now becoming apparent. I felt myself stiffening, getting colder. I tried to whistle, pursing my lips, but I had no spit. My thoughts were becoming darker again. I began to worry about all the noises *Grimalkin* was making. I tried to figure out which noises meant what. I flashed back to earlier in the day, when I had considered unclipping Gerry and letting him go. This filled me with mixed emotions: guilt that I had thought of it and relief that I hadn't done it. There was so much going on in my mind. I suddenly craved a cigarette. I checked the outside pockets of my oilskins and found some. They were pulp.

My throat was sore, my mouth dryer than ever. I craved chewing gum. I craved anything I could chew, anything that would stop my jaw shivering, get the lingering taste of salt and bile out of my system. I thought about drinking my own urine – of which there was a seemingly endless supply. Where was it all coming from? It must have been my intake of salt water both above and below deck. I knew drinking urine could extend life by a day or so, but I also knew that urine was saline, which in my case would only increase the speed of dehydration.

Desperate to rid myself of these revolting tastes, I looked around the cockpit for the umpteenth time. Not one source of moisture, fresh and uncontaminated. I sucked on the draw-strings of my hood, rolling the plastic toggles round my sore gums. Wet but salt. I spat them out. I picked up a whipped end of rope tail and sucked on it, thinking it would help. It only worsened the taste.

To windward, to the west, the sun was beginning to make its slow descent. Was there anyone else out there with us in this empty sea? Probably not. Feeling abandoned and very, very alone, even with Gerry by my side, I began to think about the evening, now fast approaching, and then of darkness and the problems it would bring. The weather might worsen again after dark. I panicked that the two of us, in *Grimalkin*, wouldn't last another night. I was at my lowest ebb.

I asked Gerry about faith, his beliefs. I questioned my own faith, God, Jesus, creation itself. My upbringing had been strict, although not as strict as my brothers' and sister's. I was the youngest and I just fell in with Ma's wishes. Faith was a kind of insurance for me; it certainly wasn't blind. As I lay there next to Gerry, pondering faith and all its implications, I spotted something in the distance. A black dot, another sighting, my imagination at work again – probably. I didn't react to it – just carried on talking, mumbling to

Gerry. The small dot on the horizon got bigger – too significant, too constant to ignore. I sat up, apologising to Gerry
for stopping mid-conversation. Blinking, rubbing my eyes
with gloved hands, I took a good look. Disbelieving, quiv-
ering, I told Gerry I was 99 per cent sure something was
heading in our direction. I kept looking. It was getting closer,
becoming very large; there was no mistaking it now. A very
large commercial vessel was coming *Grimalkin*'s way.

'Bloody hell, Gerry, it's a boat. It's a frigging massive
boat – to hell with faith. This is real.'

I jumped for joy, waved my hands, unclipped and climbed
onto the deck to gain a higher vantage point – to make us,
Grimalkin, as visible as possible. From up there I blew my
whistle like a maniac and used what CO_2 was left in my
foghorn to sound an alarm. I shouted frantically to Gerry
that even if *Grimalkin* foundered right now, we would be
rescued. Slightly hysterical now and light-headed, my voice
started squeaking, like the Donald Duck quack Gerry had
been doing for fun early on in the race.

Then I stopped short – my stomach fell away – the vessel
wasn't slowing down. It wasn't heading our direction any
more – its course had changed before even reaching us. It
was passing us, steaming on, moving away from *Grimalkin*.

'What the hell's up, what's going on?' I yelled at Gerry.
Then it clicked. Of course – it was obvious. I could see
the much larger boat, but they couldn't see us – floating so
low in the water, without even a mast to spot, how the hell
would they? My instinct was to jump in and swim to it, swim
to the receding boat – let them know, whoever they were,
that we were in need of help, that we needed rescue. But what
if I didn't make it? What if while I was out there swimming

to the boat, *Grimalkin* went down, taking Gerry with her? What if I drowned? I'd miss my twenty-fourth birthday – only eight days away.

Tantalised, I hung onto the guardrail. As the vessel passed its nearest point to us, my knees trembled, my breath came thick and fast, my head hammered. As it ploughed on away from us, I looked at Gerry. If one boat had missed us, sailed right past, others would too – it was inevitable.

The dot on the horizon – a boat that had every possible method of rescue available to us – disappeared to nothing. Had we – Gerry, the boat and I – become invisible? Were we now in some make-believe world that nobody could see? Maybe I was dead? Maybe we were both dead and already in hell.

Sixteen

In My Mind's Eye

I sat back down again and stared at nothing in particular, first to the horizon, then around my feet, at the rubbish, the lines, the water in the cockpit.

'Is someone playing tricks on us, hey, Gerry? Does someone think this is funny?'

How could we possibly have been left here for so long? I belched; God, what an awful taste. I licked my lips but lacked saliva. My tongue felt numb and cold against the cracks in my mouth.

The surface of the water in the cabin had risen. It was creeping, biding its time, waiting to drag us down. I wondered if *Grimalkin*'s name had now completely disappeared into the sea. If her name vanished, surely we would too.

Wasn't *Grimalkin* the name of a character in one of Shakespeare's plays? I looked back at Gerry.

'Do you know which play it is? Come on, mate, I bet you do. *A Midsummer's Night Dream*? *Much Ado About Nothing*? *Twelfth Night*? *The Tempest*? Ha-ha! No, none of those, is it? Maybe it's *All's Well That Ends Well*. No? It'll come to me, I know it will.'

Chatting away here to Gerry, it occurred to me how little I knew about him. How weird was that? I had shared some of my most intimate, emotional, life-changing moments with this man and I had no idea what he even did for a living.

'What do you do, Gerry? How long have you been doing that for? Do you enjoy it?'

I couldn't stop myself from bombarding my crewmate, my friend, with inane questions, for which it appeared I needed no answers.

'How do you get to work? Do you walk, drive or cycle? You lucky bugger, at least you can drive if you want to . . . I've got to walk or cycle everywhere.'

Laughing hysterically, I told Gerry how I nearly ran over a cat once. 'I was pissed . . . pissed out of my head . . . a pissed epileptic on a bike! Imagine that, hey, Gerry?'

Of course! A cat. That's who Grimalkin is – the witches' cat in *Macbeth*. I read that play in Mr Moseley's class in 4G. That thought reminded me of my old school song. I hadn't forgotten a word of it.

> '*Hamble, our school, we have made thee*
> *What thou art today*
> *Foundation strong for adventure*
> *Out onto life's highway*
> *Hamble, we will honour thee*
> *In thought and . . .*'

I stopped mid-song and called over to Gerry. 'Come on, mate, join in. Got a problem with that, have you?'

I could feel a resentment building up against Gerry and his dumb presence. I was itching, gunning for a row.

'You don't know the words, do you, Gerry? You don't know the frigging words.'

Unable to reason, my thoughts and anxieties accelerated.

'What have you done to help our situation, eh? You haven't bailed, you haven't found food, water . . . nothing. Not a bloody thing.'

I went berserk. Looking him straight in the face – Christ, it had turned a funny purple colour – I asked him why he had missed the spotter plane. Why had he stopped me from swimming to the other boat, to safety? I accused him of seeing lifeboats, helicopters, even other yachts while I was down bailing, trying to save the boat.

'You just couldn't be bothered to tell me, could you, Gerry?'

I stopped. A disturbing image flashed through my head. An image of my crewmates leaving on the life raft. I didn't know, but maybe Gerry did. Or maybe they hadn't left at all? With my dehydration-fuelled paranoia, I managed to convince myself that the screams I had heard earlier in the day, which I had put down to imagination, were in fact real. My crewmates were still on the boat, trapped up in the bows somewhere. I stood up, shakily.

'Come out, come out, wherever you are!'

There was no answer. I caught sight of Gerry's green Puffa jacket, poking out of the top of his oilskins. My paranoia escalated. Green, that colour, that's what caused all our bad luck. There was no doubt in my mind now – this bloody jacket is what caused the storm, caused us to have been left alone together. About to launch into yet another undeserved tirade at the unfortunate Gerry, I hesitated – there was a warm, wet feeling on the right side of my mouth. I pulled my glove off and wiped my mouth, and was shocked to see bright red blood smudged across my hand. Wiping again, I realised that my ranting had caused my cracked lips to split and bleed.

Christ, what the hell was I up to? What was I doing to myself? I needed to get a grip. I forced myself to sit back down. Dropping my head into my hands, I wheezed, inhaling deeply, shaking. I was the one at fault. Not Gerry. It was me.

Slowly, with immense mental effort, I finally felt a sort of level-headedness return. The heightened feelings of the last hour or so evaporated. My emotions were deadened, and for this I was thankful. Less alert, but calmer, I was able to reason better. I knew I had all the signs of dehydration and hypothermia: light-headedness, confusion, irritability. I didn't need a doctor to diagnose it. I could also rationalise that it was these symptoms that had driven me into a state of angry paranoia.

There was no need to apologise to Gerry. I knew he understood. Scanning round *Grimalkin* I saw that the weather was no longer as evil, as threatening. Over the last hour or two it had greatly improved. The wind had subsided and it was now quite bright. There was still a long, deep swell – that hadn't changed. But the waves were slower, not as steep. Judging by the height of the sun it was late afternoon, early evening.

I looked out across the empty nothingness. Then I saw movement. Were my eyes deceiving me? Whatever it was, it vanished between the crests of the waves. Keeping my eyes directly on the spot, I tugged at Gerry's oilskin.

'Christ, there's something out there, Gerry . . . I'm sure of it. I saw it. It's about a mile away, swerving in and out of the swell.'

My heart rose at the sight of the white of a sail. This was a lone yacht – no doubt about it. I stood up on the cabin roof, and from there I shouted down to Gerry. 'It's a yacht! I can't see any crew, but it's there all right . . . it's there.'

It vanished again behind a swell. Who were they? Who was on board? Were they waiting for rescue, or could they rescue us? Then an awful thought – maybe this lone yacht had already been abandoned. Maybe it was floating free, the crew already saved. As panic mounted, I remembered the white sail. Of course, there was crew. Their raised sail showed that the mast was intact, and without a working crew how could the sail have been hoisted?

With that, I put my whistle to my mouth and blew the hell out of it. I waved my arms, jumped about, yelled, then stopped. I had spotted a yacht again but in an entirely different place. It was closer so I got a better view of her. I saw what looked like the name *Frayola*, and by the size of her rig I guessed this was a class-four yacht. She then disappeared. What the hell was going on? Were there two boats out there? It wasn't possible for one yacht to have moved position so quickly. This was too much. Was any of this real? Then, sure enough, two yachts came into view simultaneously, for the briefest of moments, before disappearing behind the swell. This was miraculous.

'Gerry, there's two of them . . . there's bloody two of them!'

One of the yachts emerged again. It was close enough

for me to see its hull clearly. It had at least two people on board. They waved frantically in *Grimalkin*'s direction. I managed to acknowledge them before they disappeared again behind a swell. It seemed an age before I saw either yacht again. While waiting, I wondered: did either yacht have a VHF radio? Could we be transferred over to one of them? I feared this would be tricky because of the swell. With no means of communication I stood and waited as agonising minutes passed. Then I watched as a parachute flare was launched. That flare was for us. We'd been seen, acknowledged. Thank God. Ma's God, anyone's God. The crew must have made contact with someone and rescue was on its way, and the launching of this flare told me it would be sooner rather than later.

I shook Gerry's hand. It was cold, colder than it had ever been before. I started crying. We were going to be saved. There was somebody else out here after all. I slumped back into the cockpit well and for the first time that day felt a vague sense of normality. These were real boats, real people. I felt elated, but impatient too. Why weren't things happening quicker? I dreamed of seeing Ma and Pa, my brothers, my sister Cheryl. But I had to calm down, be patient and just wait.

Out of nowhere, I turned to Gerry and announced, 'One day I'd like to get married and have a family, and settle down in the village.'

I continued talking to Gerry about my hopes for the future. Intermittently I stood up to get a sighting – wanting some reassurance that rescue was imminent. Time was really beginning to drag now. Minutes seemed like hours. Or maybe hours had passed? This was all taking an incredibly long time.

Standing up again I felt faint, but I managed to keep looking, and finally I caught sight of one of the yachts. Relieved, I sat back down. I was getting colder and more numb. I could feel my initial elation beginning to fade. I had this overwhelming feeling that we were in for another huge disappointment.

I needed to do something to help the time pass. I decided to clear up some of the mess in the cockpit – it looked awful. Christ, so did Gerry. I had to fix him up a bit too. I decided to deal with him first in case rescue came quicker than I thought. With my sodden glove I began to wipe the dirty, congealed blood from round the gash on his forehead.

'There's no need for Margaret to see you in this state, hey, mate?'

I had to shift him into a better position, where I could get at him properly, give him a really good clean-up. I was dragging his six-foot-two frame upwards when an agonising pain shot from the pit of my belly right up into the back of my chest, forcing me to drop him again. As he slid back down into his original position, I slumped back into mine. This was horrific – every breath I took was cut short by a knife-like pain. Lying back, completely knackered, I felt the pain gradually ease. That was the end of that idea. Gerry was staying as he was, as was I. I stared out into the seas. Couldn't the ocean lie flat for just one minute and allow us to see what the hell was going on? Where everyone was?

The sun was beginning to set. It must be at least 8pm now. Had the yachts just let off a flare and moved on? Had rescue come by lifeboat? Were they having difficulty in finding us? Had I lost them? Had they lost me? Why didn't they send air rescue? We were so low in the water they probably couldn't see us and maybe they had presumed we'd sunk.

Once night fell, *Grimalkin*, without illumination or navigation lights, would remain undiscovered. I thought about securing a length of chain to a sail and chucking it over the side, allowing it to act as a sea anchor. But this would have required a physical effort I no longer possessed. Even as I thought it, I knew I could never have done it.

I found it very difficult to think, let alone talk. I drained my bladder to warm myself, thinking that if ever I was found, dead or alive, I'd stink. My fingers were blue and bloated. This scared me senseless but I could do nothing now apart from wait.

Above me the skies had cleared further. The sun, that yellow ball of fire, missed for so long, was luminous as it made its descent. It was so low in the sky it lit up the cabin and I could see what looked like the surface of hell boiling beneath us. I watched as water occasionally spat out over the bridge deck and into the cockpit well, filling it up. This was no optical illusion – the levels were rising. I was bucket-less, having thrown it back into the cabin, and had not one ounce of energy left in my body. Retrieving the bucket, let alone using it, was an option no longer. Gerry's legs were being covered by water – I saw his other boot floating off. Automatically I untied and unclipped myself ready for the struggle of putting it back on. Then I thought, why? Apathetic, I tied myself back on, tighter, putting an extra round turn in my clove hitch for luck. Jesus Christ – luck. That was something I could have done with hours ago.

Gerry, very much within my dipped vision, sadly looked even more dead than before. I found talking to him more difficult now. I felt he had gone, not physically but certainly spiritually. I thought back to that conversation with him about my future, but now I thought about the possibility of no family, no wife and no children – no future whatsoever. I wanted to ask him what death was really like. I had been close to it once before, almost tasted it, but Gerry knew the reality.

Wearily I gazed at him, thinking about the inevitability of our remaining together, drifting undiscovered in the darkness. Resting my head on the sleeve of my quilted jacket, I began to envisage what now appeared to be inescapable – I began to picture *Grimalkin* foundering, sinking into the depths of the Irish Sea. These thoughts gave me a sense of control. This was a reality to be faced up to. Put simply, when *Grimalkin* sank, what would I do? I looked from my life into the emptiness of my own death.

I closed my eyes, then in my mind's eye I pictured myself and Gerry still clipped securely to *Grimalkin*. She was beginning to founder, and we were both being sucked downwards. The water was now up to my chin. It was cold, icy cold. I was struggling, my head bashing against the cockpit's sides. My lifejacket was doing its best to keep my head above water. My harness was holding firm, fighting the buoyancy of my lifejacket. Gerry's head was cradled in my arms – I could smell death on him – it pervaded his lank hair and coarse stubble. Why was I clinging to him? Because I had to – there was no way I was going alone.

Grimalkin's deck canted steeply then plunged vertically under the surface and she began her final journey into the depths of the Irish Sea. Underwater, removed from reality, I pictured myself aware, eyes smarting but open, looking around at *Grimalkin* travelling fast, gathering momentum. I saw her dragging Gerry and me by our safety harnesses ever downwards, bubbles of air surrounding us. I saw the surface of the water now 20 feet above us. As the last rays of light disappeared I wondered how long I should hold my breath for. I heard myself wanting to ask Gerry: When do I drown? How long before I die? He would know – please God, make it quick. I didn't want to be alive when I hit the seabed.

I opened my eyes and found myself still above the surface, with Gerry three feet from me. I had scared myself almost to death. What was I doing? I had to get these scenarios out of my head. I felt fainter, more disorientated and bewildered than ever before. I saw the sun's top just above the horizon. The light was about to disappear. I tried to stand up to scan the seas – just one last time, before the light went – but couldn't. Had I even seen the yachts at all? Or like so much else were they imagined?

I was as cold as death. My breathing had become quick and shallow. My brain seemed to be shutting down, along with other vital organs.

'I must not fall asleep, I must not fall asleep.'

But wouldn't it be better if I simply fell asleep? Why not? Yes, now was the time. My eyelids closed. I began to drift off. I craved sleep. I thought of home, family, familiar noises, warm clean sheets, soft pillows and eiderdowns. All was serene. I was alone but comfortable and safe. I heard the strains of a wonderful symphonic tune. God, what was that tune? I lost it, no longer able to focus. The beautiful tune changed into a pulsating beat, an unwanted mechanical sound effect – bloody rock music. The last thing I wanted to hear now was Pink Floyd. I wanted it out of my head but its beat quickened: chop, chop, chop, increasing in intensity, ever louder, ever nearer. I opened my eyes and looked up. I saw a blurred light-grey thing hovering, suspended in the sky, no more than a quarter of a mile away, maybe less. It was getting louder, closer. Was this another trick? I couldn't cope with another knockback.

Then the powerful downdraught from rotating rotors created swirling shapes on the surface of the heaving sea beneath its fuselage and I knew this was no delusion, no daydream – it was the unmistakable metronome beat of a helicopter. Something tangible, authoritative was here – Royal Naval help had arrived. My calmness, my acceptance of my fate was abruptly and thankfully shattered.

'Gerry, look, mate, look . . . it's a helicopter, it's a Sea King.' And in my bemused state I pointed to the sky and wept.

The navy-grey helicopter circled us. The noise was extraordinary. I could see the pilot clearly, and the winchman standing at the open door. A crewman waved down to me, to let me know he was coming. I'd been waiting for this moment all day but I felt unprepared, as if I had been caught off guard. What would the crew think? Gerry was lying in a precarious position; he was bloodied. I was bloodied; it was down the front of my jacket – and Gerry's.

'That won't come off.'

What would they think? I thought of washing it off, thought of trying to move my friend, prop him up. I realised, finally, that none of it mattered. We were being rescued; they'd understand.

Within moments the crewman was descending on a cable towards the cockpit, but with *Grimalkin* still rising and falling some 20 or 30 feet it became evident that his descent was going to be hindered. As he got lower he began to swing

Clockwise from left back: Dave Ferrarotto, Tony Russell, Nick Ward, James 'Jimbo' Davies (1st Mate), Ian Kirton, Anna Kastanias-Kirton, Emily Caruso (2nd Mate), Simon Bradley (Skipper), Nigel Beacham, and Penelope Rance.

The full kit for Fastnet 2009: three layers of comfortable, breathable, waterproof clothing, so different from 1979. My combined lifejacket and harness shows twin crutch straps which prevent it from riding up over the wearer's head – a cause of death by drowning in 1979.

Introduced after 1979, these double action hooks cannot open or straighten under load. The twin hooks can be opened with one hand and are stitched or looped to a flexible 2-metre tether and clipped to a soft loop on the harness.

Designed to cut tethers under load, and fitted as standard to my combined lifejacket and harness, this cutter is one of many safety innovations which could have saved lives back in 1979.

Motor sailing to the start line *Ariel* prepares to hoist her huge Yankee jib off Osborne Bay.

Off Cowes before the start. *Grimalkin*, the boat which saved my life in 1979, came out to see me off. 'Good luck from *Grimalkin*' is the message strung from her stanchions.

Action aboard *Ariel* as we tack to cross the start line. The wind is light and the huge Yankee jib is manhandled over from starboard to port tack. I am out of the way aft, timing the start. Taken from *Grimalkin* there's an Isle of Wight ferry and supporter's RIB in the background. White discs on *Grimalkin*'s guardrail aid the genoa over it when tacking.

With crew wearing lifejackets along with all other 274 entrants, *Ariel* passes through the starting gate flying her orange tri-sail and storm jib. This has been a requirement since 1979.

Yachts flying orange coloured storm sails follow *Ariel* into the start gate to be checked by the Royal Ocean Racing Club (RORC).

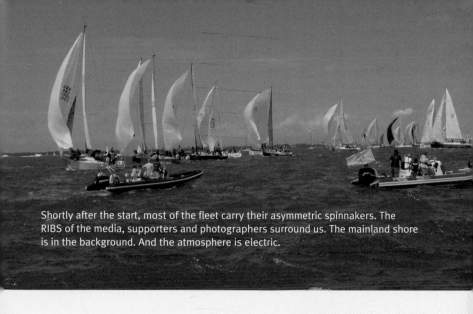

Shortly after the start, most of the fleet carry their asymmetric spinnakers. The RIBS of the media, supporters and photographers surround us. The mainland shore is in the background. And the atmosphere is electric.

Trying to get every ounce out of the light winds, we take it in turns trimming. It's my favourite job. Concentration is no problem.

An amazing horizon and a vast expanse of sea. With no competition close to *Ariel* I realise that on this day I will round the Rock. As my watch ends I stay above deck to savour the moment.

As *Ariel* approaches the iconic Fastnet Rock, I fulfil my 37-year ambition, see it in the flesh and take *Ariel*'s helm to round it. I feel tired and very emotional, but it's a brilliant moment as it closes the loop for me.

3pm Friday 14th August, on the way home. We are approaching the area where, on Tuesday 14th August 1979, I was picked up.

A new day dawns. On rounding the Rock the weather forecast is ominous and *Ariel* flies her medium-weight spinnaker and looks forward to some stronger winds – we want to surf home to Plymouth under full sail. This sky reminds me of another time and another place, not far from this point.

more violently, rotating on what must have been well over a hundred feet of cable. His target, his landing area, was tiny. The pilot was trying to adjust height and pitch to suit the rise and fall of the yacht, but watching this crewman, my rescuer, struggle in the crosswind and with the downdraught, trying to reach his mark, I panicked again. What if he had to abort the landing? Perhaps I could help him – pull his legs over the pushpit.

But this young man required no help from me. He was purposeful, strong and deliberate in his movements. His black boots hit the deck with some force. The light reflected off his visor so that I couldn't see his eyes. I was elated, shocked, ecstatic to see someone else. I stared at him. He began shouting and gesticulating but I couldn't hear what he was trying to say. Finally I understood – he was going to lift Gerry first – Gerry's purgatory was over.

It looked as if I'd become a survivor.

Seventeen

Horizon to Horizon

With urgency and authority, the crewman unclipped himself and asked if I was OK. I wanted to hug this man, wanted him to hold me and let me tell him everything – all that had happened to me and to Gerry, but I just nodded and said, 'Fine . . . fine, thanks.'

This guy with all his gear had a huge physical presence and commanded instant respect. The very opposite of me – filthy, bloodied, smelly and unkempt.

One glance and I felt sure he knew that Gerry was dead. With Gerry's unearthly posture no further confirmation was needed. I felt guilty, embarrassed that I hadn't been able to position my friend in a more dignified, upright way as he deserved. I began to murmur an apology, try to explain, but the crewman was so busy doing his thing he didn't hear. With his harness in hand he unclipped Gerry first, then turned him over onto his back, just as I had tried and failed to do a short time ago. *Grimalkin* was still moving severely with the swell and he was forced to stop several times to counter the unpredictable movements. Finally he managed to loop his heavy webbing strop round and under Gerry's armpits. I watched as he manipulated Gerry's stiff upper limbs into a position where he could be lifted off the boat. What a heart-wrenching sight, poor Gerry – I had to turn away. Unable to stand any longer I fell backwards and found myself sitting in the furthest corner of the cockpit. I held onto the tiller and shook. Weak, cold, I wondered again if I was the only one of the crew left alive.

Bloody hell, this was noisy. A thick shiny steel wire was being lowered towards the boat – it took several attempts before the heavy, swinging wire was secured. I watched in awe as this young man managed to hold on to Gerry's $14^{1}/_{2}$ stone dead weight and secure the wire before attaching it to them both. This was it then. With a sharp cracking noise they were snatched off the deck. Gerry's unbooted feet hit the guardrail heavily. I wanted to yell out as they disappeared up towards the underneath of the helicopter, 'Hey, be careful with him,' but of course I didn't.

The sadness and the remorse I felt at watching Gerry leaving *Grimalkin* was overwhelming. Events were now over-taking me. Everything, including Gerry, was out of my hands. As Gerry was swallowed up by the Sea King, I wondered where they would put him, whether they would administer mouth-to-mouth. Maybe they had a doctor on the helicopter?

With the constant downdraught, I was shivering violently. My teeth felt as if they might fall out of their sockets. Waiting, I became uneasy. How long could it stay, hovering above me, before having to return to base to refuel? What was its range? Heart racing, I huddled further into the corner of the cockpit – it felt smaller, harsher and bleaker than ever. I needed a drink, water.

Then, just as quickly as the crewman had disappeared, he reappeared. He was on his way down to me. Once more, it took a few tries before I heard an almighty thump as he landed on the deck. The helicopter moved away and he began to pull me to my feet. I reached up, trying to clutch the wire.

'Don't touch the safety wire – it's static,' he shouted.

I simply wanted to hold on to something other than *Grimalkin*. What harm was a bit of static going to do me? But he was emphatic, impatient to get me off the boat. Once on my feet, I remembered.

'I have to get my gear, my money.'

As soon as I said it, I saw what I recognised as emotion coming from this, up until now, detached professional. It was a look of sympathy, pity even. Christ, I felt pathetic – this request was stupid and unnecessary.

Squeezing my arm gently he said, 'There's no time, she's going down. We have to get off the boat.'

These were his orders. I was his casualty, and for him to do what he needed to do I had to let him take control. As he worked quickly, assuredly, making hand signals to the aircraft, I wanted to ask if there was any news of the others. I didn't. Before I knew it, his strop was looped round me and under my arms, just as it had been with Gerry. Strapped to him now, I could see his face clearly. I wondered if he could smell me? He shouted for me to try to be still, then edged his way off the deck. The strop tightened round my chest; my armpits hurt like hell as I was lifted off the deck. I didn't care. I lay there, passive for the first time in hours. The view from this vantage point was amazing. The ferocious seas looked almost benign and inviting, the last of the sun's rays reflecting off them. Looking from horizon to horizon – 20/20

– I saw the two boats. I was amazed at the clarity of the view I got of them and their waving crews. Not so long beforehand I had wondered if they were a figment of my imagination. There they had been behind the swells, all the time, right up until the last moment. I felt immense gratitude that they must have waited all those hours for our rescue, had seen it all.

About 50 feet up, looking straight down, I saw our abandoned boat and how ravaged she was. Her deck was strewn with the wreckage of the felled mast, boom and sails. Damn, I had left her companionway open, with no washboards in place to keep the seas out. Staring directly down into her cockpit – the shelter she had provided me and Gerry for all those hours – I wondered how long it would be before she foundered. Only a miracle could keep her afloat through the night. The water level had risen so much her name wasn't visible at all.

The open side door of the Sea King helicopter appeared in front of me and I was pulled in to safety. My legs wobbled uncontrollably as they guided me to a bench seat. There I sat, speechless. One of the crew gave me a blanket. Gerry was not far from me – he had been laid out behind a bulkhead and covered by a blanket. Someone placed ear defenders over my freezing ears. This softened the relentless noise but left me so isolated. One of the crew signalled for me to deflate my lifejacket. I was bizarrely unnerved by this request. This lifejacket had saved my life, time after time. Deflating it made me feel insecure. I felt I was outside of, not part of, what was going on. Everything around me looked technical, alien. I looked towards the windscreen. I saw a radar screen and my eyes followed its bright green indicator, tracking like a single clock hand, round and round its black screen.

We were headed off somewhere – where, I had no idea. I was desperate for sleep, water and food. My teeth were chattering again. I felt anxious, disorientated and cold. I needed to pee but stopped myself, realising I couldn't – not here.

I wanted to ask questions about my crewmates and my family but apart from a few hand signals there was no conversation between us. The engine noise was too loud. The lack of communication made me paranoid and suspicious. I felt sure there was more bad news to come. I could see the blanket that covered Gerry, but not Gerry himself. This was very distressing. Anguished and full of guilt I felt helpless that out of a crew of six I was probably the only one to survive. I needed to talk to Gerry. I needed to find out what he really wanted me to say to Margaret – were those few words enough? I wanted to feel for his pulse, just in case. I was still uncertain, even though I knew. This unfamiliar, noisy environment compounded the confusion I felt.

Then there it was – the coastline of England, home. This first sight of land gave me a great boost of adrenaline – my panic subsided and turned to elation as the land got bigger, noises got louder, the crew sat down and braced themselves and the helicopter began to bank. This was like no other landfall I'd made before. I felt like whooping with joy. From a side window I saw hedgerows, two tractors, a horse grazing. I saw a railway viaduct in the distance and nearby some grey chimneys, tin mines. The boundaries of an airfield and then grey tarmac came into view. As we got lower I clearly saw a large yellow H painted on the tarmac. Lower still I began seeing dots scampering around. The dots became bodies. There was a bump and then the sliding side door opened.

A military ambulance stood by. I tried to stand up but

couldn't – my legs were like jelly. One of the crew gestured to me to stay seated. I now knew that Gerry was going to be the first to leave. He was lifted and laid onto a stretcher, then put into the ambulance. His head was covered; his exit was dignified. The ambulance door closed and I watched as it drove away from us. Gerry and I were now separated – I hated that.

I was helped out of my seat, out of the Sea King and into a waiting wheelchair on the tarmac. From there, I saw the pilot, high up in his cab – he put his right thumb up. I wanted to acknowledge him, thank him, thank everyone, but I couldn't. Everyone was smiling – broad smiles – as though we were all long-lost friends. I was whisked past everybody, away from the Sea King, away from the tarmac towards what looked like the entrance to a sick bay. Over the door was a sign that read 'RNAS Culdrose Naval Base' – I now knew where I was.

Once inside I was transferred from the wheelchair onto a trolley, where I was laid flat but with my head propped up. Everything was white, gleaming white. A bath was being filled – Christ, I craved water. As though she had read my thoughts a nurse held a glass to my mouth. That first glassful didn't touch my throat. Despite the pain, I drank more. Three, maybe four before the nurse said, 'Enough.' Anxiously I told her that I was epileptic and that I needed phenobarbitone as quickly as possible. She assured me that this would be arranged.

She then put some ointment on my lips, and with that the naval doctors and the Wrens stripped me. There was no messing around, no embarrassment. The room was hot. Briskly they rubbed me down with starched white towels. I wondered why on earth I was being dried off so vigorously, so thoroughly, when I was about to be plunged into a bath of steaming water. Again as if reading my thoughts the nurse smiled at me and said, 'We have to get your circulation going.'

I nodded, now too weary and bewildered to question any more. They knew what they were doing. They immersed me in the huge white bath full of very hot water, almost too hot to bear. This is standard practice for victims of hypothermia: to get the core body temperature up. During this procedure I was asked various questions about my condition and how I felt – serious faces wrote every detail down. I was hot but still shivering, trembling, at the same time. I asked a nurse if Ma and Pa had been contacted. She didn't know – nobody seemed to know. I asked if anybody else had been brought here – nobody answered. Staring at my blue toes under the almost scalding water, I again feared the worst. I knew only too well that in sailing terms no news meant bad news.

A doctor came in, carrying a clipboard. He called me by my name, my full name. I knew that this man would know the fate of my four missing crewmates. I immediately asked if anyone else had been recovered or rescued from the yacht *Grimalkin*. He flicked through his clipboard – two or three pages – then ran his finger down the names.

'It's kilo five six three seven,' I said, willing him to find the names quicker.

Without lifting his eyes he carried on. My gaze switched to the white tiles in front of me – this wait was killing me.

'Yes,' he said calmly, matter-of-factly. 'Three other men were recovered.'

I knew this must be Matt, Dave and Mike. 'And the fourth man? David Sheahan . . . the skipper. What of him?'

The doctor shook his head. 'Still missing, I'm afraid.'

Christ, poor David – he was dead and I knew it. Everyone in the room knew it. I could tell by the uneasy faces and the intense silence. I stared at the white tiles – shocked but at the same time relieved – the others were alive – thank God, they had made it. I was going to ask how or where they had been recovered. But instead I sank back into the bath. Not now. Something told me the implications of this good news would be too much to handle right now.

After soaking for what seemed like ages I was helped out of the bath. As the nurse dried me off I felt warmer, better, but more emotionally raw than I'd felt for hours. I was dressed in warmed regulation pyjamas, then taken to a side room where I was helped into a preheated iron-framed bed. Alone now, lying in my bed, resting, I was sure I saw, through the half-open door, Gerry, sitting in his warm bath, just as I had done, with a young doctor beside him with a clipboard, writing notes. I wanted to call to him – tell him that Gerry was dead and had been since early this morning – that must have been about fourteen, maybe fifteen hours ago. Poor Gerry, he looked as if he was just asleep. And then the door to my room was pushed shut.

That was the last time I saw Gerry.

My door opened. A trolley came in, pushed along by a smiling nurse. I saw a steaming plate, piled high. I smelt eggs – I'd forgotten how hungry I was. It had been over 24 hours since I'd last eaten. It felt more like a month. The friendly-looking nurse propped me up in bed with about five pillows. A table was brought and I ate – scrambled egg it was, piled high on buttered bread. Frustratingly, I had no strength to grip the cutlery, to cut then raise the yellow fluffy nectar to my lips. It was cut for me and I managed to fork lumps of it in – my right hand shook as I held the fork.

'There's more if you want it.'

It was enough, more than enough. Slowly I ate; slowly I drank warm milk, lots of it. I felt better. My whole body still prickled, stung, but the hot bath had washed away the smell. Eggs and milk had purged the rancid taste from my gullet. I suddenly thought of Ma and Pa. With everything that had gone on, they had slipped from my shattered mind.

'My parents . . . do they know? Has anybody—'

The nurse smiled reassuringly. 'Don't worry, Nick. Everything's been taken care of. Those who need to know, know.'

Warm, nourished, I began to relax. There was no watch to keep, no water to bail, no bucket to worry about.

I recall being monitored quite closely and finding the constant flow of people in and out of my room reassuring after all those hours alone. Finally, resting my head on soft pillows, I drifted off, knowing I was safe. Sleep came easily but was laden with thoughts and disturbed by images of Gerry and David. The next morning I awoke with a start. I thought I was fitting but then realised I had been dreaming. In this dream I had seen and heard Gerry mumbling through his abnormally coloured lips, repeating something over and over, something important. How could I forget? Those words were etched on my brain.

I saw crisp, folded sheets, I was in a bed. No cockpit, no deck, no boat – no Gerry. Slowly, full awareness of my new surroundings registered. A rescue, a helicopter,

Culdrose, safety, dry land – all these images returned. The windows in my room were high; I couldn't see out. A nurse appeared.

Later that morning I was taken to Treliske Hospital in Truro. The medical staff continued to be very professional, very matter-of-fact. Accompanied by an ambulance man, I was still dazed. I recall seeing countryside as we slowly made the short journey to Truro. After being admitted and assessed by doctors, I was visited by a journalist from the *Herald Tribune* newspaper. This man, this journalist, although courteous and understanding, was a stranger and I wished he'd go away. In brief, I told him what had happened. I couldn't tell him everything. That was impossible. At this point all I wanted was to see my family. The journalist left and a short while later I was informed that Ma, Pa and my brother Simon were already on their way. They had had to wait for news of where I was being transferred to before travelling the 150 miles from Hamble. It was now early evening and even though I guessed it would be the following morning before I saw them, I was reassured.

Despite this, I still had a nagging anxiety that I found impossible to shift – no matter how hard I tried, I couldn't think of anything other than Gerry, Margaret, David and my crewmates. I knew that in order for me to explain anything to my family, to officials, to my surviving crewmates, but mostly to myself, I would have to write it down – as it had happened, chronologically, watch by watch, knockdown by knockdown. What I needed now was paper and a pen. Christ, I was thirsty. There was a glass, fresh water, by the bedside. With a dozen sheets or so of paper before me, I drank, then wrote. I wrote with a will – motivated by guilt for not being

<u>Crusalkin Fastnet Race 1979</u>

13.20 11th Aug Cowes. SAT

Extremely good start, first across the line with "Green Dragon".
3rd place through the needles. Watch started at 20.00
1st 12 hrs I was off watch, duty cook and general dogsbody.

12 th Aug (SUN)

Poor Visibility — on watch with Mike Doyle 4hrs on 4hrs
off etc, was able to sleep well. David was quite ill. came up
on Portland Bill still doing well in the light airs we were
amongst many larger class II III & IV boats. "Green Dragon"
was nowhere to be seen, so we assumed we were ahead of her.
Good humour on board, David made contact with Graye
through start point radio everyone well. Fog again during
the night, no wind for a time during 12 – 4 watch

13th Aug (TUES)

Through the Lizzard and Lands' End by 10.00
Fog clearing and we see yachts all around us mainly class III
& IV. Glorious spinnaker reach during the afternoon doing
8–10 knots over the water.

Extracts from Nick's notes written in Treliske Hospital on 15th August 1979.

left leg, which at the time I thought was broken.
I was unable to helm the boat, leaving that to Dave
I sat in the cockpit with Mike, Jerry sat forward
looking out for a Nimrod. David & Matthew
radioed to "Morning Town" who said she would
arranged a rendezvous with a "Sea King."
David gashed his head down below when we
rolled yet again. It was a bad gash, and although we carried a comprehensive first Aid kit
the best we could do was spray on antiseptic,
lint & Plastic skin protected by his hood &
wollen balladava.

Every thing was wrecked below — the engine
& its housing, chart table, V.H.F. & Companionway
ladder. David & Matthew returned on deck
with great difficulty, and we again gathered in
the cockpit, knowing that one more knock-down
would be fatal — David kept loosing consciousness
& had to be supported, every one was calm — I think

able to save Gerry. I had to write it down to prove that I'd tried – a hard-copy proof for myself and for others.

So I began at Cowes, with the start, with all I could remember. The weather, the crew, David, Gerry, Matt, the boat – all so fresh in my head. I wrote all of it down. This came easily, but the sequence of events just before I woke up in the water, that would have to wait – for later? As far as I knew – I'd heard someone mention it last night – *Grimalkin* had gone down. Nine, non-stop pages later, I'd run out of things I knew. I felt cleaner, as if by writing, I'd washed. I put the sheaf of paper and the pen in the top drawer of my small bedside table, to keep it safe until I knew what to do with it. I had a disturbed but less painful sleep that night in Treliske.

The next day, Thursday 16 August, after having been woken at 8am with a breakfast of porridge, I was given a bed bath then a shave by a kind young nurse. This same nurse soon had me sitting in a chair, next to my bed. I ached so much that as soon as my bed was made up I had to lie back on it. The nurse then left me alone with my thoughts and I soon found myself drifting off again. Intermittently, while dozing, I heard her come into the room to check on me.

Later that morning I heard more than one set of foot-steps approaching – instinctively I knew who it was. I opened my eyes and saw Ma, Pa and Simon walking up the aisle of the small ward towards me. I didn't know whether to smile or cry. Poor Ma, she looked distraught, and so tiny as she stood there between Pa and Simon. There was a total loss of words so we just hugged. Ma wept, then so did I. It was such a relief to be in their presence. A short time later the young nurse brought in tea and biscuits and things slowly began to feel more normal. Ma told me our black cat Tom had gone missing for the whole time I had and only reappeared after they had received the phone call to say that I had been found safe. Pa reckoned Tom had been hiding from the storm but Ma was adamant it was a sign. I found myself talking but it was small talk about all sorts of things that had nothing what-soever to do with why we were here. Eventually Pa looked me straight in the eye.

'What happened out there, son?'

I shrugged my shoulders. It was clear to Pa that it was not so much reticence on my part as ignorance – I simply did not know. Then I listened carefully as Pa filled me on the sequence of events and quickly realised that he and the rest of my family knew far more than I did. They had heard radio broadcasts, spoken to race control, to Gay, to Margaret, and others too.

Pa told me that Matt, Mike and Dave had left *Grimalkin* on the life raft and been air-rescued at about 9.30am on Tuesday 14th. I went numb. As the information filtered into my brain, I felt more alone than I had done at any time on *Grimalkin* with Gerry. I began to tremble. Although Pa continued talking, I tuned out – his words now indistinct as the realisation dawned on me. At the time my three crew-mates had been rescued – 09.30 – Gerry was still alive.

I was overcome with nausea. I felt emotionally sick. I told my family that that was enough, please, no more. I knew now what I wanted to do with my handwritten notes from the previous night. I opened the top drawer of the bedside table and handed Pa the nine sheets of paper, asking him to read them later, when it was quieter. He nodded and carefully put them in his coat pocket.

Later that day Gerry's wife, Margaret, visited me. We

were alone in the room; she sat on a brown plastic, metal-framed chair. Even though I'd spent hours alone with this woman's husband, I was terrified. I do not recall much about her visit, only that we both, obviously, found it distressing, particularly when I passed on Gerry's last words to her. I'd been rehearsing them to ensure that what Gerry had told me came out right – exactly as he had said it to me on the boat. Margaret wiped her eyes; she looked drawn. I wanted to hug her but couldn't. I felt I was imposing on her grief. If she were my sister, a relative or someone I knew well, I could have. I wanted to know if she was taking Gerry home with her, but there was no way I could have asked her that kind of detail. Her grief was such that she asked no other questions of me. I had no idea at that time if she knew the full circumstances under which we had been found. I did not know if she had seen or spoken to Matt, Dave or Mike; if she'd had an explanation from them of what had gone on. I knew nothing and did not ask. Margaret squeezed my hand and as she left I felt emptiness, a pit in my stomach, and a slight sense of shame, wishing I could have said more to comfort her.

On Friday 17 August I was released from Treliske Hospital and the next day I was back in Hamble – it was so great to be home. I got lots of phone calls from concerned friends and relatives. I was still finding it difficult to talk about what had happened to anyone, even my own family. So home was where I stayed. Wednesday, 22 August was my twenty-fourth birthday. Four friends of mine, good friends, wanted to take me out sailing. I wanted to go too, very much – but I knew that physically I wasn't up to it yet.

The day after my twenty-fourth birthday I learned I had

been the last survivor taken from the water or off any boat during the Fastnet Race. That same day I received a newspaper article, sent by my aunt. It was about Peter Harrison – a young naval midshipman and crewmember of Sea King 819. The headline read:

SHY PETER – *Brave Hero of the tragic yacht race*

It was Peter Harrison who had come down on the wire to rescue me. In this article he described how, after two hours of patrolling, the crew had spotted a dismasted white yacht with a black transom on which was written: *Grimalkin*, Southampton, RAFYC. He saw that two motionless men were sprawled in her cockpit. It was now just after 8.45pm and getting dark so rescue or recovery of the bodies was going to have to be executed quickly. Before he made his descent, he saw that one of the men was moving. He landed on the deck and this man, the younger of the two, had tears pouring down his cheeks and kept saying over and over that he had to get his clothes from the cabin below. Peter then described how the other man, lying in the bottom of the cockpit, said nothing and it took a moment for him to realise that he was dead.

Strangely, I remembered the clothes but not the tears. It was quite surreal reading this. It felt as though this article was about somebody else – not me, not Gerry.

In another report I found out that the aircrew had been unaware there was anyone still alive on board *Grimalkin* – until they saw me in the cockpit. This made sense of Peter's description of seeing 'two motionless bodies'. This is what he expected to see – two dead men. Their mission at that point was search and recovery, not search and rescue. Confused by this new information, I contacted the RAF and requested a trace on the radio logs to try to piece together the events between the time I was spotted and the time I was rescued. Unfortunately the radio logs of the aircraft involved did not go into such detail. The two yachts were not mentioned, so I can only surmise that while it was they who made the mayday call, they were unable for some reason to relay that there was a person alive on board. On reading this I felt all the luckier for being alive.

Eighteen

Aftermath

Early the following week I found out to my absolute surprise and delight that *Grimalkin* had not foundered after all. A friend of Pa's called to tell us. At first I found this hard to believe – especially after all those hours spent aboard her in the certainty that at any moment she would go down. It seemed almost miraculous that she was not at the bottom of the Irish Sea, but in the end it was manpower that had saved her. A Royal Navy helicopter crew had found her drifting not far from where Gerry and I had been lifted and had made her as watertight as possible. She was then salvaged and towed by a commercial vessel to a safe haven – where I did not know.

Fastnet '79 was the biggest peacetime sea-and-air-rescue operation that had ever taken place. By the time the race was over, there had been 15 fatalities, 24 crews had abandoned ship, 5 yachts had sunk, 136 sailors had been rescued and only 85 of the 303 yachts managed to finish the race. Many different organisations were involved, including the Royal Navy, the RNLI, the RAF, Her Majesty's Coastguard, and others. I heard that the Royal Western Yacht Club in

Plymouth had been overwhelmed with enquiries from all over the world about relatives or boats. There were no computerised switchboards in 1979, just a team doing its best to give out accurate information. Ma described it as being like the war, waiting for news to come in.

Pa and I were shocked to hear that, with this un-precedented loss of life, the future of the Fastnet Race was in jeopardy. Despite all I had been through, I did not want to see this great race brought to an end. But there were realities to be faced. Unlike *Grimalkin*, many of the smaller yachts in the competition had not been equipped with a radio and were therefore unable to report their positions. Life rafts had broken up and safety harnesses snapped, causing crew to drown, or die of hypothermia as Gerry had done. People wanted answers. Inevitably most of the blame was put on the Royal Ocean Racing Club, who had organised the event. With the levels of criticism increasing, an inquiry into the disaster was commissioned jointly by the RYA and the RORC.

Over the couple of weeks that followed, more calls and letters from the press and local TV stations arrived at my home. An intrigue was beginning to build around the events that had taken place on *Grimalkin*. This was confirmed by my sailing mates, who were being asked if they knew, through me, what had happened. Why had we been left? It was not long before national newspaper articles appeared, detailing our two separate rescues. After reading accounts in the press and my nine-page handwritten document, Pa wanted answers. My whole family, my friends wanted answers too. As I got stronger, better, so did I. But this was not proving easy.

Since my rescue from *Grimalkin* on the evening of 14 August, not one of my three surviving crewmates, Matt,

Dave or Mike, had contacted me, not even to see how I was. Any information I had got so far was through word of mouth or in the press. The effect of this was to create even more questions in my mind. I found myself asking people at my sailing club, colleagues and other people who had done the Fastnet that year if they knew or had heard anything. But nobody could add to what I had been able to deduce myself. It was bizarre, embarrassing, to have to go to these lengths.

I wanted to know more but I felt it was inappropriate for me to make contact with my crewmates. But their seeming lack of concern nagged at me constantly. What had I done to them? If they thought I had wronged them in any way, why didn't they have the guts to pick up the telephone, talk it over with me? I felt isolated. In the circumstances, as I understood them so far, it was they who had left the boat at some point when Gerry and I were unconscious. Matt, the only one I knew at all well out of the three of them, was grieving for his still missing, presumed dead father, whose body was yet to be recovered – how could I call him?

In early September, an unexpected thing happened. Gay Sheahan telephoned and asked me to accompany Matt to locate *Grimalkin*; she had been found in the Irish seaside town of Waterford. I was ecstatic at the prospect of being reunited with the boat that had saved me. I was never really sure why Gay asked me – maybe it was the fact that I was older than Matt – but I was touched by her request. I was a little anxious at the prospect of spending time alone with Matt, but I thought this was perhaps part of the journey that had to be taken. I hoped I could finally find out what had taken place on *Grimalkin* between the time I lost and then regained consciousness on that horrific morning of 14 August. It was one of the last parts of the puzzle.

Gay arranged for me to travel up to Camberley and stay overnight with the Sheahan family. I did so a few days later, and slept in a spare bedroom. I couldn't help but feel I was imposing on their grief but Gay was extremely kind. It was strange seeing not only happy family pictures around the house, but pictures of *Grimalkin* in happier times too – David's smiling face in all of them. The next morning Matt and I caught the train to Fishguard in Wales to catch the ferry across the Irish Sea to find *Grimalkin*.

At first there was much uncomfortable small talk and skirting round the issue on both our parts. Then I bit the bullet and pressed Matt. He told me his account of what had happened in the time that Gerry and I were unconscious. When *Grimalkin* had capsized, he'd been thrown clear of the boat and was pinned just beneath the deck because his harness line wasn't quite long enough to get his head totally out of the water for breath. From this position he was only able to grab the occasional lungful of air.

After a couple of minutes the boat started to right herself and Matt was flung back into the cockpit. The first thing he noticed was that the boat had been dismasted. Then he saw Gerry and me lying in the cockpit covered in rope and debris – unconscious or possibly dead. Dave and Mike were hanging on outside the boat so he had to help them back on board. It was then that he saw a body face-down in the water. The boat was drifting away from the body and he knew it was his dad, but there was nothing he could do. His dad and the boat were headed in opposite directions. Hearing this from Matt was shocking. I really felt for him. But why had this happened? Why had David's harness not saved him?

Matt told me that his dad, who was unconscious, had got

trapped underneath the capsized boat, and a crewmember had been forced to use his pocket-knife to cut the line to free him in order to bring him up for air. The crewmember then lost hold of David, who was washed away. This explained the cut line, and confirmed that my image of David being washed away was very real indeed. Whoever had cut the line did it to save David's life, but in doing so there was always the risk that he would be washed away. This dilemma is not unheard of for crews caught in heavy storm conditions. Matt made it clear that he felt it was the right thing to do. Put in that position, I, we, any one of us would have cut the line to try to save David. He did not say who had cut the line and I respected him for that. I may have been wrong, but I felt sure that it wasn't Matt himself.

Matt continued. He was faced with a decision – Dave and Mike wanted to leave the boat on the life raft. Gerry and I were in the cockpit buried under lines and all sorts of debris. He told me they tried to move us, but couldn't. To the three of them – Matt, Mike and Dave – Gerry and I looked dead. He told me that it had not been an easy decision – the most difficult of his life – but what was he to do? Stay on a sinking boat alone with two crewmates he thought were dead? He made the decision to go. My three crewmates launched the life raft and left *Grimalkin*. After an hour or so of what he described as sheer hell, they were rescued from the raft by helicopter. My sympathy for Matt began to diminish somewhat. He sensed the change in me towards him and closed down.

This latter part of the explanation was, to my mind, vague. It was also not exactly the one I wanted to hear. I wanted to hear that he, Dave and Mike had tried to resuscitate Gerry and me. I wanted to hear that they'd checked our pulses to determine whether we were alive, that they'd tried to give us mouth-to-mouth, that they'd tried to transfer us to the life raft. But no. It seemed that they had collectively decided to leave us.

I didn't quiz Matt further. I wanted to ask him why he, they, hadn't tried harder, but something prevented me from doing so. Maybe I was protecting Matt, a young man grieving for his father; maybe I was protecting myself from answers I could not bear to hear.

I didn't go into any detail concerning the hours I spent alone with Gerry. Matt didn't ask – I didn't offer. But I thought it strange he didn't want to know. I wanted to pour my guts out to this young man sitting opposite. I wanted to tell him what we'd been through when they had left us. But I couldn't. I knew he had enough to think about. I also felt that if I took things any further, our already strained companionship might turn into open animosity. So that was that. It was all small talk after that – but with an underlying air of tension.

We caught the night ferry across the Irish Sea to Rosslare and from there we went on by single-decker bus to Waterford, via some beautifully soft, verdant countryside. Near the quay in Waterford, sharing space in a compound with jeeps and trucks – there was *Grimalkin*. She stood out. There were no other boats as classy as her around – not even in the harbour. She was sitting on a trailer. It was upsetting for Matt to see her again – I saw it in his eyes. She looked out of place and sad. We climbed the ladder set against *Grimalkin*'s stern and my first thought was: What a bloody awful mess.

Matt and I were both taken aback by what we saw and found. This was the one time on the trip when we felt at ease with each other – during our reunion with *Grimalkin*. Above deck, particularly in the cockpit, metres of ropes and lines were still strewn all around. Down below, the washing-machine action of *Grimalkin* during the storm was amply demonstrated when Matt discovered that one of her main batteries – the size of a car battery – usually strapped and lashed securely beneath the companionway ladder, was wedged right up in the bows. It had travelled a distance of around 20 feet, taking a chunk of the boat with it on its way. God only knows what damage it would have inflicted if flesh and blood had barred its path. The forces generated by the knockdowns and pitch-poles were tremendous – it was testimony to why we had all stayed above deck.

Grimalkin's port topsides were badly scratched and damaged – her pulpit and most of her stainless-steel stanchions were gone or badly bent. The starboard side of the coach roof was staved in, its cabin windows smashed, caused, obviously, by the final B2 capsize and subsequent dismasting. We were able to recover a few personal possessions, which was some small comfort, but almost everything aboard smelt of diesel oil or was damaged.

As I took photographs of her below and then above deck I noticed that the cut and abandoned safety harness lines had been removed from their strongpoints in the cockpit – probably by the local guy who was looking after the boat. I wanted to tell Matthew, to explain in detail how these lengths of blue braided rope had added so much confusion and trauma to that day with Gerry, but I didn't – it was inappropriate.

Nearing the end of our inspection I was very moved to hear Matt say how determined he was to get *Grimalkin* back to the south coast of England and get her sailing again. He was sure that that was what David, his father, would have wanted.

During these days away from home, during the two

four-hour train journeys, the night spent in single beds at the hotel and the two overnight ferry crossings, Matt and I didn't converse much. Apart from the chat we had on the train, talk of what had gone on a month before was avoided. Finding and assessing *Grimalkin* were our objectives. There had been no time for anything other than getting from A to B, England to Ireland, and back. I wished we'd been able to bring *Grimalkin* home with us there and then, but there were many arrangements to make before that could happen. I'd seen her, though, and she was being looked after. We travelled back home and went our separate ways, Matt to Camberley, me to Hamble.

Several weeks passed but David's body was not recovered. A memorial service for him was arranged. On 28 September 1979, Ma and Pa travelled up with me to attend the service, which was held at St Michael's Yorktown church in Camberley – a very private affair. The large church was packed, and although it must have been of little comfort to Gay, many people spoke of David's open, friendly nature, and it was obvious that, well beyond his family, David would be sorely missed.

It was an emotional, dignified memorial service. My heart went out to Gay and her young family. Although I didn't see either Dave or Mike there I made a point of looking out for them but there was such a throng of people in attendance I could easily have missed them. I felt disappointed. At least Matt and I had talked, had a closure of sorts, even if an unsatisfactory one. I was saddened by not being able to meet up with them. We had been through something huge, all of us. But this was a celebration of David's life, not the time or place for recriminations or pointed questions. But this did not quell my desire for answers.

We drove back home that afternoon and on the journey

I became very upset. It is hard to describe but I can only suppose I had a realisation that I found unacceptable, almost unbearable – it would appear that no one was going to add to the somewhat vague details I had been given by Matthew earlier that month. I felt blanked, isolated by my crewmates. I needed no sympathy from them, but there were so many unanswered questions, questions only they could answer. I wanted answers, face-to-face answers, from all three of them – but there was nothing I could do. Pa assured me that an inquiry would examine all aspects of the disaster. As hard as it was, for the moment I had to try to put it all to the back of my mind.

On my return to work at the chandlery, I decided I had to clear my head of these negative thoughts, and I did this by taking some positive action. I decided to set about finding the two yachts that had discovered *Grimalkin* and secured our rescue. I wanted to thank them, and also others who had aided my rescue.

In the weeks that followed, Pa and I wrote many letters of thanks to those involved in the finding of *Grimalkin*, Gerry and me, including a very personal letter of gratitude to Peter Harrison and his parents. It was not easy to trace the two yachts, however. I remembered that I had seen what looked like the name '*Frayola*' written on the stern of the smaller one. I checked the official entry list and there was no yacht of this name, but there was a class-four French-owned yacht named *Fragola*. She was owned by a G.J.C. des Glenans, and had retired from the race. I felt sure that this boat had retired as a result of assisting *Grimalkin*. This made me even more grateful, and determined to find and thank them.

I made every effort to find an address for Monsieur des

Glenans and the home port of his yacht *Fragola*, but could find nothing. This being nearly thirty years ago, everything was by letter or word of mouth. I also asked locally, at my sailing club, the HRSC, and the RSYC – but nobody knew. I contacted RYA and the RORC, but with such vague information and probably because of their ongoing inquiry they couldn't help me. I visited all the Hamble and Cowes marinas in my quest but came up with nothing. My family and friends had by now joined in the search, asking people wherever they went if anyone had heard of this yacht.

As a last resort I began to read through all national and local press reports about the race. I even wrote to relatives in different parts of the country asking that they check their local newspapers. While this search was proving fruitless, I did come across other information, including details about Gerry, some that surprised me. He had been advised by his doctors not to sail on the Fastnet – I was quite shocked by this but was also reminded of Margaret's anxious face as she saw Gerry off on the morning of the race. I found out that he was the son of Mr and Mrs David Winks who lived in Dublin, Ireland. I had had no idea that Gerry was Irish, but with that wild mop of red hair it made sense. All his family still lived in Ireland including one sibling, a sister. Gerry had lived in London for nearly 13 years where he ran an employment agency. Saddest of all was an article from an Irish publication – it reported that Gerry had married a Waterford girl, Margaret Hallissey, the previous year. They'd had only a year of married life together before he was cruelly taken from her. Reading this personal detail about Gerry was odd. Being with him during his final moments had left me with the feeling I knew him well. But the reality was I barely knew him at all.

For some time after Fastnet I experienced what would now be labelled as post-traumatic stress. The most common symptom was waking up in the middle of the night seeing images of Gerry and David. I also began experiencing more seizures, some of which were severe. Ma would knock on my door in the early morning to wake me for work and sometimes find me writhing, half asleep, in the middle of a fit. Most of all, no matter how hard I resisted, I could not help myself from being drawn back, in my sleep and in my waking hours, to Gerry.

I never found those two yachts I owe such a debt to. During races after Fastnet '79 I kept an eye out for *Fragola*. But it is more than likely that the two boats were sold on, and have new names and new owners. Although I never located them, just trying to helped me get back into the swing of things. I wanted to know how the storm came about, why there was no warning, and how so many boats – such as *Grimalkin* – got caught up in the middle of it.

I did a great deal of reading on the subject. I learned that the 1979 Fastnet storm began its life on the other side of the Atlantic Ocean, in the USA. I was well aware of storms occurring in the western approaches but was surprised to read that storms of similar ferocity had occurred before: in 1917, 1923, 1931, 1957 and 1975 – all in the month of August. But the speed at which this force-10 storm swept across the Atlantic Ocean confounded forecasters.

Of the many articles I have read the best was by Robert B. Rice. It first appeared in American *Sail* magazine in October 1979, and it described in detail the start and the finish of this storm that had changed everything – for me and for so many others.

'TRACKING A KILLER STORM' by Robert B Rice
– October 1979

Severe storms can be found raging over the earth's surface nearly every day. Usually their development, movement and strength can be predicted in advance, allowing people to take the steps necessary to protect life and property. From time to time, though, a severe storm develops quickly and attains a place in history. Such a storm developed late Monday, August 13th 1979 and continued into Tuesday, August 14th, exploding almost without warning in the middle of the Fastnet fleet.

The strongest winds caught the fleet strung out across the Irish Sea. As British meteorologist Alan Watts observed, 'There is no kind of shelter in that box of waters between southwest England and southern Ireland. The weather is worse than oceanic because of the interaction of Atlantic wave-making processes with the developing shallows of land masses.'

The story began across the Atlantic on Thursday, August 9th, as a weak disturbance moved eastwards across the United States into the Gulf of Maine on August 10th. Although the storm system was small and relatively weak at this point, it had already begun its history of death and destruction by spawning tornadoes and severe thunderstorms across the Ohio Valley on Thursday and over southern New England on Friday (killing two people in Massachusetts and socking the J24 worlds off Newport, Rhode Island, with winds of up to 35 knots).

As a preceding storm system became stationary southwest of Iceland, the weak storm raced eastwards across the Atlantic over the weekend, reaching a position near 48°N, 19°W by 1200 Greenwich Mean Time (GMT) Monday, August 13th, with a central pressure of about 1007 millibars (Fig 1). At this time, the system gave only subtle hints of what was to happen in the next 12 hours. The only tangible clues were the vast amounts of cold air in the associated upper-level low-pressure trough and the storm's climatologically dangerous surface position. Aloft, the air temperature was of the order of −25° to −30°, which is comparable to winter normals. It is this presence of cold air over warm, moist surface air that often feeds storm development.

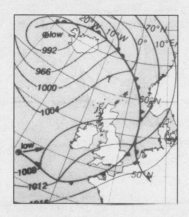

FIG 1
1200 GMT Monday
Storm centre 1007 millibars

Climatologically, all waves or minor storm systems approaching these waters around the edge of a depression in the Icelandic region must be viewed with suspicion. Even so there is nothing in the 1200 GMT reports to warrant a forecast for conditions as severe as those that were experienced. During the six hours from 1200 to 1800 GMT, the storm began to intensify and move rapidly east-northeast. By 1800, the central pressure had dropped to about 995 millibars and the storm centre was near 51°N.13°W (Fig 2). It was between 1500 and 1800 GMT Monday that questions about the storm's potential development were answered. The development rate of two millibars per hour, although not extreme, indicated that the rapid development just beginning would be likely to continue. At 1625 GMT the Meteorological Office issued a force-8 gale warning for Plymouth, Fastnet and the Irish Sea, which was broadcast on the 1650 BBC shipping forecast. Soon thereafter, at 1705 GMT, the warning was upgraded to 'southwest gale force 8 increasing severe gale force 9 imminent'. (The term 'imminent' in British forecasts means 'within six hours'.)

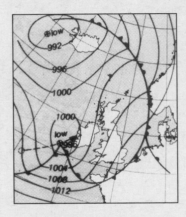

FIG 2
1800 GMT Monday
Storm centre 995 millibars

The weather map for 2100 GMT (Fig 3) shows the truly explosive development that was under way within the decelerating storm system. Valencia on the southwest Irish coast reported a pressure of 989 millibars and winds gusting to 48 knots. The rapidly developing pressure gradient suggests that gusts of 50 or 60 knots were already being felt over the water south of Ireland, eastward to 7°W. At 2145 GMT, as the wind really began to freshen on the course, the Meteorological Office issued a new warning: 'Southwest gale force 9 increasing to force 10 imminent.' Although the leaders (including the overall winner, Tenacious) had already rounded Fastnet Rock and had the wind abeam, most of the fleet was still spread out behind, struggling to beat into a rising wind and sea.

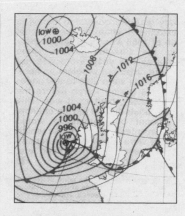

FIG 3
2100 GMT Monday
Storm centre 983 millibars

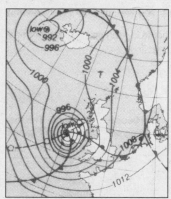

FIG 4
0000 GMT Monday
Storm centre 979 millibars

By midnight GMT (Fig 4) the storm centre was off Galway Bay with a central pressure near 980 millibars, which then held fairly steady for the next six hours. At 0250 GMT Tuesday, the Meteorological Office issued a further warning that the strongest winds were yet to come – force 9, locally gusting force 10 – veering westerly over the next six hours. Just over three hours later, at 0600 GMT, the storm centre had moved to a position near Londonderry, while its attendant cold front had whipped eastwards into the coastal sections of Scotland and England. As often happens, the front had accelerated out of the

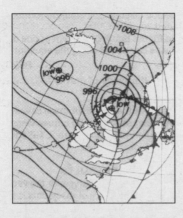

FIG 5
1200 GMT Tuesday
Storm centre 983 millibars

principal low-pressure trough, which extended across eastern Ireland and out to sea east of Fastnet. The rapidly rising pressures behind this trough created what Alan Watts calls 'the most potent feature of this tragedy'. As the principal trough sped east, Watts says it created 'a wickedly confused seaway as the force 9–10 winds ahead of it were suddenly replaced by an almost right-angled shift to the north-west. It is this feature, perhaps more than the wind strength that had so many craft in terrible trouble.' Reports of rogue seas of 50 feet and wind gusts to 80 knots can therefore be accepted as realistic, despite the relatively short duration and fetch of the wind.

By 1200 GMT Tuesday, the storm had moved on to the Moray Firth off northern Scotland, heading for the Shetland Islands (Fig 5). The squares to the north of the storm centre in Figure 5 represent the continued six-hour plots as the storm moved on toward the Norwegian Sea. This retreat from the scene allowed sea conditions to subside over the area, which permitted the widespread deployment of air/sea rescue units to aid the stricken yachts. Had the storm lingered on for several days, the toll would very likely have been even more staggering.

Since the storm of 1979, technology has moved on apace. Depressions are tracked now in 'real time' from on board yachts, via sophisticated weather prediction and forecasting computer programmes, gaining information from shore stations, weather satellites, via e-mail and weather buoys. But one thing we can be assured of is no matter how accurate weather predicting has or will become, mother nature can always overturn it in an instant.

In October 1979 I received a questionnaire, posted to me as part of the Fastnet Race Inquiry. I wrote my own experiences down – I felt, though, that some answers I gave might not be believed. Some questions were almost unanswerable, as the conditions we had experienced at the height of the storm defied belief. It was difficult to simply answer yes or no – or even to put a height or a figure to waves, wind strength, etc. Some questions, subjective questions, I felt could only be answered objectively. Later that month Bill Anderson, one of the inquiry officials, paid me a visit at the chandlery and put more questions to me. I felt better able to describe what had happened, as far as I knew, in this more personal, one-to-one way.

In late 1979 the official report was submitted to the RYA and the RORC by Sir Hugh Forbes, Sir Maurice Lang and Lieutenant Colonel James Myatt, and then subsequently published. It was welcomed by everyone. Much of the information it contained came from race competitors, who like me had answered a questionnaire. Much of the detailed report referred to the technical and safety elements that were lacking in the race. No boat or crewmember was specifically referred to.

The report was sent to me directly, and I had been

waiting for it. I went up to my bedroom to read the report alone, without Ma and Pa around. Sitting on my bed, I scrutinised the 76-page document, reading it cover to cover twice, then re-reading specifics. I read about the times of the broadcasted weather reports to try to determine if we could have avoided the storm. I read of the rescue of survivors, the abandonments, the accounts of what had happened on boats other than ours, about losses of life. Here it was – the official version, for all to read.

EXCERPTS FROM FASTNET RACE INQUIRY 1979
– Relevant to *Grimalkin*
WEATHER

From Page 14 – 2.16:

> The gale warning broadcast at 1830 and 1905 was the first to indicate that anything more than force 8 could be expected. It is unfortunate that the Meteorological Office issued the first two gale warnings just too late for inclusion in shipping forecasts. The force 10 warning broadcast at 2300 was the first to indicate the true nature of the winds which would be generated in area Fastnet by low Y.

This extract confirmed to me that forecasters had insufficient evidence to broadcast any earlier warning. David Sheahan could only protect and prepare *Grimalkin* by means of information available to him. It also confirmed to me that *Grimalkin* was just one of many yachts that inadvertently sailed into the eye of the storm.

Most of all, of course, I had been looking for the extract about David, Matt, Mike, Dave, Gerry, *Grimalkin* and me and what it had to say. When I found the relevant section, then the page, then the paragraph, I read it, alone, sitting on my bed. On close analysis I worked out which fatalities related to relevant boats. When I came to the following paragraphs I knew immediately that this was what I had been looking for, waiting for. I read it carefully, slowly. I wanted to fill in the gaps in my story. I found my finger tracing and retracing the account, line by line.

From page 44 under Fatalities in 4 G: (d)

> The exact sequence of events is difficult to ascertain. During the early hours of 14 August the yacht was heavily knocked down several times and then ran off under bare poles with warps streamed. The entire crew remained in the cockpit for most of the night but the skipper went below to make a distress call. While he was doing so he was struck on the head by an item of loose gear believed to have been a tin of food. He was concussed and thereafter lapsed into unconsciousness from time to time.
>
> The yacht rolled through 180° and remained upside down for a period of time estimated by various members of the crew to have been between two and five minutes. Two of the crew were thrown clear but remained attached by their harnesses. A third crewman extricated the skipper by cutting his safety harness, but after bringing him to the surface he lost his grasp on him and the skipper was washed out of reach. One of the three crewmen in the water climbed onto the upturned hull and the yacht then righted herself, dismasted.

The three conscious survivors were able to climb back on board. They found that two crewmembers who had been trapped in the cockpit throughout the capsize were lying motionless in the bottom of the cockpit and assumed they were dead. They launched the life raft and abandoned the yacht. They were unable to do anything about recovering the skipper and they were subsequently rescued by helicopter.

One of the unconscious casualties came to some time later, in the water alongside the hull. (It seems that the yacht may have capsized again while he was unconscious.) He was able to climb back on board and with the aid of a winch he pulled his semi-conscious companion into the boat. His companion was still alive and responded to resuscitation but died about three-quarters of an hour later. The one remaining survivor spent some 12 hours bailing the disabled yacht and keeping a lookout for rescue before being lifted off by helicopter.

Although Matt had given me his account of what had happened, it hadn't really sunk in until now. Everything that I pieced together on *Grimalkin* had indeed happened. As for our being left on the boat, much though I wanted to deny it, I could no longer do so – we had been abandoned. We had been left for dead – that was fact. But there was still something unaccounted for. If I had managed, on my own, injured, to pull Gerry back on board, to resuscitate him, then why couldn't they have done the same for me and Gerry when the boat was upright with us in it? There were three of them, and unlike me not one of them was injured.

The report was not easy reading, and while I felt it was

well put together and accurate, I found its impartial language deeply frustrating. Those who'd been there, who'd submitted the questionnaires, had seen it all for real, smelt it, heard it and felt it in every painful, terrifying detail, but this report did not tell the whole story of the storm or explain in detail the events that took place on *Grimalkin*. I didn't even know whether all three of my surviving crewmates had been interviewed when the report was being compiled. Looking back now I realise that each individual death, including Gerry's, should have had its own separate inquest. That way all the questions would have been answered.

As for safety precautions aboard *Grimalkin*, from my point of view there were no issues to account for. *Grimalkin* had qualified, by sailing the required mileage; she was equipped with more safety equipment than the rules required. She had three radios, two for two-way communication. (Some boats had none.) David Sheahan had provided the right tools for the job. He saw to that. We were simply not able to deal with the storm. The storm dealt with us.

Although the race fleet was spread out between Land's End and the Fastnet Rock, most of the helicopter activity was within a 40–45 mile radius around 70 miles north-west of Land's End. At 6am on 14 August, *Grimalkin*'s reported position was 30 miles north-west of Land's End, based upon the previous evening's fix; she was described at this time as being capsized. An hour and a quarter later her position was reported a further 35 miles north-west, by whom I am not sure, possibly another boat. So there was some confusion over her exact position, which led to me and Gerry being left undiscovered for so long.

There were some questions that remained unanswered,

but what could I do? Dwell on this for the rest of my days? Unlike my shipmate Gerry, I was alive, and I intended living my life to the full.

I have been asked many times how I managed to survive. I can link it to three things. The first and the most obvious is that at the age of 15, I survived a near-death experience: my brain haemorrhage. I had to relearn many basic skills, such as walking. I took things stage by stage. I set goals and targets for myself. I learned to think with a portion of my brain that would otherwise have been left dormant. I had been told by the surgeons that when parts of the brain are destroyed their function can be recovered by neighbouring areas. I didn't waste any time. I retrained the fingers, the toes, the muscles of my body's left side, laid waste by paralysis. It took months; it was painful, but, young and determined, I managed. My ultimate goal was to be able to sail again. What I had to work on, work hard on, was dexterity. It has been proved that someone who has had a near-death experience is more likely to survive a subsequent one, and I can see that this was true for me. I used similar methods to survive aboard *Grimalkin* as I had done during and since my illness.

My brain haemorrhage and subsequent surgery left scarring – the result of which was epilepsy. This is the second link. I took, take, daily medication. Fits, convulsions, once considered a stigma, once seen as a form of mental deficiency, disabled me. But with the love and support of my family I was forced to, and learned to, cope. Some weaknesses are in fact strengths. These strengths, learned at a young age, helped me to survive on *Grimalkin*.

Gerry was the third, the most important link, in this chain of survival. I wish that I could have said this to Margaret, to her face, when I had had the chance, 25 years ago. But at that time I was in such deep shock that I was unaware of exactly how big a part he had played. It is simply this: without that man, I would have perished. Even in death, he brought me life.

Nineteen

Revisiting *Grimalkin* – 26 years on

I began writing a book in September 2004 very soon after meeting Sinéad. I found it hard; it made sense in my head but not on paper. So I stopped – feeling that maybe I was not yet ready for it, wondering if I ever would be. A few months went by, and during this time Sinéad and I kept in touch as she researched for the documentary. She often mailed me with questions and sometimes with information that she had found while researching. Although the events that took place were never far from my thoughts, I had avoided thinking deeply about them. The process of being asked questions by Sinéad was invigorating, and it also forced me to face things I had blocked out for so many years. At times I felt myself becoming angry, even bitter – worryingly so. The bitterness was mainly brought on by the action my three crewmates took in the early morning of Tuesday, 14 August 1979.

During Christmas 2004, my son Sam celebrated his birthday. He did the obligatory birthday-cake thing with all the family. And after politely listening to me, his mother

Chris and his younger sister Elizabeth sing 'Happy Birthday', he wolfed down some cake and was gone. Fair enough – he had just turned 17 and wanted to be out with his mates.

It was then the realisation hit me. I pictured Matthew as the carefree young man I'd known at the age of 17, the age my son was turning now. Back in 1979, to me, Matthew had been a man – self-assured and capable of decision. But he wasn't. He had been a teenager like my own son, still maturing and understanding. He has had to live with so much, including the knowledge that he would never spend another Christmas, another birthday, with his father.

As the weeks went by I also began to think more about Mike and Dave. Despite my bitterness and anger towards them, I was beginning to see their situation in a different light. They had been so young too, Dave not much older than Sam. All six of us were in an impossible position. Survival in a force-10 storm is determined by each second that passes. Rash decisions are made when your life is in danger. They were quite simply terrified – I can see that clearly now. My crewmates had gone through a hell of their own; of this I was now convinced. And apart from the horror of the storm, one of them has had to live with the consequences of cutting David's line. That day was no picnic for any one of us. They were blameless, and I bear them no ill-will.

I set about writing the book again, but I still felt blocked. The following year something happened that changed this. In July 2005, I had a phone call from a man called Keith Grainger, one of the present owners of *Grimalkin*. Keith said he would be honoured if I came to visit the boat. Before I

knew it, we had arranged a suitable date to visit. My wife
Chris took time off work and Sinéad flew over from Dublin.

On the morning of 25 July, Chris and I picked Sinéad
up from Southampton airport and we drove west to
Weymouth, where *Grimalkin* was moored. We parked a
distance from the marina and walked along the quayside in
the sunshine. I felt slightly detached. As we got closer, I began
asking myself if I was doing the right thing. Was this not a
bit bizarre, even macabre?

We reached the locked marina gates. I couldn't see
Grimalkin immediately. I had been told she was moored bows
on in one of the first berths, port-side to – but I couldn't see
her. Then, there she was! Keith Grainger waved a hand and
let us through the marina gate and onto the pontoons. I could
not go aboard straight away. Instead I paced up and down
the pontoon alongside her, noting her neatly moored position. I smoothed her topsides with the palm of my hand,
rather like grooming a well-remembered thoroughbred mare,
getting to know her again. Sinéad had a video camera in her
hand and was following my progress up and down the
pontoon; she asked me if I was OK. Apart from slightly moist
eyes, I was fine. This was the renewal of an old friendship.

Keith greeted us with gusto. It had been a while since I
had been welcomed aboard a boat in such a generous manner
and with such a firm handshake. Then he left us, to 'pop up
to the shop' for a bottle of wine. It was a gracious excuse,
leaving the three of us alone with *Grimalkin* – and me with
my thoughts.

I noticed that apart from a few minor details, such as
her new shaped windows, she was much as I remembered.
Her hull was still white and her decks still light blue. I leant

over her gorgeously shaped stern and noticed that although her name was there still, it had been painted over. '*Grimalkin*' was only just visible under the newly applied dark-blue paint of her transom.

Taking all of this in, I moved into the cockpit: there were the same four winch-handle pockets but a lot cleaner. I lifted the cover to the cockpit well. The well was empty. There was no life raft. My heart missed a beat – and it all came flooding back: the noises, the braced knees, the effort to stay in one place long enough to breathe. All the moored yachts around me disappeared and I was back in the western approaches, back in the Irish Sea. I felt nausea, experienced a strange smell, almost an aura. Seeing how I was affected, Chris sat me down.

I quickly came to my senses. Sinéad sat alongside me, and I began to explain where everyone had been sitting in the cockpit, how high the waves had been. Things that had been difficult to convey before were easier to describe with us both on *Grimalkin*. And then I felt ready to go below. I climbed down the new, stronger, stainless-steel companion-way ladder. *Grimalkin* smelt the way she was meant to, that special odour of seasoned wood, fibreglass, salt and stowed sails combined, the unique smell of a yacht that has some stories to tell. Her bunks had been replaced with substantial, more comfortable ones. Her navigation table was to port, not to starboard as it had been. The thoroughbred, lightweight racer/cruiser I had known and loved over 25 years ago was still a serious vessel. *Grimalkin* still stood out, turned heads, held her own in any company.

We spent an hour or so with Keith, joined by his lovely wife and daughter, drinking white wine in the late afternoon sunshine, in the cockpit of this boat I knew so well, which had saved my life. Keith told us that hardly a day passed when people didn't ask him about *Grimalkin* and what had happened to her in 1979. Some people asked about the crew and what became of them. I recounted some of what had happened on the race, some of what the storm had been like – and I told Keith about what I had experienced after lifting the cockpit cover. He apologised profusely, explaining that the life raft was being repaired.

But there was no need for him to apologise. This moment had been fated. It made me want to go back, retrace my steps – relive the hours I spent with Gerry on *Grimalkin*. Walking back to the car I recalled the flashback I had experienced and the thoughts it had provoked. Sinéad suggested I write down what I had seen exactly as I had described it to her on the boat. Two days after Sinéad's return home, I sent her what I had written. She saw immediately that my motivation came from a different, more basic, emotional place. Not exaggerated thoughts, but thoughts that had been harboured, neglected for years.

There and then we decided to collaborate in turning my story into a book. I put my journal on the back burner and Sinéad did the same with her documentary and emails were soon flying between Hamble and Dublin.

Recently, and with the manuscript almost complete, I met up with some of my old sailing colleagues, good friends from the past. Through them I learnt more of the hearsay around the events that took place during the race. One piece of information was new to me, and shocked me. Apparently the crewmember who cut David's safety line had to cut his own first. It was the only way he could get to David. I have no reason to believe this is not true. I saw only one clearly cut line, but with the state the boat was in – and the state I was in – it is possible that another line showed evidence of having been cut too and I didn't notice it. To cut his own safety line was an act of great bravery. This crewmember had endangered his life in an attempt to save someone else's. It brought home to me all the more that the four of us – Matthew, Mike, Dave and myself – had experienced horrors that we have had to come to terms with. We all went through our own hell during and after this race – I see that now.

I have never heard a version of what had happened from either Mike or Dave directly. It was never offered and I never asked. But what I do know is this. I have finally achieved what I had thought impossible for a quarter of a century – acceptance.

7 August 2005

I realised that I wanted to do something I had not done since 1979 – experience a Fastnet start. My 1979 experience had never destroyed my love and respect for the sea and all things about it and I felt I was ready for this – more than ready. A good friend of mine, Simon, offered to take me out in his ex-Coastguard launch; Sinéad and Chris came along too. It was a bright day, warm and sunny, blowing around a force 3 or 4 – conditions not unlike the start 26 years before. Sailing into Cowes Roads and being there in the throng was amazing, and so very familiar: the chop, the atmosphere, the press boats, the spray on the face and the fresh sea breeze. It felt superb – little had changed since 1979. This was as I remembered it – Fastnet electric, truly uplifting – a race of such importance that it is now an integral part of any yachtsman's life. The race is tradition. Thank God it was not stopped.

Men and women would forever be pitting themselves against the elements, attempting to win races and set new records, alone or with crews. But one thing is for sure: however hard they try, however experienced they are, however many weather forecasts they hear, the thing that cannot be changed is Mother Nature. As Ted Turner, the winner of Fastnet 1979, said of the disaster: 'Every time you go in an airplane you risk your life. Every time you get into a car you risk your life. Who'd have thought the *Titanic* would go down? If you stay ashore you die – eventually. Storms like that happen.' He was right. I would much rather have been taking part than watching.

Standing in the cockpit observing it all was not so different from when I stood, at seven years old, alongside Pa aboard *Snapdragon*. I swear I smelt the tobacco of a Senior Service cigarette waft by as a voice in my head said, 'One hand for yourself, one for the boat, Nicholas.'

Later that day as we motored home I thought that maybe one day I would sail west out of the Solent again. Who knows? Never say never.

Epilogue 1

The Pact?

It was 20 March 2007. For two years my mind had been filled with memories of towering seas, fear, companionship and death. But now the end was in sight. That morning the proofs of *Left for Dead* had arrived in the post. I cannot deny the sense of pride and achievement I felt upon holding them. Reliving the horror of that terrible time had somehow been worth it.

Jointly Sinéad and I completed the lengthy process of proofreading before approving the book cover and selecting photographs. I understood there was much at stake for our publishers, but I have to admit to being taken aback when asked to sign a confidentiality agreement. A subsequent discussion, and things became clear – worryingly so. Earlier in the year, unknown to me, Matthew Sheahan had contacted the offices of A&C Black, asking to see a copy of the book before it was published and saying he had concerns over the content. The publishers assured Matthew that the book was in no way libellous to him or his father, and neither did it inaccurately recount events that had taken place on *Grimalkin* during Fastnet 1979. Thus, they declined his request; I have been told he expressed a level of unhappiness over this. Consequent provisions were put in place in order to protect the story from untimely exposure. The book was strictly embargoed until a week before publication, and confidentiality agreements were signed not only by the authors but by all who had or were about to read it. Furthermore, correspondence had to be channelled through the publicists.

The sheer elation, the unrivalled sense of achievement I had experienced on finally finishing the book was short-lived – the news of Matthew's discontent unnerved me greatly. My morale plummeted, bringing with it doubts and uncertainty. I began to realise that the world Sinéad and I had immersed ourselves in while writing the book had cocooned me from the reality of what lay ahead – exposure, in its rawest form. That far from being the end, this was merely the beginning. I began to wonder, usually on waking, if I had been naive when I undertook to make public what previously had been known only to me. All around it felt as if a storm, altogether different in nature, was gathering. The momentum that the book and its publicity were gaining daunted me – it was inexperience on my part, but the feelings I had were wholly unanticipated. My innermost worry was: would all this exposure be more than I could cope with? After all, the only person who could corroborate my story was dead.

Before publication, my wife, Chris, arranged for us to spend a week on Sark, the smallest and most beautiful of the Channel Isles. Never had I been so relieved to slip away. I had sailed past many times but never once landed. The island, its stillness, its lack of tarmac roads and cars, the cream teas and the pure civility of its 600 or so inhabitants gave me the chance to reflect. With no television, no mobile, no email, I felt somewhat detached, and, best of all, Chris finally had the chance to read the manuscript in full. Line-by-line she read of things I'd never before been able to tell her. My wife, my friend, my closest confidante was shocked at the graphic detail, at what we had all endured. Reading the manuscript cover to cover in a matter of hours she sometimes just reached out to squeeze my hand, stoically silent. Finally, when she finished, she cried – and didn't stop for some time. Then she told me that what had moved her most was the part about Gerry's passing. Words cannot describe the comfort I felt upon hearing my wife, a nurse with 25 years' experience, tell me that she doubted if Gerry had suffered at the end.

This really was the first time I'd been able to talk to Chris about it all, yet her words, her absolute endorsement of the book, did little to give me the composure I longed for. I guess that deep down I knew my wife would be the kindest of critics. Instead, in the calm sanctuary of Sark, my fears escalated. The silence, the stillness were having a contrary effect – they became suffocating. I began to picture, with quite a level of paranoia, that there would be others out there much less understanding, less willing to believe me. But how could I explain this? How could I expect sympathy, for I had agreed to all of this – too much time and money had been invested by other parties for me to pull out now. I suspected I might well be the author of my own meltdown. Maddeningly, my sleep was broken by sweat-drenched bouts of panic, but, most worryingly, I was now beginning to silently question my own story. I closed off from Chris, and Sinéad. I knew that I had to get a grip, somehow restore belief in myself, but this was proving to be the greatest obstacle I had faced since being abandoned with Gerry on *Grimalkin* all those years ago.

My return to Hamble worsened this underlying sense of dread. I ignored my full email in-box for a day, then two days, fearing there could only be more news I wouldn't want to hear. When I finally looked, I had a wonderful surprise. Within those mails was a message forwarded by my publisher from a man by the name of Christian Schaumloffel. This man, based in Virginia Beach, USA, claimed to have been on one of the yachts that made the distress call that resulted in my rescue. Not *Fragola*, but a yacht by the name of *Tai Fat*. Attached to his mail were photographs he thought I would be interested to see. I opened one, and just as when Sinéad had first showed me the streamed video a couple of years before, hairs on the back of my neck stood up. It was of *Grimalkin* wallowing alone in the high seas, so low in the water that it was implausible, almost miraculous that she had not sunk. Apprehensively, I opened the next image. The sight of it sent a chill down my spine. It was of poor Gerry – I recognised his orange oilskins immediately. He was in mid-air, being lifted up into the belly of a green Royal Navy Sea King helicopter. I felt suddenly queasy. Strangely, I was overcome by an unpleasant odour, all too familiar … it was the dank, rancid stench that drifted up from the cabin. These colour images were so vivid, so real, I was compelled to speak to whoever took them immediately.

Bearing in mind the confidentiality agreement I had signed, I was bound to confirm the credentials of this person before I contacted him. I 'googled' the name *Tai Fat* and an image popped up that was instantly recognisable – it was the larger, red-hulled yacht that had circled *Grimalkin* at a distance before my rescue. I checked my Fastnet competitor index and saw she was a class-three yacht, ten feet longer than *Grimalkin*, which had retired from the race. A subsequent search provided confirmation that Christian was a navigator and one of the helmsmen aboard. I had never really doubted it myself, but I could now show others that this guy was for real. Amazing! There was a number in the email, and without further thought I lifted the phone, dialled and introduced myself.

The man on the other end of the phone sounded charming and self-possessed. First off he told me how he found out *Left for Dead* was being published when researching for a presentation on his Fastnet experience. While dialling the number my head had been spinning with questions, but now I felt tongue-tied. I became emotional, then embarrassed; unable to explain that this was a momentous event for me. Christian proved to be a most lovely man – both calm and compassionate in voice. Clearly aware of my lack of composure, he suggested that he just tell me what he remembered. I knew now that I was talking to a man who fully understood and empathised. After all, he had been there – he had encountered and survived the very same storm as me.

He described his own experience leading up to their discovery of *Grimalkin*. Overwhelmed by the sheer violence of the storm, Christian decided to turn his yacht downwind, as *Grimalkin* had, to save the nine-man crew and the boat. It was early in the morning but before light – probably 5am. Six of the crew, including Christian, were down bailing the waterlogged cabin. He described how the high humidity in the closed cabin coupled with the violently rocking boat had emptied several of the crew's stomachs – I understood that only too well. With sea heights escalating at a fierce rate all they could do was ride out the storm, but some time later three crewmen above deck lost control of *Tai Fat* and she pitch-poled over a forty-foot wave. I remembered the complete terror, the noise and confusion of pitch-poling in *Grimalkin* in complete darkness. It was late morning when this occurred, 11am he reckoned. By then I had been alone for at least four hours, Gerry was dead and the storm was evidently still peaking. He described how by mid-afternoon the weather had become gradually less aggressive, just as I'd experienced – then by late afternoon the skies had begun to clear and the swells, while still at about 20–25 feet, were more the big rolling type – less steep, less dangerous.

Later that day *Tai Fat*, having retired from the race, was sailing back towards Plymouth. Visibility was almost perfect when about a mile ahead of them one flare then another shot into the evening sky. Immediately they changed course in that direction, assuming that whoever had just fired the flares needed help – and fast. About half a mile ahead they spotted a mast and altered course towards it. Christian himself went below and relayed the mayday rescue call. This proved extremely difficult for they, like everyone else, were unable to give an exact position – nothing more accurate than plus or minus a ten-mile radius. Knowing that this could be a significant moment, Christian grabbed his camera. When he returned to the deck the rest of the crew were engaged in heavy discussion: they had glimpsed something else between the waves. It took maybe another ten to fifteen wave cycles before it became visible again and suddenly they realised that the yacht which had sent up the flares had done so not for herself but for a dismasted, far smaller yacht nearby – *Grimalkin* – which was clearly in serious trouble. They saw one man – me – sitting at the stern of the boat, and presumed the rest of the crew were either lower in the cockpit or down in the cabin. Thoughts of a boat-to-boat transfer were discussed but quickly abandoned as collision in these conditions was inevitable and could have caused *Grimalkin* to sink within seconds. Wasting no time, they made a further mayday call for rescue.

From that point on *Tai Fat* stayed back, well clear of *Grimalkin*, as her 55-foot mast would have been hazardous to oncoming rescue, but although visibility was excellent, keeping watch over *Grimalkin* was not an easy task, for she was almost permanently hidden beneath or behind the swell. This information in particular was overwhelming. It was at this point that all hope of rescue had faded for me – I imagined both yachts, *Tai Fat* and *Fragola*, had gone. Now I knew that *Tai Fat* had been watching over me. I cast my mind back to the imagined sinking, to me and Gerry being lost, the utter bloody madness.

Christian did not know the exact time of rescue, only that it was very late in the day. He remembered this clearly, as the sight of a fast-approaching naval aircraft set against the backdrop of clear skies and a luminous orange sunset was bizarre, almost surreal, after all they had been through in the previous 24 hours.

As the aircraft hovered over *Grimalkin* it became evident to Christian almost at once that placing a man on board was going to be difficult. In normal circumstances keeping a footing is tricky, but a yacht without the stabilising pendulum effect of its mast is completely unpredictable in its movements.

The Sea King approached several times but failed. There was a unanimous sigh of relief among the crew when the airman was finally placed successfully on *Grimalkin* and, despite losing his footing several times, he managed to stay on board. Some time passed when they could not see what was happening. Then Christian described how they saw one man being winched from the yacht – it was Gerry, just as I had seen in his photograph. My memory had failed me; in my delirium I'd thought Gerry had been taken up by Peter, who had then returned for me. In fact, Gerry's poor lifeless body had been winched up alone.

The next piece of information sent a chill through me. While watching the lift, although Christian had noticed Gerry was limp, it never for a moment occurred to him or anyone else on *Tai Fat* that he was dead. As far as they were concerned, if somebody was still on board he or she must still be alive – injured possibly, but alive. Listening to him reason this, I had to agree, for I would have concluded the same myself. After a second man (me) was airlifted and vanished inside the hovering aircraft with the winchman, they all waited for the wire to be dropped again, but to their utter amazement the Sea King turned away from the rescue scene and disappeared off into the horizon. At once a strange eeriness descended on *Tai Fat* and her crew. Without a word being spoken, they all knew that something must be dreadfully wrong. It was obvious that two people had been picked up – Gerry and me – but more obvious and shocking was that there should have been at least five or six people on board a yacht of this size. Where were the others?

As they journeyed on to Plymouth, endless theories were discussed by the *Tai Fat* crew as to the fate of *Grimalkin*'s missing crew – though Christian admitted that none of them came anywhere near guessing what had really occurred; they only found out well after the event. Despite the emotions this conversation conjured up, and the upset it caused me, it was enormously comforting to speak to someone who had been there on that same tragic, almost unreal August evening in 1979. It was at this point I wished I could have opened up to Christian, to tell him, man to man, what had happened to me and Gerry. I didn't, why I don't know, but as I listened, I thought, Christ, there were nearly 2,500 sailors other than Mike, Matthew and Dave on this race – why did I wait till now to talk to one of them?

While the bigger issues of abandonment could not be addressed or explained, the effect of this chat was immediate relief – for apart from the recovery of Gerry's body, every-thing Christian had said was how I remembered it. Christian's revelations, and his photographs, were too late for inclusion in the hardback version of the book, but his verification of events during our opportune, reassuring conversation, gave me reason to believe in myself again. This was the true nature of seamanship: everything he had said was exactly how helping offshore sailors in distress works. What Christian and his crew, and for that matter *Fragola*, had done, was come to the aid of a stricken vessel – an unwritten law of the sea. I was so happy that Christian and I had spoken, that I was at long last able to thank him, to thank someone personally.

Just two days after this, another incredible thing happened. Peter Harrison – the man who all those years ago had come down the wire to save me from the madness of the Irish Sea – also made contact via my publisher. Again, as I'd done with Christian, thinking it almost too good to be true,

I telephoned him, and another remarkably detailed conversation ensued. Peter, being a naval officer, was pragmatic in tone. As he saw it, he had simply been doing his job. In fact, one of the first things he told me was that as the winchman he was known in naval terms as 'the dope on the rope'. Amazingly, of the five crewmen aboard the Sea King, Peter's undertaking was considered the most rudimentary.

He remembered taking off from Culdrose and going due west. It was late in the day and conditions had eased considerably. At this stage the crew were really just locating and reporting back names of the many abandoned yachts that littered the Irish Sea; a rescue mission was not expected. It was some time around 8pm that they received a request from a Nimrod to check out a position at closer range. Having noticed a tiny speck on the radar, the Nimrod had descended from 9,000 to 500 feet and seen what appeared to be a small dismasted yacht, but from that height was unable to identify anything else. Peter and his crew set off to investigate the position given, assuming it would be a straightforward boat name-check to report back to headquarters. What amazed me about this was that I had not seen or even heard Nimrod engines so close above me, as I had earlier in the day when the noise and mayhem of the storm had been at its peak. By this time I must have slipped into a semi-conscious state.

As the Sea King approached with about half a mile to run they noticed one man (me) slouched at the stern of the small yacht and knew at once this was a rescue mission. Peter described how he sat on the helicopter floor looking down directly at the barely afloat, devastated yacht with the name *Grimalkin*. It was only after he had landed and balanced himself that he saw what he described as a crumpled heap in the footwell of the yacht and realised that there was someone else on board. Poor Gerry. Peter knew at once there was no need for mouth-to-mouth. With one glance it was obvious to him Gerry was dead.

While Gerry was airlifted alone up and into the Sea King, Peter stayed with me. He said that with the level of exposure I had experienced, everything had shut down and that my state was as close to catatonic as he had ever witnessed in a casualty. I was obsessed with finding my passport, he told me, refusing to leave without it. I had remembered being anxious about getting my gear, though not of being so stubbornly irrational and needing to be talked out of it. Eventually, up in the Sea King, his job was done and another crewman took over minding me. Peter went back to his radar for the return trip to Culdrose, but just as the crew of *Tai Fat* had, he could not help speculating about where the rest of the crew from *Grimalkin*, which was clearly not a two-man boat, were.

In the weeks prior to and since publication I have met many wonderful people who have helped me fill in the gaps. One of those was an ex-naval officer by the name of Charlie Thornton – he had been the pilot of the helicopter that had rescued Matthew, Dave and Mike from the life raft early on the morning of 14 August. He was put in touch with me, bizarrely enough, by his near neighbour Keith Grainger, the present owner of *Grimalkin*. The world I now inhabited was proving to be very small. The first question I had for him was: what did they say? Did they report myself and Gerry as dead or possibly alive?

Charlie could not answer that. He had not had a direct conversation with them, but he did clarify other things for me in the same pragmatic way that Peter had done. He knew that whatever the others reported of *Grimalkin* would have been passed on to another team anyway as they had already been out for three hours and needed to refuel. He also confirmed that any plot or position given by the others at this time would have been of no use. Given the horrific conditions, position plotting had been all but abandoned – it was quite simply impossible to tell any area apart in that sort of weather. In fact, at the beginning of the day they could see nothing on the radar; the only thing it was useful for was finding their way back to Cornwall.

Although it was not funny at the time, he did in a rather humorous way tell me that most of the yachts had no idea where they were and reported some very odd plots – some of them thought they had been blown as far as the French coast when they had not gone any distance at all. He did tell me that my three crewmates had been picked up earlier than I had first thought, however – he knew this because once back at base he went straight from the aircraft and did a slot on the *Today* show, which finishes at 9am. Although I said nothing to Charlie about it, this information saddened me greatly – I could have done without hearing it at all. It meant the others had been rescued at least an hour before Gerry had died. It was fruitless to dwell on this, selfish even, but I could not help it. In the chaos of the final capsize of *Grimalkin*, it seems it had not taken my three crewmates very long to decide to leave Gerry and me.

Another fact I had been unaware of was that for most of the day, until well after the storm had begun to level out, it was those in life rafts or in the water who were given first attention. Of course this made absolute sense, and it was now easier for me to see that being on *Grimalkin*, a yacht still afloat that had not made an SOS call, had inadvertently pushed me down the priority list. The Nimrods and spotter plane had most likely spotted *Grimalkin* earlier in the day but their priorities lay with those likely to be in greater danger.

Although the question of what Matthew, Dave and Mike had said upon being rescued remained unanswered, talking to Charlie had been great. He clarified so much for me. Even in the calmest of conditions search and rescue is fraught with confusion, so during a catastrophe on the scale of the Fastnet Race that year, everything had been out of control. Charlie told me that any rescue is akin to three-dimensional chess. You are trying to drop something on to a moving target: sometimes it works – sometimes it doesn't. Ironically, the first lift he did the crewman landed straight into the life raft next to the survivor. And such were the horrific conditions during those early hours of 14 August, the survivor hadn't even realised there was a helicopter overhead.

The book was published at the beginning of June 2007 and I spent the summer promoting it by means of press and media interviews, which at first was strange to me; as someone who had been working on or around boats all his life, I was not in the least media savvy. But I learned, and learned quickly, to do just as Pa had taught me years ago, to shake hands firmly, look people in the eye and be dead straight. And while these next few months were enjoyable in many ways, it was relentless. So by October it was a relief to have some home time, some quiet family time. Chris and I rarely go out, but this long overdue break was a good reason to go for some celebratory drinks. We ventured down to the Bugle Inn on Hamble High

Street. During the evening I got chatting to Mike Swain, an old friend from the marine trade, a skilled yacht painter. During the course of our conversation I mentioned that *Left for Dead* had been published. He told me he knew, and then he gestured to a man of around my age sitting at the bar. I glanced over but did not recognise him.

'It's Mike Doyle,' my friend told me. I took another look and there was no denying it – Mike Doyle, sitting not more than 20 feet from me. This was such a surprise that I had no idea how to react, so I just carried on chatting about everything and nothing, all the while wondering – does Mike know I am here, in the same bar as him? It did occur to me that if this man had not been pointed out to me, I would not have recognised him. After all, I hadn't laid eyes on him in nearly 30 years. Therefore, it was feasible he had no idea who I was either.

By now I wanted to go over and talk to Mike, but Chris in her wisdom and calm advised against it, particularly as the busy bar was full of locals, many of them friends or acquaintances of ours, and maybe Mike's too. Chris decided, and I agreed, that she approach him as an intermediary to get a sense of whether this was a good time to talk. She went, and arrived back far more quickly than I expected. She told me that she had spoken with Mike but that because he was with friends now was not the time to talk. I was a little disappointed, but relieved there was no confrontation, no obvious animosity. Shortly after that we finished up and returned home. It was only then that Chris related what had really happened:

She had introduced herself to Mike and asked if she could shake his hand. They shook hands, and Mike said, 'Do you know who I am?'

Chris nodded. 'Yes, that's why I wanted to shake your hand.'

Mike then told her that he did not agree with the book being written, that he felt it was not an accurate account. The lady beside him said that Dave Wheeler felt the same way. It was at this point that the situation became, for want of a better word, uncomfortable. I wondered what part of the book Mike was referring to when he claimed it was inaccurate. The fact of their having left the boat with me and Gerry on it was a matter of official record. Mike also told her that he had visited me at my home after the race. I have to accept his word on this but I genuinely do not recall it. Pa was extremely protective and may have deterred him from seeing me, or like so many things concerning the race, I may have blocked it out.

But it was the next thing Mike told Chris that I found staggering. He said that we, and I presume when he said 'we' he meant all four of us, had agreed never to speak about the events that had occurred aboard *Grimalkin* or make money from it. I was quite simply astounded. This sounded to me like a pact, something agreed on during a meeting after the event. No such meeting took place, and more importantly no pact was made. Certainly not one that included me – I was flabbergasted. Before things became too tricky Chris said it was clear everyone was 'a bit worse for wear' but that she would be happy to give Mike her mobile number so maybe he and I could get together and talk at a later date. He ignored her offer.

My initial reaction was shock and upset, but I have since had the time to think about what occurred with, I hope, a greater level of understanding. If, like us, Mike was out for a quiet drink, in a busy Hamble pub on a Friday night, I can surmise now that being confronted by a virtual stranger about something that happened nearly three decades ago would have been hugely uncomfortable for him. The very last thing I had expected that evening was an encounter with this man, once a friend – so he too would have been taken by surprise. Perhaps if we had met in a less noisy, less public place then perhaps we could have spoken rationally. I'd have been able to listen to his point of view and then had the opportunity to explain things from mine.

Something on which Sinéad and I had placed great importance was letting those closely concerned with the book's content – in particular Margaret and Gay – know that *Left for Dead* was being published. I wrote personal letters, sending them via my publishers. I sent letters to Matthew, Mike and Dave, too. I tried to place myself in their position. What would I do, how would I feel, if I felt myself misrepresented in an account of something that happened almost 30 years ago? The last thing I wanted to do was hurt anyone's feelings. If anything, my intention was to make clear that there was no bitterness on my part towards my crewmates. In those letters I stressed that the book was written entirely from my own point of view, my perspective. Matthew's approach to my publishers before publication was understandable. However, he had no qualms in posting online his own memories of those three days. He did not consult me or, as far as I know, Mike or Dave before doing this. About a month ago, I contacted Matthew Sheahan again to see if he felt the same as Mike and Dave – that my account was inaccurate. As yet, there has been no response. I do not know whether this silence means acceptance or total disagreement.

The book is my account of events. I stand by what I have written, absolutely. Sinéad and I have sought out and talked to the service personnel and officials who had a direct involvement in my rescue and the recovery of Gerry, as well as those involved in the rescue of Matthew, Mike and Dave from *Grimalkin*'s six-man life raft. This research, fact-checking and interviewing was essential for a book of this nature. I do, however, understand an opinion offered me by a friend, that by recounting in such detail what happened on those three days in August 1979, I may have put my three crewmates in a untenable position, a position where it was impossible for any of them to respond without leaving themselves open to criticism.

Reaction to the book has been astonishing. I have received many personal letters of support and feedback from strangers, both yachtsmen and landsmen, all bearing essentially the same message: 'Well done, it needed to be written.'

I have received approval from family and friends, all of whom had little or no idea of what I'd endured and survived. Reviewers have been extremely generous, and even more amazing was that *Left for Dead* was short-listed for the William Hill Sports Book of the Year 2007, and then named the *Sunday Times* Sports Book of the Year, as well as receiving other unexpected plaudits from the media, both at home and abroad. I never expected such a reaction. Now, at last, I know that I did the right thing in telling my story.

Publication of *Left for Dead* has changed my life. It has given me the freedom to talk about what happened on 14 August 1979, and the three days before, in a way I never dreamt possible. No longer do I wake in a cold sweat or blind panic. None of this would have been possible without Sinéad.

I have so much to thank her for since that day she first phoned me in September 2004, but it is her creative input on the writing of *Left for Dead* that must take priority. Her innate style of phrasing and tremendous use of language have given the narrative a level of drama that would never have been achieved otherwise. And one thing that has surprised me, apart from faith in God and in myself, is that during the writing and research of the book and in particular this epilogue there have been moments when, all of a sudden, things fell into place. Chance encounters or events all seemed to mesh, to link to one another – leading me to believe in a synchronicity of sorts.

One last thing. Perhaps I was naive to have hoped for a response from my crewmates, but I did hope for one. If their recollections conflict with my own, then I wanted to know. I am sorry not to have heard from them. If their feelings have been hurt by the book's content, then I guess I am sorry about that too – but it happened, all of it. I take consolation in the thought that I've been Gerry's advocate, that my story has been a memorial to him. Anyway, I have come too far to turn back now. Just like *Grimalkin*, I will weather any storm. It doesn't matter what other people think. As far as I am concerned, we're all survivors and we've coped with survival in our own ways.

Nick Ward, 2008

Epilogue 2

Never Say Never

I threw my packed rucksack into the boot, closed it over and joined Chris in the car – then, pulling out of the quiet cul-de-sac where we had lived for 17 years, I thought of Pa. Our detached house is one of many in a large estate built on what was once Hamble's North Airfield, where my father had been Chief Engineering Instructor for many years. Funnily enough, our property was built nigh on where the airfield's control tower once sat and where Pa had worked. This is perhaps the reason I have such an affinity with our home and would never choose to live elsewhere. The late afternoon sunshine reflected off the windows of houses and as usual in good weather there were youngsters playing in and around the mature trees and shrubs that had been no more than saplings when my two children were that age. As we pulled out of our estate we passed the School Lane turning that led to Hamble Point Marina and I could feel a familiar rush of adrenalin sweep through me – the very same I had experienced leaving my childhood home on 11 August 1979, waved off by my mother and driven by my father to the same marina, where *Grimalkin* waited for her crew. Suddenly a small smile spread across my face: today was the day. I was finally off to realise my dream, to complete some unfinished business.

2009 was a year of many celebrations, anniversaries and commemorations. Forty years since man landed on the Moon, forty years since Robin Knox-Johnston became the first man to sail non-stop around the world. But most poignant for me, it was thirty years since the Fastnet disaster, which I had so narrowly survived. Never say never – that's what I wrote at the end of the first edition of this book, hoping that one day I might sail west out of the Solent on a Fastnet Race. But to be truly honest, I never saw this as a real prospect. Then, quite unexpectedly, in September 2008 I was asked to compete and race in Fastnet 2009 aboard *Ariel*, a 60-foot-long clipper yacht with her skipper, two mates and seven other crew: eleven in total. Despite reservations about my health, my age and general lack of recent offshore sailing experience, I felt compelled to close the loop, to finish this legendary race. And so once more I found myself drawn to that start line, nine miles from my home, on the west bank of the Medina River, Cowes, Isle of Wight.

As Chris turned onto the M27 motorway headed towards Gosport where *Ariel* was berthed, we finally picked up some speed. Neither of us spoke for this part of the journey – I think Chris must have sensed I needed this time to centre myself. In my mind I began to repack my rucksack exactly as I had done the night before. Over the years I had got used to packing for sailing: absolute essentials only, including my medication, and nothing coloured green, but this time I had included two extra things. I brought a candle to light at some point in remembrance of Gerry, David and all who perished in '79's race, and I brought the brown leather wallet I'd recovered from *Grimalkin* when, with Matthew, we found her in Ireland. This old watermarked wallet, one of the very few belongings that made it with me back to Hamble, was to be my lucky charm.

As we reached Gosport the rising adrenalin was now accompanied by the anticipation that comes just ahead of any offshore race. Driving towards the docks we passed by what was once Camper and Nicholsons boatyard – the place where *Grimalkin* had been built. Seeing this now abandoned yard brought more feelings to the surface – this was the place it had all begun, the very yard that had produced the boat without which I would not have survived. I now knew just how crucial to my psyche it was for me to get round the rock that lay 11 kilometres south of the mainland of Ireland in the Atlantic Ocean.

After showing Chris my bunk and all that *Ariel* had to offer, I carefully handed her back down onto the pontoon. We hugged and I watched as she walked back up the ramp to the security gate, turning back just once to wave. And so it was that Chris and I said our farewells. Now I knew how it felt – a happy marriage and two grown-up children puts a different perspective on going offshore, out of sight of land. I had not expected to feel so unsettled, and it took me a good hour to calm down after she had left. Later that evening our skipper and the rest of the crew went off to the pub, leaving me alone on the boat. I took this time to sit out on deck and observe my surroundings. The sun shone brightly as it began its early evening descent into the western sky. Apart from the occasional rap of halyard wire against alloy, everything was still.

This place was as unlike Hamble as any place could be.

My home village is timeless, its river beautiful, whereas Gosport, part of Portsmouth Harbour, one of this country's main naval bases and commercial ports, is filled to the brim with ships, aircraft carriers and ferries. Three centuries of seafaring in this historic dockyard offered a glorious back-drop to the August sun setting over the yardarms of Nelson's flagship. In the foreground, moored alongside the quay, was a modern aircraft carrier. Shoreside I could see the evening's last rays blending in with the soft red hue of the seventeenth-century bricks of maritime offices. From my position perched on one of *Ariel*'s primary winches, I felt a world away from the commotion we were expecting tomorrow.

I observed the length of *Ariel*'s deck, pushpit to pulpit, stern to stem, looking at the size and diameters of her running and standing rigging, her spars, mast and boom – everything belonging to this clipper was more substantial than *Grimalkin*. As an ex-chandler and a yachtsman I can tell you for sure that racing in a port and starboard situation you would take a chance on crossing *Grimalkin* on port tack, whereas if *Ariel* was steaming towards you, you would tack quickly and stay well clear. Having three times circumnavigated the globe, *Ariel* was tough and well founded, built to withstand the worst weather any of the five oceans could throw at her. *Grimalkin* was half the length of this clipper. God, however did we cope?

By now dusk had fallen but there was still no sign of the rest of the crew so I decided it was time to go below. For a while I lay in the tranquillity of my bunk, alone with my thoughts. I heard the sound of late arrivals – another crew to another boat – their feet treading the planks of the marina pontoon, their voices jovial. It reminded me of a happy time three decades before, when a merry *Grimalkin* crew returned in high spirits after shoreside drinks to celebrate a brilliant pre-Fastnet-qualifying St Malo race. We were all so young, my skipper then younger than I am now, and none of us had any idea of what was to come. Leaning back on the soft pillow of my sleeping bag, I recalled how thirty years ago I had been so excited to be setting out, sailing with Matthew and his dad. And I cursed as I felt the old, unwanted bitterness rising within me once more.

In the distance I hear the soft laughter of my skipper and crew as they return from the pub, a timely distraction from my darkening mood. Rubbing the small of my back with the palm of my right hand, I try to relax. As I wait to drift off to sleep, I visualise our start and *Ariel*'s course westwards, down-channel towards the Scilly Isles. It's the same pre-sailing ritual as ever. The only difference is that now I picture everything through digitised charts – the watches we keep, the lighthouses we pass and the course we steer.

I wake the next morning at 05.30 to the sound of Radio 4 and the shipping forecast. The boats, the gear and the technical side of sailing may have changed radically since my first Fastnet but the familiar sounds of a busy marina and the BBC have not. Even from below deck, snug in my bunk, I can feel the excitement. Today, Sunday morning, will be the last opportunity to use the marina's facilities and I jump at the chance of getting ashore to shave and shower in relative luxury. I know too that others will be thinking the same, so the earlier I am up and off the boat the better for everyone. The deck is covered in dew but it is a beautiful morning and the warmth of the rising sun is burning that away in no time at all. I take my tablets then pick up my washbag and spend

20 minutes enjoying the last shave and shower for goodness knows how long. Back aboard *Ariel* and under the direction of our skipper I help to prepare this 60-footer for business.

Teamwork is all. With my crewmates I help carry *Ariel*'s massive sails and her long, huge diameter sheets up and out on deck. We rig and sheet over the top of *Ariel*'s huge yankee and mainsail the two smallest sails in her wardrobe, the trysail and the storm jib. Both of these heavyweight storm sails are bright orange and have to be hoisted before the start for the RORC to check – one of many safety implementations since 1979. It is hard work but fun. Every lead, every knot has to be checked and checked again. And so an hour later *Ariel* is fully prepared, rigged and ready to the satisfaction of her skipper – and, after all, the wellbeing of the vessel and crew rests with him. Just as, in 1979, it did with David.

At 09.20 our skipper hails us to cast off under the watchful eyes of his first and second mates. As *Ariel*'s bow and stern spring ropes are slipped I hear the gentle lap of water beneath her bow and I am happy we are no longer tethered to the shore. Not yet clear of the marina, I grip the backstay and stare behind me at the berth we've just left. There are three people standing there – two women and a child – waving someone off on another yacht just ahead of us. I observe the huddle on the pontoon and a vivid image engulfs me – it is of Gay Sheehan standing with Margaret, and it's chilling. Those two loving wives thought they would welcome David and Gerry back into Plymouth the following week. But it was a last goodbye for them both. I can't stop myself thinking of Chris and our own farewell. Did I say enough? Did I say the right things?

Almost overwhelmed with sadness I have to work hard

to shake myself out of it and concentrate on holding onto the wire shroud as *Ariel* motors out into the mouth of Portsmouth Harbour, past the forts marking and protecting its entrance. We sail the ten miles over to Cowes, with many yachts and spectator craft making the same journey. Then the familiar sight of the Medina River emerges, the entrance to Cowes, which brings us to our start line. Looking around me at the melee of yachts, waiting, like us, for their start, I know I am back. I am back in that atmosphere – Fastnet electric – and this, three decades later, feels no different. And at that very moment, just as I feel things could be no better, I spot an old friend in the distance – one who has come across from Hamble to see me off, one who three decades ago saved my life. Seeing this 29-foot-7-inch-long yacht complete with banner proclaiming 'Good luck from *Grimalkin*' is incredibly emotional. As she edges towards us I observe her more closely, and in doing so think again of Pa and something he said to me after the Fastnet Disaster Report and its findings had been released. Back then I had felt depressed. I had been holed up in my bedroom for a week when Pa finally insisted I get out of the house. We walked from our home down to Hamble and onto the marina and sat together on the very bench I had so often in my childhood used as a vantage point, when I was recovering from the brain haemorrhage.

For a long while we said nothing – silence between us had always come easily – but before we left he turned and quoted that well-known phrase of Churchill's: 'Those who fail to learn from history are doomed to repeat it.' He went on to explain that while the report fell short for me on a personal level, it was important I try to take something positive from it. Looking around me I now know that in the case of the Fastnet Disaster 1979 the lessons had most definitely been learned. Most of the recommendations outlined in the enquiry had been implemented. And one thing is plain – seeing *Grimalkin* here on the start line it's all too apparent that without modification she would not be allowed to race under the safety standards set today. It is all too telling that there is only one yacht of *Grimalkin*'s length here today, the shortest boat in the fleet.

As our start gets ever closer, with 20 minutes to go, I can still see *Grimalkin* keeping vigil. There is so much goodwill out here and I am absorbing all of it, every last bit of it. It is palpable. Finally there is wonderful silence as the engine is killed and the yankee jib hoisted. All I can hear are hails, the countdown from the shore – ten, nine, eight, seven, six ... two, one, BANG! We make a clear and safe start, which is not easy on a crowded Fastnet start line, and we are westward bound towards the Needles, first passing Hurst Castle and its narrows. We tack several times, none as close fought or as hectic as thirty years ago but I am still loving the spectacle.

Even though my concentration is focused on the race, I am in my own little memory bubble, busy drawing comparisons between the conditions then and now. This is the same course I sailed three decades ago marked by the same evocative lighthouse names. One by one I will check these off, just as the folks back home can check our progress online, because *Ariel*, along with every other Fastnet entrant this year, carries a tracker lashed to her backstay which every half an hour or so pings a position – the wonders of modern technology.

Of course, nothing is simple or straightforward when it comes to offshore racing, particularly along this Fastnet course. Our westerly progress on day one is halted by doldrum-like winds. By day two we hear that some have thrown in the towel, fed up with stemming a tide or waiting for wind. Luckily for me, all aboard are determined to complete the course. There is no turning back.

Monday morning's freshness drifts seamlessly into the windless kedging of Tuesday. The weather continues to play mind games. We keep frustration at bay by concentrating on the day-to-day shipboard routine. Then at last the wind fills, the tide turns and once more we make our way westward, squeezing up and through the gap between the mainland, Land's End, and the Scilly Isles. On Tuesday afternoon we pass by Land's End and the GPS readout confirms in stark numbers that I am in exactly the area where on the afternoon of 13 August 1979 *Grimalkin* began to surf and we, her crew, enjoyed the thrill of setting out into the Celtic Sea. We pass the points on the chart where back then sunset came early, that dreaded ochre sky that was at once beautiful and terrifying. It spooks me, and I am now feeling removed from the crew, more so than I did at the start. In my mind's eye I recall in vivid detail how back then death was possible on the face or back of every malignant wave, then I bring myself back to the present and look at the open sea so calm around me. There is no comparison between then and now.

Wednesday the 12th is a difficult day too. The wind keeps coming and going and it takes all of our skipper's guile to keep *Ariel* on track for the Rock. After long periods spent fighting the tide, I am suffering the familiar weariness of having been a few days offshore. The watch system is beginning to take its toll. But I'm driven; my objective is clear. At 04.30 on Thursday morning, *Ariel* is cutting a deep furrow through the darkness towards the Fastnet Rock. Somewhere in the night I know that 274 other yachts are converging on this Rock, but huddled in the cockpit, ducking the spray and dodging lumps of cold Celtic saltwater, *Ariel* may as well be alone in the North Sea or the Southern Ocean. There's not another yacht in sight, not even a navigation light. The visibility is not good, it's cold and I feel instinctively that I am right here – in the death zone of 1979 where 15 people perished. With a strengthening breeze and a rising swell, a fine drizzle chills my bones, bringing memories flooding back. I'm happy it's dark and no one can see my spray-filled tears.

By 8am the rain has gone and a grey dawn is rising. Mainland Ireland is shrouded in mist but I'm excited knowing that we are edging closer. Cape Clear comes into view and then there it is, the infamous Fastnet Rock – more spectacular than I ever imagined, this icon of yacht-racing history, which from my early childhood has taken on mythical proportions, and which through an act of God changed my life.

I am handed *Ariel*'s wheel. And so it is, at 10.20 on the morning of 13 August, that I finally round the Rock. As I do so, I say some words, they tumble out – I feel self-conscious, embarrassed even, in front of the crew, who are all on deck for this significant moment. I keep talking about Gerry and David, how their souls rest in peace now. I am torn apart by the thought of how overjoyed all of us would have been back then to see this sight. And in spite of everything I am happy finally to be here and to have made it with this boat, this skipper and this crew. They are all deservedly in a great mood, happy to have ticked their own Fastnet box, and apart from a face that's wracked with emotion, I am no different.

The weather, the weather! What I'd have given for a perfect, aft-of-the-beam reach in which *Ariel* could excel, lift her heavy skirts and surf her way home to an ideal finish. It was not to be. It is a long slow journey to the finish. By midday *Ariel* is almost in the spot where in the late evening of Tuesday 14 August 1979 I was rescued. If you had looked up into the sky, say at 21.15, not only would you have seen a dark green Royal Navy Sea King helicopter and heard the amazingly loud clatter of its rotor blades, but dangling from its rescue cable you'd have seen the distressing sight of a single man, clad in orange waterproofs, whom you would not have known was dead or alive. He was dead. That man was Gerry. Diverting your gaze to the white, dismasted, half-swamped sloop, watching the swollen crests and the deeply cut valleys of troughs, you would have noticed the other seemingly lifeless orange-clad man slumped and tied in to the rear of this yacht. That was me – a man full of madness and shock. But I lived. And that's why I'm back doing this race – because I can.

I wake early the next day, still full of emotion and anticipation, for I have one more moment to honour. I am not on watch but it is 14 August 2009 and I know that shortly I must go on deck. At ten past ten I find myself alone, leaning against the rail, gazing yet again out into the vast ocean. Although not flat, the sea allows me to spot other yachts who, like us, are homeward bound – some are near, others far, but no matter, they are there – and the sight of them offers me a security that I would have given anything for that morning when Gerry and I found ourselves alone on a damaged yacht in a storm no one had seen the like of in sailing history. I withdraw the candle from the pocket of my smock and light it for Gerry, who had died in my arms at around this time on Tuesday 14 August 1979. Today there is no spray from the sea nor shield of darkness from the night sky to disguise my tears – they simply pour down my cheeks unhindered for all that has passed and for all that can never come back.

Night falls and Plymouth, our finish line, is only 75 miles away. The sky is cloudless, the moon bright and all along the Cornish coast the picturesque village lights twinkle in the darkness. If I have one complaint it would be that dawn comes too late to allow me to see the finish line clearly. At 05.00 we cross the line in the dark, unseen, but I am delirious at having rounded my Rock, for I can say it now – my ambition has been achieved. Thirty years after my last attempt and 46 years since first dreaming of completing this race my dream has come true, and with it some ghosts have been laid to rest. As we cross the line I see Chris in the distance waiting for me, my own rock. I believe I have now, at last, found the peace I have so long desired.

Nick Ward, 2009

Appendix 1

Grimalkin's Layout and Plans

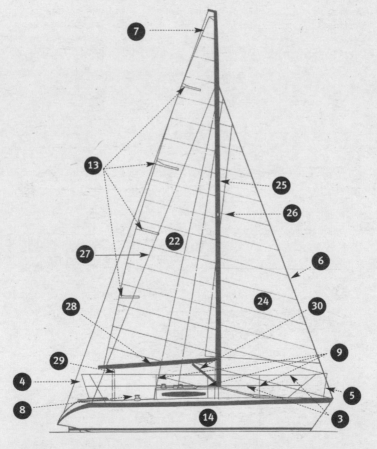

Reproduced courtesy of Ron Holland, designer, and Jeremy Lines,
Camper & Nicholson's Archivist

KEY TO PLAN OF *GRIMALKIN*, NICHOLSON 30: ABOVE & BELOW DECK

1	Cockpit	12	Tiller	23	Cabin ladder
2	Cabin	13	Sail battens	24	Genoa/jib
3	Guardrail/lifeline	14	Topsides	25	Mast
4	Pushpit	15	Toilet	26	Spreaders
5	Pulpit	16	Keel/fin	27	Backstay
6	Forestay	17	Cooker	28	Boom
7	Topping lift	18	Sink	29	Mainsheet
8	Winch drum	19	Fore hatch	30	Kicking strap
9	Stanchions	20	Life raft well	31	Navigation table
10	Rudder	21	Bulkhead	32	Bunks
11	Transom	22	Mainsail	33	Bow

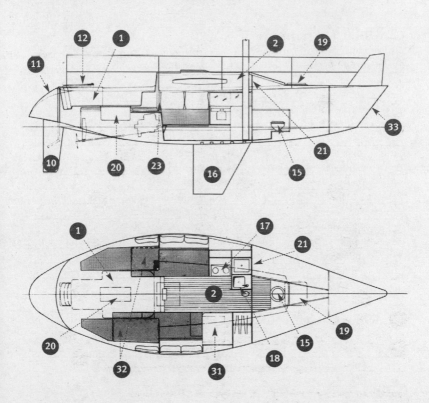

Appendix 2

Fastnet Race 1979: Retirements and Finishers

CLASS 0 (14 starters)

CLASS PLACE	YACHT NAME	OWNER (sailed by)	
1	Tenacious	Ted Turner	Finished
2	Condor of Bermuda	R Bell	
3	Kialoa	JB Kilroy	
4	Mistress Quickly	W Whitehouse–Vaux	
5	Siska	RL Tasker	
6	Gitana VI	E de Rothschild	
7	War Baby	WA Brown	
8	Travel	RT Gustafson	
9	G3	P Facque & M Loiseau	
10	Boomerang	GS Coumantaros	
11	Whirlwind V	NAV Lister	
12	Il Moro di Venezia	R Gardini	
13	Endeavour	J Callow & M Dunham	
	Battlecry	JO Prentice	Retired

CLASS I (56 starters)

CLASS PLACE	YACHT NAME	OWNER (sailed by)	
1	Red Rock IV	E Mandelbaum	Finished
2	Acadia	B Keenan	
3	Gregal	M Peche	

CLASS I (cont.)

CLASS PLACE	YACHT NAME	OWNER (sailed by)	
4	Sleuth	S Colgate	Finished
5	Vanina	V Mandelli	
6	Formidable	PW Vroon	
7	Yena	S Doni	
8	Ragamuffin	S Ficher	
9	Carina	RS & RB Nye	
10	Williwaw	S Sinett	
11	Moonduster	DN Doyle	
12	Rose Selavy	B Bonadeo	
13	Matrero	T Achaval	
14	Vanguard	DTV Lieu	
15	Togo VI	Dr T Yamada	
16	Indigo	S Eotelho	
17	Uin-Na-Mara IV	Mr & Mrs H Ross	
18	Apollo IV	J Barry	
19	Aries	M Swerdlow	
20	Morning Cloud	Rt Hon Edward Heath	
21	Toscana	E Swenson	
22	Hadar	YK Stal (Z Perlicki)	
23	Blizzard	EG Juer	
24	Noryema	RW Amey	
25	Hamburg	Hamburgscher Verein Seefahrt	
26	Cetus	YK Stal (J Suidy)	
27	Incisif	A Loisse	
28	Dorothea	WC Petersen	
29	Festina	N Mooney	
30	Midnight Sun	J Pehrsson	
31	Alliance	Naval Academy Sailing Squadron	
32	Carat	V Forss	
33	Nauticus	YK Kotwica (T Slewiec)	
34	Milene IV	A Mirlesse	
35	Parmelia	RJ Williams	
36	Lutine	Lloyds Yacht Club	
	Adventure	MOD (Navy)	Retired
	Abacus	DK Clark	Retired
	Big Shadow	S Bjerser	Retired

CLASS I (cont.)

CLASS PLACE	YACHT NAME	OWNER (sailed by)	
	Quailo	TD Parr	Retired
	Kukri	MOD (Army)	Retired
	Dasher	MOD (Navy)	Retired
	Tina	T Friese	Retired
	Tyfoon 6	G Versluys	Retired
	Jan Pott	N Lorck-Schierning	Retired
	Scaramouche	H Blane Bowen	Retired
	Yeoman XXI	RA Aisher	Retired
	Silver Apple of the Moon	B Guttinger & G Noldin	Retired
	Casse Tete V	DH Johnson	Retired
	Marionette VII	CAF Dunning	Retired
	Golden Apple of the Sun	H Coveney	Retired
	Schuttevaer	Dr JCW Van Dam	Retired
	Scaldis	ST Nauta	Retired
	Magic Eliza	Mr Schuldt-Ahrens	Retired
	Oryx	E Adams	Retired
	Chastanet	NA Brick	Retired

CLASS II (53 starters)

CLASS PLACE	YACHT NAME	OWNER (sailed by)	
1	Eclipse	JC Rogers	Finished
2	Jubile VI	H Hamon	
3	Impetuous	G Lambert & J Crisp	
4	Police Car	PR Cantwell	
5	Imp	DW Allen	
6	Schollevaer	W Dearns & F Eekels	
7	La Pantera III	C Ostenfield & E de Losala	
8	Assiduous	N Beger	
9	Marloo	Dr NS Girdis	
10	Campsa	J Cusi	
11	Magistri	C Bentley	
12	Koteru Teru II	T Yamaguchi	
13	Sur II	DP Ramos	
14	Darling Dee	A Nelis	
15	Rubin	HO Schümann	

CLASS II (cont.)

CLASS PLACE	YACHT NAME	OWNER (sailed by)	
16	Loujaine	Sir Maurice Laing	
17	Dagger	JL Dolk & TEW Vinke	
18	Inishanier	G Bramwell & B Buchanan	
19	Pinta	P d'Andrimont	
20	Sarabande	JJ Hozee	
21	Tornado	W Singleton	
22	Charlatan	RW Appelbee	
23	Quickstep	SR Johnson	
	Nick Nack	N Langley-Pope	Retired
	Belita VII	JS Bouman	Retired
	Suca	W Kurt	Retired
	Farthing	Mr & Mrs ET George	Retired
	Amarante	L Maisonneuve	Retired
	Fair Judgement	DC Dillistone	Retired
	Caiman	G Jeelof	Retired
	Telemaque II	L Delacou	Retired
	Grune Sec II	J&J Leguelinel	Retired
	Evergreen	D Green	Retired
	Animal	FD Hogan	Retired
	Gekko VI	S Namiki	Retired
	Pachena	J Newton	Retired
	Standfast	J Hass	Retired
	Double O Too	RL Hay	Retired
	Pepsi	A Milton	Retired
	La Barbarella	M Hervey	Retired
	Blauwe Dolfijn II	C Wargnies	Retired
	Sophie B	BH Owen	Retired
	Golden Leigh	L Kertesz	Retired
	Wild Goose	J Ayres	Retired
	Yachtman II	R Montagut	Retired
	Regardless	K Rohan	Retired
	Accanito	S Poli	Retired
	Impromptu	J Ewart	Retired
	Maiton IV	KB Merron	Retired
	Dugenou I	J Pajot	Retired
	Lancer	GR Fuller	Retired
	Goodwin	JN Van Drongelen	Retired
	Spica II	WL Riviere	Retired

CLASS III (64 starters)

CLASS PLACE	YACHT NAME	OWNER (sailed by)	
1	Revolution	J-L Fabry	Finished
2	Blue Bird	A Gerard	
3	Ceil III	W Turnbull	
4	Solent Oyster	JAS Bassett	
5	Flycatcher	JW Roome	
6	Xara	DC Barham	
	Mickey Mouse	K Robinson	Retired
	Pordin Nancq	J Lamouric	Retired
	New Brig	Sir Frederick & Lady Coates	Retired
	Innovation	Sir Peter Johnson Bt	Retired
	Moonstone	D Chatterton	Retired
	Rock On	P Farrar	Retired
	Ailish III	B Foulger	Retired
	Croix Du Cygne	K van Exter	Retired
	Delnic	L Rousselin	Retired
	Silver Apple	G Cryns	Retired
	Cavale	PL Dorey	Retired
	Tai Fat	Hamburger Regatta Gemeinschaft	Retired
	Griffin	RORC (N Graham)	Retired
	Gorm	S Brandstedt	Retired
	Checkmate	RJC Barton	Retired
	Windswept	I Godfrey	Retired
	Bernard II	University of Louvain	Retired
	Vigilant	SRG Jeffery	Retired
	Oyster Catcher	RB Matthews	Retired
	Jolie Brise	W Jansen	Retired
	Peau D'Bouc	A Simon	Retired
	Zeehaas	MJF Vroon	Retired
	Veronier II	CJ Vroege	Retired
	Combat II	D Gilliam & G Bottomley	Retired
	Sundowner	B'Odonnell	Retired
	Polyhymnia	OV van Tijn	Retired
	Ballydonna	RJ Hogson	Retired
	Asterie	R Jeanty	Retired
	Gallivant II	WR Binks	Retired
	Amandla Kulu	S Polliack	Retired
	Allamanda	M Campbell	Retired

CLASS III (cont.)

CLASS PLACE	YACHT NAME	OWNER (sailed by)	
	Andiamo Robin	J Harding	Retired
	Samurai III	RG Jordan	Retired
	Zap	W Stewart-Ross	Retired
	Live Wire	DD O'Brien	Retired
	Poppy II	JM Dean	Retired
	Juggernaut	A Cassell	Retired
	Tam O'Shanter	JC Butler	Retired
	Hoodlum	CJ Evans	Retired
	Tiderace IV	DEP Norton	Retired
	Crazy Horse	C Goater	Retired
	Good In Tension	CW Billington	Retired
	Festina Tertia	N Mooney	Retired
	Pepsi	JJ Smith	Retired
	Carmargue	AF Moss	Retired
	Victride	A Lanoue	Retired
	Mutine	Cdr EA Morrison	Retired
	Finndabar of Howth	JP Jameson	Retired
	Trophy	AW Bartlett	Retired
	Autonomy	E Bourne	Retired
	Charioteer	Dr J Coldrey & J Lindsay	Retired
	Assassin	NG Watson	Retired
	Steady Tension	RS Havens & GW Havens	Retired
	Passing Cloud	PB Morgan	Retired
	Angustura	WW & AW Oliver	Retired
	Palamedes	AJ Sheldon	Retired
	Firanjo	Gp Capt R Wardman	Retired
	Hindustan	Lt Cdr Steele	Retired

CLASS IV (58 starters)

CLASS PLACE	YACHT NAME	OWNER (sailed by)	
1	Black Arrow	Royal Air Force SA	Finished
2	Samsara	Madame O Tran-Van-Dom	
2	Lorelei	M Catherineau	(time allowance)
3	Mahuri	GM Lowson	

CLASS IV (cont.)

CLASS PLACE	YACHT NAME	OWNER (sailed by)	
4	Kalisana	HMS *Sultan* (Cdr Watson)	
5	Karimata	E Blokzyl	
6	Tronador	RMH Edwards	
	Dai Mouse III	DWT Hague	Retired
	Challenge	FM Murray	Retired
	Bertheaume	Brest Syndicate	Retired
	Kamisado	MJW Green	Retired
	Fragola	GLC des Glénans	Retired
	Golden Princess	A Hagnere	Retired
	Scattered Magic	J Chuter	Retired
	Cheesecake	D Hopkins	Retired
	Contentious Eagle	Barclays Bank Ltd (B Roberts)	Retired
	Cosmic Dancer	RG Warren	Retired
	Minipyge	M Merfabruge	Retired
	Baradozic	M Ganachaud	Retired
	Nepthys II	Y Bodin	Retired
	Prairie Oyster	CFR Purchase	Retired
	Goniocoque	P Barriere	Retired
	Virginie	Ecole Navale	Retired
	Drakkar	R Morelisse	Retired
	Quixote	E & IJ Watts	Retired
	Sigmania	Major P Scholfield	Retired
	Electron II	HMS *Collingwood*	Retired
	En Passant	M Postman	Retired
	Hullabaloo	AJ Otten	Retired
	Cassiopee	R Hubert	Retired
	Rhapsody	JA Hughes	Retired
	Cote De Beaute	M Amiant	Retired
	Dumonveh	G Messink	Retired
	Thunderflash	Royal Naval Engineering College	Retired
	Copernicus	A Morton & B Jackson	Retired
	Impetus	DJC Longstaffe	Retired
	Carronade	Mr & Mrs P Clements	Retired
	Alvena	Y Dreo	Retired
	Scenario	A Fitton	Retired
	Maelstrom	MA Bolson	Retired
	Lipstick	C Clarke & D Seabrook	Retired

CLASS IV (cont.)

CLASS PLACE	YACHT NAME	OWNER (sailed by)	
	Sandettie I	K Krygsman	Retired
	Fiorinda	PB Eyre	Retired
	Detente	CK Bond-Smith	Retired
	Locomotion	EA & JA Clegg	Retired
	Flashlight	RN Engineering College	Retired
	Hestrul II	DA Lewis	Retired
	Gringo	A Morgan	Retired
	Callirhoe III	P Bouyssou	Retired
	Ariadne	FH Ferris	Retired
	Polar Bear	JC Clothier	Retired
	Pegasus	PGA White	Retired
	Ocean Wave	(J Toler)	Retired
	Cabadah	Capt G Greenfield	Retired
	Odyssea	M Guichard	Retired
	Mezzanine	K Hancock & L Chapman	Retired
	Elessar II	WPJ Laros	Retired
	Clarionet	G & N Playfair	Retired

CLASS V (58 starters)

CLASS PLACE	YACHT NAME	OWNER (sailed by)	
1	Assent	W & A Kerr	Finished
	Fluter	Ministry of Defence (Army)	Retired
	Spreadeagle	Barclays Bank Ltd (F Sanders)	Retired
	Morning Rose	Bank of England	Retired
	La Negresse Blonde	J Cruette	Retired
	Tikocco	C Caillere	Retired
	Mosika Alma	J Forrester	Retired
	Phynnodderee	Dr JK Hinds	Retired
	Sarie Marais	Cdr D Gay	Retired
	Rapperee	B Kelly	Retired
	Festina	GP Green	Retired
	Green Dragon	Mr & Mrs B Saffery Cooper	Retired
	Valross	TH Bevan	Retired
	Kate	Mr & Mrs F Ellis	Retired
	Silver Foam	JA Mehigan	Retired

CLASS V (cont.)

CLASS PLACE	YACHT NAME	OWNER (sailed by)	
	Beep Beep	G Cornier	Retired
	Morning Melody	Y Prieur	Retired
	Espirit	B Lesieur	Retired
	First of April	O Goguel	Retired
	Thunderer	Royal Ordinance Corps SA	Retired
	Right Royal of Upnor	Corps of Royal Engineers	Retired
	Marina	Dr JH Van der Waals	Retired
	Flamingo	B Chapman	Retired
	Redskin	P Van Tongerloo	Retired
	Hurricantoo	AB & N Simms	Retired
	Mordicus	C Volters	Retired
	Gunslinger	National Westminster Bank	Retired
	Trumpeter	Ministry of Defence (Army)	Retired
	Option II	J Desfeux	Retired
	Gay Gannet V	General Sir Hugh Beach	Retired
	Tamasin II	RT Bishop	Retired
	Contessa Catherine	Royal Engineer Yacht Club (Brigadier R Dowdall)	Retired
	Golden Thistle	AWF Russett	Retired
	Sissytoo	RL Hill	Retired
	Maligawa III	G Foures	Retired
	Alpha II	HS Axton	Retired
	Morning Glory	FA Davies	Retired
	Pinball Wizard	PT Lees	Retired
	Billy Bones	Ms Boudet & Seuly	Retired
	Skidbladner III	HA Hansell	Retired
	Xaviera	RA Woodbridge	Retired
	Korsar	RE Mollard	Retired
	Ossian	P Ratzel	Retired
	Gan	J Hercelin	Retired
	Magic	PT Whipp	Retired
	Grimalkin	D Sheahan	Retired
	Bonaventure II	Ministry of Defence (Navy)	Retired
	Arkadina	AJ Boutle	Retired
	Tarantula	P Le Floch	Retired
	Little Eila	SR Field	Retired
	Congreve	(Major P Crump)	Retired
	Corker	GT Davies	Retired

CLASS V (cont.)

CLASS PLACE	YACHT NAME	OWNER (sailed by)	
	Explorer of Hornet	Ministry of Defence (Navy)	Retired
	Humbug	NR Palmer	Retired
	Illusion	K Watson	Retired
	Enia V	M Touron	Retired
	Karibario	J Legallet	Retired
	Skat	Dr N Southwood	Retired

* Tinted entries are yachts mentioned in the book.

SUMMARY OF SINKINGS AND ABANDONMENTS

Class (IOR)	Length	Starters	Finishers	Retired	Crew lost	Abandoned and recovered	Sunk
O	59–79ft	14	13	1	0	0	0
I	44–55ft	56	36	19	0	1	0
II	39–43ft	53	23	30	0	0	0
III	34–38ft	64	6	52	6	4	2
IV	33ft	58	6	44	6	7	1
V	28–32ft	58	1	48	3	7	2
TOTAL		**303**	**85**	**194**	**15**	**19**	**5**

LOSS OF LIFE

Boat name	Fatalities	Class	
Grimalkin	2	V	Gerald Winks & David Sheahan
Trophy	3	III	P Everson, John Puxley & R Boyer
Ariadne	4	IV	Frank Ferris, WCL Le Fevre, David Crisp & RL Robie
Flashlight	2	IV	R Brown & C Steavenson
Gunslinger	1	V	Peter Baldwin
Cavale	1	III	Peter Dorey
Festina Tertia	1	III	Roger Watts
Veronier	1	III	Gerit-Jan Williahey
TOTAL	**15**		**15**

Acknowledgements

Nick Ward:

Special thanks to my dear wife Chris, my own steady rock. Special thanks also to my son Sam and my daughter Lizzie, for listening, always.

And to my dear sister, Cheryl and her husband, Bob Drury. Simon Ward, my brother, and his wife Jane for giving me confidence and assistance with the photographs in the book.

I thank John Rousmaniere and Bob Fisher, good men, examples of how to write clear, understandable books and articles on yacht racing.

Thanks to my niece Sarah for sound advice.

To Andy Hussey for being a good friend, and for directing myself and Sinéad to Janet Murphy.

To Glyn and Bill Foulkes of Aladdin's Cave Chandleries.

Also to Simon Sheehan, Jane and 'Albi'.

Thanks to Liz Saunders of Hamble Sailing Services, Hamble School of Yachting.

Thanks to James and Mark Grainger, Keith Grainger

and Andrew Howard, current owners of *Grimalkin* – great sail – and thank you all for being so welcoming.

Thanks to Marianne and Patrick, literary agents, and to all at Adlard Coles and Bloomsbury: Jill Coleman, Janet Murphy, Rosanna Bortoli, Liz Piercy and Nicola Mann.

Thanks are due to my dear friends David and Nikki Madsen for their friendship and seamanship. Also for Nikki's great images of *Grimalkin* racing in the Solent.

For standing by *Grimalkin* in 1979, I extend my enduring gratitude to the crews of *Fragola* and *Tai Fat*. And for allowing me to publish his amazing photographs of my rescue, to Christian Schaumloffel.

To Charlie Thornton and Commander 'Harry' Harrison RN: thank you.

For their support and encouragement, special thanks to Simon, Jim and Emily, Nigel Beacham, and the crews of *Ariel* and *Blackadder* – you are the best. Also to Jez Rowles of Spinlock, Dave Ellis and Amy of Henri Lloyd.

Finally, to Rosanna and Janet for their added help, encouragement and support before, during and after 2009's Fastnet. Thank you.

Sinéad O'Brien:

Thanks to four amazing women:

Our agent, Marianne Gunn O'Connor – for your absolute belief in this project and for all you have achieved with it.

Our publisher, Janet Murphy – thank you for your patience, your inspiration and your input – it has been a complete pleasure working with you.

To our book editor, Mari Roberts – you are fabulous and your contribution to this book has been tremendous.

And to Chris 'the trojan' Ward – you are the best and deserve to be canonised.

Thanks to Liz Piercy, all at A&C Black Publishers and Nick Trautwein of Bloomsbury US for your support and belief in this book.

Special thanks to Noel Pearson – you have been a great friend to me.

Thanks to Pam Buckley for first telling me of Nick Ward's Fastnet experience as she remembered it – the very next day I began my search for Nick.

Thanks to Patrick Lynch at Marianne Gunn O'Connor Literary Agency.

Special thanks to Nick Ward for asking me to collaborate with him on the writing of this incredible story.

I would like also to thank Christian Schaumloffel, Charlie Thornton and Peter Harrison for the time they gave me – without them the final chapter could not have been written.

Very special thanks to Katie O'Brien, Peter O'Brien, Eoin Spencer, Aisling O'Neill, Niamh Byrne, Jill O'Neill and Ian McCarthy for your love and support.

And most of all – thank you to the light in my life – my beautiful daughter, Eve Buckley.

Photos, Excerpts and Article Acknowledgements

All reasonable efforts to trace the copyright holders have been made.

Photographs courtesy of the Ward Family, Stanley Ward,

Simon Ward, Chris Ward, Miss Eileen Ramsay, John Eagle, William Payne, Mary Borrett, Gary Griffin, David Cobb, Beken of Cowes and The Royal Navy (© British Crown Copyright/MOD and reproduced with the permission of the Controller of Her Majesty's Stationery Office).

Article 'Tracking a Killer Storm' by Robert B Rice, first published in *Sail* Magazine in 1980.

Boat plans and layout courtesy of Ron Holland, Designer, Stuart Roy, Marine Architect and Jeremy Lines, Camper & Nicholson's Archivist.

Extracts from the Fastnet Race Inquiry 1979 published by The Royal Yachting Association and the Royal Ocean Racing Club.

Excerpt of *Desiderata* by Max Ehrmann.

Excerpt of *Footprints in the Sand* by Mary Stevenson.

The Authors

Nick Ward:

As an energetic youngster Nick Ward took on many part time jobs including helping out on Hamble River's ferry, all to finance his enduring passion – sailing. After finishing at Fareham College Nick worked full time at Solent Yachts in Warsash, then at Camper & Nicholson chandleries in Southampton and Gosport. In 1975 he began delivering sailing yachts and motor vessels across the English Channel and further afield to Spain and Portugal.

Back ashore, in 1976 Nick joined Hamble-based Rank Marine at their two riverside chandleries, and became a partner in the chandlery at Mercury Yacht Harbour. The business was sold in 1993 to Aladdin's Cave Chandleries, for whom Nick worked for eleven happy years, imparting his knowledge and enthusiasm for sailing.

Nick still remains close to the Hamble River where he lives with his wife Chris, a nursing sister. They have two children, Sam and Elizabeth.

Sinéad O'Brien:

Sinead O'Brien is an award winning documentary maker and dramatist. Since her first documentary *Dusk 'til Dawn* (1999) she has written and directed seven further documentaries including the multiple-award-winning *Luke. Left for Dead* is her first non-fiction collaboration. Sinead O'Brien lives in Dublin, Ireland.